THE ALL-AROUND HORSE AND RIDER

THE ALL-AROUND HORSE AND RIDER

DONNA SNYDER-SMITH

HOWELL
BOOK
HOUSE

Howell Book House
Published by Wiley Publishing, Inc., Hoboken, New Jersey
Published simultaneously in Canada

For general information about our other products and services, please contact our Customer Care Department within the United States at (800) 762-2974, outside the United States at (317) 572-3993 or fax (317) 572-4002.

Wiley also publishes its books in a variety of electronic formats. Some content that appears in print may not be available in electronic books. For more information about Wiley products, visit our web site at www.wiley.com.

Library of Congress Cataloging-in-Publication Data:
Snyder-Smith, Donna.
    The all-around horse and rider / Donna Snyder-Smith.
        p. cm.
ISBN 0-7645-4974-X (alk. paper)
    1. Horsemanship. II. Horses. III. Title.
    SF309.S635 2004

                                                        2003018788

Printed in the United States of America

10 9 8 7 6 5 4 3 2 1

Photography by Donna Snyder-Smith unless otherwise credited
Illustrations by Bethany Caskey and Susan Harris

*This book is dedicated to the special horses in my life—
Kopper, Karmah and Falcon*

*To my horse friends, since only they can understand
what it means to need to be in the presence of these
unique creatures*

*And to my many clients, who have allowed me to
participate with them in their journey toward their
equestrian dreams.*

Contents

Foreword

s I began to read Donna Snyder-Smith's *The All-Around Horse and Rider,* I found myself constantly nodding in agreement, thinking, "Yes! Yes!" For what Donna has brilliantly accomplished here is to have taken a highly complex subject and, without downplaying its complexity, made it appear possible.

Possible, not easy—an important distinction. It's a truth-telling book, not necessarily a feel-good book for those with low goals and meager aspirations. For the truth is that while there are many gradations of riding skills, and it's possible to "ride" a horse very badly, good riding requires physical and intellectual rigor.

Donna uses phrases like "biomechanical action," "basic cognitive program" and "auditory, visual and kinesthetic learning channels." This is clearly a book aimed at the serious student, but that's not to imply that it's a "heavy" book—just one that is uncompromisingly correct.

Correct is a term that can be used very narrowly, as in "That is a correct half pass," but that isn't the "correct" I mean. Horses, for all their variety, have skeletons and muscles, tendons and ligaments, which move in certain ways that are relatively constant. They have central nervous systems that have been programmed by eons of evolution to respond to certain stimuli in ways that are also relatively constant.

When riders are in tune with these movements and responses, that is "correct" riding. The horse feels less pressure, less duress, less discomfort. When the rider's incorrect posture, or rough hands, or abusive temper puts her out of tune with the horse's natural physical and emotional pathways, that is incorrect riding.

The really good, all-around riders can ride lots of different horses in a multitude of disciplines because they harmonize correctly with the movements of the horse in ways that also do not trigger the horse's fight-or-flight mechanisms. It doesn't matter whether the saddle is Western or

English, or whether the rider foxhunts or trail rides, as long as she maintains that fundamental correctness.

I've spent much of my life in close proximity to some of the truly great riders in the world. Almost universally, they aren't one-dimensional riders. Eight-time Olympic three-day veteran Mike Plumb won the Maclay equitation class as a child and placed second in the Maryland Hunt Cup. Frank Chapot, six-time grand prix jumping Olympian, placed third in the Maryland Hunt Cup.

Great riders are great riders—something Donna recognizes and encourages in this marvelous book. She says to us, in essence, that we need to learn to ride correctly, and then take that riding wherever we wish to go, in any direction that sparks our passion. *The All-Around Horse and Rider* is a road map, an intellectual exercise and an inspiration that deserves a prominent place on the bookshelf of every serious rider.

Denny Emerson
Tamarack Hill Farm
Member 1974 USET World Championship
Gold Medal Eventing Team
USCTA National Leading Rider

Introduction

*R*iding, in its simplest form, is nothing more than keeping a horse between you and the ground. Competition, on the other hand, is an expression of skill and athleticism, and has as its ultimate goal—winning. Riding as art is much like Zen—an enlightenment (of the rider by the horse) by direct intuition (communication done through bodily contact) achieved through meditation (upon the horse, by the rider). Good riding is good riding, regardless of the clothes, the saddle or the century.

To become an all-around horseman or horsewoman requires education. Whether that education is self-taught or gained with the help of experienced teachers and mentors, the rider who wishes to attain the title of all-around must be prepared to challenge themselves mentally, as well as physically. The first challenge you will meet is finding a jumping-off point for your journey. Intelligent adults can select a goal and proceed toward it in a successful way on their own time schedule if they are provided with reliable information and an overall context.

Forty years of working within the equestrian industry as an instructor and trainer has impressed upon me that the value of context is often underestimated, and it is not unusual for that particular piece of the puzzle to be missing all together. I see riders and owners making diligent efforts to seek knowledge but finding it only in isolated segments. Not having an overview is as much of a handicap as is trying to piece together a puzzle without first looking at the image you are working to bring together. Seeing the journey as a whole gives context, which in turn gives greater meaning and clarification to the content you are seeking.

Today's rider faces many landmines in the search for context as well as content. For instance, it is currently fashionable to recommend that you look to the horse to evaluate input. But if you lack the expertise to read him accurately, you will be unable to rely on his input as your primary guidance system in the search for a safe and satisfactory route to your destination. On another front, there is a lack of continuity within the equestrian industry that makes it, at best, a flimsy launching pad to success. It is a sad fact that within any state, even within a single county, riders exhibiting identical skills can be classified so differently that one is named a novice by one instructor and the other is named advanced by another instructor. This poses a serious problem to both the individual and the industry, and is, in part, the reason this book was born. Over the course of your riding lives, you and your horse can try many paths; you don't have to choose just one. In order to do this, however, you will need an overview of the equestrian world that allows you to see and understand that the various disciplines function on the same principles. Loving horses all my life, I wish to see them live happy lives, and I know that the better you ride, the happier your horse will be. My second goal is to see the level of equestrian knowledge in this country constantly evolve to a higher and higher standard, and I believe that today's caring, adult amateur riders can become the standard bearers in this cause.

In the past 50 years, performance tests have tended to underscore differences and emphasize specialization. This trend has resulted in practices in training and showing horses that are ultimately injurious to the health and soundness of the animal. Horses in western pleasure classes are forced into head sets so low that they are known as "peanut rollers." The exotic Arabian horse that appears in the show rings today is shaved to the skin around his eyes and muzzle and coated with oil, to "enhance" his beauty. Tennessee Walking horses have been subjected to leg irritants and devices on their feet to promote "natural" movement.

Specialization has even crept into the breeding shed. Stallions and mares are being selected with one purpose in mind. That is, Thoroughbreds, which are bred for racing on a groomed track, are selected for speed, not the structure and strength of their feet. As a result, many in the breed now have thin walls and shelly feet that often won't hold up to the wear and tear of normal riding. Similar problems haunt the Quarter Horse, whose notoriously small feet are simply not engineered to support their large, muscular body. As a result, many of the breed are plagued with soundness problems during their performance lifetime.

As we enter the new century, I believe the pendulum of specialization has finally reached the end of its negative arc and is beginning to return toward center and balance. Riders and owners want more for their horses, who have become companion animals rather than toys or tools. Events in our nation's recent past have encouraged many to revisit their sense of identity, and, awakened by the piper's song of our country's equestrian heritage, riders are reaching for a new vision—one in which the team of horse and rider forms a deep and historical partnership.

The American urge to "be all you can be" will continue to challenge riders, but the standards many strive toward today are the standards of the men, women and horses whose mastery of multiple skills is the reason our nation exists. We want to ride the cavalry mount; the companion and trusted friend who braved the roar of cannon and the rattle of sabers to carry his rider obediently into battle; the one who would gallop great distances, leaping barriers and swimming rivers at his rider's request, to arrive at their destination; the horse who stories tell was known to stand guard over his rider fallen in battle rather than return to the safety of the stable. Or the cow pony, the horse who stood quietly at the end of a rope for the cowboy while the branding iron was applied to the calf, moved readily to full gallop if an animal broke from the herd and returned to a relaxed walk when the errant critter had been returned to its place, who stood without being tied while his rider strung fence, and brought him safely back to the home corral on the darkest night, in rain or snow. That horse, the all-around horse, is our heritage, our privilege and our prize.

Chapter 1

The All-Around Horse, an American Heritage

*T*he history of the horse seems to holds a tenacious influence on man's future. Doubters may want to consider the case of the solid rocket booster fuel tanks, a part of the propulsion system for NASA's Space Shuttle, which is arguably, the most advanced form of transportation of the age. Made by Thiokol in Utah, their size is influenced by horses who lived and served their owners in Imperial Rome! Deeply imbedded ruts made by the Roman war chariots dominated wheeled design specifications for centuries, influencing the prototype for the British railroad gauge (the width between the rails on railroad tracks is 4 feet, 8.5 inches, derived from the specification for an Imperial Roman war chariot), and Englishmen helped design and build the American rail system. The shuttle's booster tanks, which must be shipped by rail from their manufacturing site to their final destination at the launch pad, could not, therefore, exceed the width of a pair of horse's haunches—or so the story goes.

It seems no coincidence, then, that the history of our country is bound up with that of the horse; the very act of riding continuing the chronicle of horsemen and horsewomen who have left their marks on history from the saddle in years past. It is fair to say the country could not have grown the way it did if it were not for the service of horses.

Used in everyday affairs from the time they were brought to the shores of this continent in 1493 by Columbus, horses were the earliest tractors, serving the farmer in the nation's agricultural fields, pulling plows and clearing the land for building. They were the engines between the traces of a great variety of vehicles, from the earliest version of UPS (heavy delivery wagons) to the forerunner of our modern bus (the stagecoach) to the RV of its time (the covered wagon). They served as engine for the family station wagon (the buckboard), sedan (doctor's buggy) and sports car (the gig).

But it wasn't until the American Revolution, when a regiment of 400 men from Connecticut known as the Light Horse reported to General George Washington mounted on their own private bloodstock, that the horse made a significant appearance in American history as a war machine. This particular group of sporting gentlemen enlisted with the agreement that they would be excused from some of the normal soldierly duties in order to have the time to care for their animals, whom they considered as valuable as their other fighting weapons. General Washington, fearing his foot soldiers would be jealous of the time these men spent with their mounts, sent the regiment home. Shortly thereafter, he suffered a major defeat at the hands of the British, whose successful strategy relied heavily on mounted troops. Washington, himself a horseman and a foxhunter, soon changed his mind, and in 1777, Congress formally authorized the formation of four regiments of dragoons. They fought with sabers and flintlock pistols, and the fashion press of the day showed them dressed in buckskin breeches and top boots with helmets of brass—their actual attire was much meaner.

As the mounts for couriers and soldiers, horses earned their daily rations by their patience, endurance and bravery. When life and death hung on the point of a saber, the cavalry horse had to respond to a rider's slightest cue, rapidly and without question.

After the end of the Revolution, as men and families from the East pushed West, it was largely the fighting skills of Native American horsemen that revived the government's interest in the cavalry in 1832. In *The Story of the U.S. Cavalry* by Major General John K. Herr and Edward Wainwright, the Indian mounts are described as scarcely 14 hands, slight in build, with powerful forequarters, good legs, a short, strong back and a full barrel (deep heart girth). Although they did not resemble the "blooded" horses from the East, it was said they had sharp ears and bright eyes, and unusual intelligence. "The amount of work he could do and the distance he could cover put him fairly on a level with the Arabian," Herr and Wainwright wrote.

The Indian pony was an example of the wild plains horses, known as mustangs, whose herds numbered in the tens of thousands and roamed throughout much of the Midwest and Southwest into Mexico. Tales of these horses carrying riders 70 miles a day without tiring or going unsound were common. In 1856, J. S. Rarey, who referred to himself as an "American horse tamer," wrote in *The Modern Art of Taming Wild Horses,* "On bringing a [wild] horse into a stall for the first time, the best way is to lead a gentle horse into the stable first and hitch him, then quietly walk around the wild colt and let him go in [the stable] of his own accord. It is almost impossible to get men who have never practiced on this principle to go slowly and considerately enough about it. They do not know that in handling a wild horse, above all other things, is that good old adage true, that 'haste makes waste;' that is, waste of time for the gain of trouble and perplexity."

By the 1850s, the United States Army Cavalry was well established, and horses continued to play a strong role in the affairs of the country with the onset of the Civil War. The Confederate Cavalry demonstrated its equestrian prowess early in that conflict. Men such as General Robert E. Lee and Major General Jeb Stuart hailed from a population where riding and hunting were an integral part of life and a focus of education, and they lived up to the title "horseman" and all that it conveyed about the ability to do almost anything from the back of a horse.

The riders of the Union Cavalry lagged behind their Southern counterparts for a time, men from the North being recruited primarily from urban areas, few having experience in the saddle or any skill in the handling of horses.

The training time for a cavalryman was approximately two years and required a high order of intelligence and initiative. A good trooper had to be equally efficient on the ground or in the saddle. The Confederate rider's knowledge of his horse resulted in better care of the animal, while the early Yankee cavalry lost a great number of its horses through ignorance of even the simplest horsemanship principles, such as the severe debilitating effects of allowing an overridden, hot horse to fill his belly with cold water.

In 1862, a Captain Vanderbilt described a chaotic scene that might easily have been anticipated by any experienced horseman in the same circumstances.

My company had been mustered into the service only about six weeks before, having received horses less than a month prior to the march. In issue we drew everything on the list, watering-bridles, lariat ropes, extra blankets, nice large quilts presented by some fond mother or maiden aunt, sabers and belts, carbines with slings, pockets full of cartridges, nose bags, extra little bags for caring oats, haversacks, canteens, spurs, curry-combs, brushes, ponchos, button tents, overcoats, frying pans, and coffee pots, etc. Such a rattling, jingling, jerking, scrabbling, cursing, I never heard before. Green horses, some which had never even been ridden, turned round and round, backed against each other, jumped up or stood up like trained circus-horses. Some of the boys had a pile in front on their saddles and one in the rear, so high and heavy it took two men to saddle one horse and two men to help the fellow into his place. The horses sheered out, going sideways, pushing the well disposed animals out of position, etc. Some of the boys had never ridden anything since they galloped on a hobby hose, and they clasped their legs close together, thus unconsciously sticking the spurs into their horse's sides. Blankets slipped from under saddles and hung from one corner; saddles slipped back until they were on the rumps of horses; others turned and were on the under side of the animals; horses running and kicking, tin pans, mess-kettles, flying through the air; and all I could do was to give a hasty glance to the rear and sing out at the top of my voice, "CLOSE UP."

The Confederate Cavalry not only took advantage of the inexperience of the Union Cavalry men, they depended largely on captured Union mounts to fill their needs. The situation gradually improved for the North when the Quartermaster Department built remount depots in convenient locations to train and furnish horses for the Union army. Records show that the government bought or captured a total of 210,000 horses in one year alone to supply the army's need. In 1861, Philip St. George Cooke wrote *Cavalry Tactics*, an instructional book on mounted maneuvers. It was this organization and education of both the horses and men of the Union Cavalry that helped turn the tide of the war.

BETHANY CASKEY

Union Cavalry riders had little horse experience.

Following the Civil War, Cavalry units were dispatched to the Western frontier, where attacks against white settlements by Mexicans and Native Americans had been on the rise. In January 1880, the War Department set the following specifications for a horse that was to be considered suitable for an army remount: "To be sound in all particulars, from 15 to 16 hands, no less than 5 years and no more than 9 years old, except when suitable in every other way for cavalry use. Colors to be bays, browns, blacks and sorrels. Good trotters and bridle wise."

The War Department continued to use horses and their riders into the 20th century, culminating in what may still be considered the nation's greatest equestrian school, the Cavalry School at Fort Riley, Kansas. Much of the information in the *Horsemanship and Horsemastership Manuals*, written in 1942 and used as a part of the curriculum at Fort

Riley, is as appropriate today as it was at the time it was written. Old photographs and diagrams show the correct seat and position for the rider who wanted to be ready to meet any contingency, from jumping a fence to sliding down a steep embankment, and I would venture to offer that any rider who aspires to become an accomplished all-around horseman or horsewoman could do much worse than to acquire a set of these old books and study them carefully, doing his or her best to follow exactly the instruction set forth in their pages.

Members of the United States Army Cavalry, excellent riders on well-trained horses, represented the United States at the Olympic Games through 1948 in the three major disciplines of dressage, eventing and jumping. Captain Guy V. Henry, who served in the Spanish-American War, World War I and World War II, was the first of many American riders to travel to France to train at the French Cavalry School at Samur. The school, notorious for the quality of its equestrian programs and its horses, left its mark on Capt. Henry, who later modeled the Cavalry School at Fort Riley on the French school. Promoting advanced courses for both riders and horses, he is credited with being the creator of the modern American doctrine of equitation.

In 1912, the United States Army Team won a bronze medal in the Olympic three-day event. Henry rode as a member of the team on a horse named Chriswell. Displaying the all-around ability of his mount, Henry also showed the horse in the dressage competition, placing 11th, then led the United States jumping team to a fourth place as well. (It is interesting to note that the Olympic dressage tests didn't require the elegant movements of passage and piaffe, but did require jumping obstacles immediately upon entering the arena and as a part of the test.) He added to his versatile equestrian career by winning three medals at the 1948 Olympics: a team silver in dressage, and an individual silver and team gold in three-day eventing.

Henry continued his passion for horses throughout his lifetime, acting as civilian director of the United States Equestrian Team, which was formed to take over the responsibility of fielding equestrian Olympic teams when the cavalry was disbanded in 1949.

In *The King Ranch*, Volume I, by Tom Lea, the origin of the term *cowboy* is credited to the men who were paid to steal Mexican cattle to feed federal troops located north of the Nueces line in Texas. Rough-riding bands of 10 to 15 horsemen would gather 200 to 500 head of wild cattle, keeping them in a punishing run for as long as 24 hours, gradually slowing their gait when they were so tired that they could be controlled. These riders were young toughs who had served in the army—gangs who referred to themselves as Cow Boys and carried bowie knives and muzzle-loading rifles. "The generic name for future practitioners of the most celebrated legend on the continent thus was given birth, in the region of the Santa Gertrudis," Lea wrote.

As the nation expanded West, American cowboys—men who made their living on the back of a horse—began to have a greater influence on the nation's style of riding. In the early 1900s, entertainment extravaganzas like the Miller Brothers 101 Ranch Real Wild West Show and early Hollywood Westerns popularized the versatile skills and expanded the legend of the cowboy, including his saddle type and his horse—the 14.2 to 15.2 hand, heavily muscled cow pony. This influence would continue to cast its spell over amateur riders around the world for more than a hundred years. In 1998, the United States Equestrian Team (whose members had previously competed exclusively in English disciplines riding flat saddles) would succumb, expanding their ranks to include the stylized discipline of reining—maneuvers distilled from the work a cowboy and his horse performed in handling cattle.

The horse best suited to life in the West was similar to the cavalry-man's mount, both horses performing many jobs. There was also another similarity: Both cavalryman and cowboy came to realize that the best all-around horses fell within a fairly narrow size range, 15 to 16 hands. Larger horses were not "good doers" and smaller horses just didn't have the length of leg for sustained speed.

It was common practice for ranchers to try to improve the local wild horse herds by turning out blooded stallions to mate with the wild mares, then harvesting the offspring to use in ranching and farming and to sell to the United States Army as remounts. Before this could be done, however, the herd stallion had to be shot, because no stallion raised in captivity was considered to be the equal to his wild cousin in a fight for herd supremacy.

Out of the forge of the Southwest emerged a type of horse eventually known as the American Quarter Horse. Founded with Thoroughbred blood, the Quarter Horse breed was also influenced by crosses to mustangs and Mexican Vaquero horses descended from the Spanish Barb. In the East, the Quarter Horse was popular primarily as a short-distance race horse, but in the West, the iron of its heritage subjected to the fire of daily work, turned the breed into steel; producing a horse strong enough to stop a 1,000 pounds of steer, fast enough to catch a "bunch quitter" and able to turn on a dime.

Open ranges meant horses and riders could be out for months working hundreds of square miles. Each cowboy might have six or more horses in his string, which he was responsible for training and conditioning. These horsemen took pride in the ability of the horses in their string, and it was a fighting offense to ride a man's horse without his permission.

Often, cowboys rode horses provided by their employers. Many ranches used rough stock, directly off the range, and a large outfit often hired a bronc buster, a rider whose sole job was to break horses to saddle. It took six to seven years to turn a horse into a top roping or cutting horse. New hands were assigned a string, but were not told anything about their horses, part of the employment test being to see if the man could sort out and ride the horses assigned to him.

In 1940, the American Quarter Horse Association was formed and the breed coalesced under its auspices. To qualify for registry, early horses

CON HAFFMAN'S PHOTOGRAPHY, TEMECULA, CA

Cowboys and horses are still at work today on many ranches.

had to meet certain bloodline standards and also performance standards, including running a quarter mile in 23 seconds. Wimpy, owned by the King Ranch, was named Grand Champion of the Southwestern Exposition and Fat Stock Show in Fort Worth, Texas, and given number one in the new stud book. Today the American Quarter Horse is known for its versatility and good temperament and has been exported around the world, where riders have used the horse in almost every equestrian discipline.

In Vermont, the daily demands of the young nation were also met by a unique type of horse, which came to be known as the Morgan. Like the progenitor of the Quarter Horse, Figure, the first Morgan, was thought to trace his history to an import sired by a Thoroughbred whose lines traced back to one of the three English foundation Arabians. The breed eventually became known by the surname of the man who owned Figure at the time, Justin Morgan.

Figure's first owner was, appropriately, as much a jack-of-all-trades as his horse was reputed to be; Morgan was a teacher, a successful composer and a tavern keeper as well. Life could be as harsh in the hills and valleys of Vermont as it was in the vast Southwest. Horses were used as basic transportation. They were ridden, but much more frequently in the East they were driven about. Since farming was more prevalent than ranching, Eastern horses proved their versatility by pulling a plow and, in heavily wooded areas, clearing the land, dragging felled trees out of the forest. Figure performed all of these jobs with such ease that his reputation spread by word of mouth, until he was known throughout the state and into neighboring states.

He was described as having small ears, a broad forehead, large kind eyes, tapered muzzle, expressive nostrils and an arch to the neck, which was set on a well-angled shoulder. His chest was broad, the back short, the body compact and muscular with flat, dense bone. Figure's walk and trot easily left other horses in the dust. The stories of his endurance ran to mythical proportions, but time and the fact that the breed has excelled in both competitive and endurance riding as well as in the demanding sport of combined driving, would suggest that the stories were firmly rooted in reality. He could also jump very well and run, yet was gentle to handle. Black Hawk and Ethan Allen, both Morgan horses, were successful harness racers, establishing formidable records early in the history of the sport of harness racing. Most importantly, Figure was a prepotent sire, a stallion who passed his many diverse abilities to his offspring down through the generations.

SUZY LUCINE

The repeat World Champion Morgan stallion Born to Boogie, owned by Lynn Peeples of Waterford Farm, Buttzville, New Jersey.

In *A Morgan History*, Sue Brander writes, "Toward the end of the [19th] century, Morgans distinguished themselves on the battlefield, when the First Vermont Cavalry was mounted mainly on Morgans and 1,100 Morgans left Vermont for the Civil War. Only 200 returned home. At the Battle of Gettysburg, the First Vermont Cavalry charged uphill and over stone walls into a fusillade of Confederate gunfire. Others had tried and failed. The Morgans took the hill. They drove through the First Texas Division, cutting General Lee's supply line. As a result, Lee withdrew from the field, ending the Battle of Gettysburg. Had the Morgans failed in that heroic charge, Lee might have continued the battle and won a clear victory. He would have had a clear march to Washington and the Civil War might well have ended sooner and quite differently."

Published in 1857, D. C. Linsley's *Morgan Horses* was the earliest book documenting the history of Justin Morgan and America's first breed. In 1907, the United States Department of Agriculture established the American Morgan Horse Farm in Weybridge, Vermont, for the breeding and preservation of the Morgan horse. The farm was taken over in 1951 by the State of Vermont, which changed the name to the University of

Vermont Morgan Farm. In 1985, a pair of Morgans represented the United States in the World Pairs Driving Championships in Sandringham, Britain, and the United States Postal Service issued commemorative stamps depicting the Morgan horse.

The individuality that so marks our nation's personality resonates today through the versatility of the horses and the riders on today's fields of "battle": the competitive arenas and the roads and trails of our land. Today's all-around horse and rider work together in the same close partnership, mastering multiple skills, pushing the limits of the athletic envelope at all its edges. They are resistant to the siren songs of awards based on fashion, unwilling to sacrifice functional form in favor of stylistic exaggeration— knowing that to do so robs them both of the ability to excel at the ultimate challenge of supreme all-around champion. They claim their entitlement to tomorrow's prize, by the virtue of survival of the fittest.

EQUESTRIAN
REPORT CARD

Safety	A
Stable Management	C
Horsemanship	B+
Equitation	C+
Training	B-
Saddlery	A-
Farriery	C+

BETHANY CASKEY

Chapter 2

Determining Where You Stand Now

*W*hen you are planning a journey, having a clear idea of where you intend to go is only a part of what you need. If you want to get to your destination without spending a lot of time being lost or stuck in a dead end, it is equally important to know precisely where you are starting from and how that relates to where you eventually want to end up—next door, next town, next state, across a continent or across an ocean.

For some, riding and horse ownership can begin as a spur-of-the-moment decision that results in either owning or being aboard a big, powerful, potentially dangerous yet wonderful, intriguing and inspiring creature. Then slowly, or perhaps with lightning speed, you discover your "casual ride" through sweet-smelling fields of innocent ignorance is at an end when you realize you need more information so you can help your equine partner, advance your skills or protect yourself from injury. And, more often then not, you needed it yesterday!

Learning about horses is a lifelong pursuit, as any well-rounded horseman or horsewoman will tell you. The fact that you can literally spend a lifetime involved with horses, and continue to learn and be taught by them the entire time, is one of the many aspects of the interaction that draws people into the relationship in the first place. Horses can be wonderful, exciting, memorable, intelligent, gentle, intuitive, demanding, frustrating, thought-provoking, frightening, exhilarating, irritating, aggressive, timid, comical, endearing, labor-intensive, heart-breaking, bone-breaking beasts. What they *never* are is boring.

To acquire the knowledge you'll need to enjoy your journey with your horse, you'll need two things. The first is a basis for comparison, and the second is a way to organize information. To begin to acquire the first, you should spend as much time as possible soaking up the sights and sounds of a wide array of horse-related activities. The images you take away with you from each event and/or discipline will form a base from which you will build your foundation of learning, or deepen and broaden your understanding. This base will provide a reference library of comparative values. While it may be time-consuming to accomplish, in most cases there is no deadline by which you must have viewed every discipline, and it is the cheapest education you will get in the field.

The second element, a way to organize information, is contained in these pages. In this chapter, you are invited to begin by getting an idea of the depth of your present knowledge. Equally important to those who seek the ultimate title of all-around horseman or horsewoman is the challenge of becoming aware of the view your present position affords you of the horse and his world. You can best begin your exploration of that question with the foundation topic of guardianship. Not owning a horse won't excuse you from this class. If you come in contact with horses, you will want to improve your skills of observation and communication. Shouldering the responsibilities of horse guardianship, even in your imagination, is an important step in your learning process. Thinking you know everything there possibly is to know on that topic is a sure indication that you have some significant hurdles to jump before you can win the title of all-around.

Guardianship

To be a good horse guardian and caretaker, there are myriad skills and layers of knowledge that must be absorbed. Some are simple to master with exposure to crucial information—for example, horses need regular dental care—then locating and contacting the professionals who can provide these specialized services for you. But who would have thought that horses need *dentists*? Don't veterinarians do that?

Well, hang on, because you are about to jump on the carousel of equestrian knowledge, where you will seldom find straight yes or no answers. The longer you ride, the more you will learn that the terms *correct, right* and *best* almost always have a qualifier attached. And if they don't, these absolutes can mislead, with the consequences being injury to you or the horse.

The Horse's Mouth

Up-to-date equestrian caregivers know a balanced mouth can affect their horse's ability to chew his food, accept and comfortably carry a bit and move in a supple, balanced manner. Head shaking or tossing, rearing, refusing to be bridled, rough transitions between gaits, inability to flex or come on the bit when being ridden, stiffness or "sidedness" when working under saddle, weight loss, poor coat, anxiety and colic can all be symptoms of problems in your horse's mouth.

An equine veterinarian and an equine dentist are *not* the same thing. All vets have limited exposure to dental procedures (commonly known as *floating*) during their training, but unless they have extended their studies into the specialty field of dentistry, most are not prepared to perform the extensive dental work of a trained equine dentist. Horses should be checked by an equine dentist once a year.

You wouldn't go to a surgeon or an internist if you needed a dental crown or wanted a tooth pulled, but unless you know the difference between what the average vet does when he floats teeth and the jobs an equine dentist can perform, you may well find yourself in the position of a loving horse owner I know whose mare was several hundred pounds underweight, despite having her teeth floated regularly for 10 years by her veterinarian. When I suggested she have the mare examined by a dentist, it was discovered her back teeth were so ramped she could hardly chew. As soon as the mare's dental problems were relieved, with no changes in diet or work, she gained back the weight she had lost, returning to the normal condition and state of health she had enjoyed in previous years.

Do You Know?

It is not at all uncommon for mature horses to have one or more hidden wolf teeth. Also called permanent premolars, these teeth lie right up against the horse's premolars and sometimes fail to erupt through the gum. Invisible wolf teeth can be the cause of great discomfort when the reins, acting on the bit, bring it back in the horse's mouth and put pressure against these teeth.

Pop Quiz

You'll find the answers to all the Pop Quizzes in this chapter in the Appendix.

Novice

1. You can get an approximation of a horse's age by looking in his mouth and examining his teeth. True or False?

2. Horses fed hay and grains rather than grazing on grass pasture need dental work more often because the silica in grass naturally grinds down a horse's teeth. True or False?

3. Drooling in horses is normal and is not an indication of a problem in the mouth. True or False?

Intermediate

1. Pressing your thumb firmly against the gum of the horse just above the front teeth to blanch the skin, then noting the amount of time it takes for the blood to return and bring the gum color back to pink is a diagnostic procedure that can indicate dehydration or shock. True or False?

2. Horses do not have temporary teeth when they are young, as humans do, but keep the same teeth throughout their lifetime. True or False?

3. Canine teeth are found in all horses. True or False?

Advanced

1. *Points* refer to the shape of a horse's tooth and are undesirable. True or False?

2. Corner incisors usually erupt around two years of age. True or False?

3. As horses age, their teeth change from rectangular to triangular. True or False?

All-around rider homework assignment: Locate and accompany an equine dentist to observe him practicing his profession for one day.

No Foot, No Horse

Not all horse knowledge is as easy to acquire as knowing the difference between a veterinarian and a dentist. If you own a horse, chances are you have him shod periodically, which means you deal with farriers. Hypothetically, it is easy to understand that not all craftsmen are created equal. But when we employ a professional, it is fair for us to assume they know their trade. And in the case of horses, we also assume they have an understanding of the biomechanics of the animals on whom they work.

That assumption, without verification, can be a critical mistake. In the case of a farrier, we are depending on this craftsman not only for our horse's shoes, but in some cases for his very soundness, since an unbalanced hoof or a misaligned bony column can make a horse lame in a relatively short period of time. In an extreme situation, it is possible for poor judgment or lack of an eye for hoof balance and/or movement to impair the horse for an entire career!

There are practitioners and there are *gifted* practitioners. The men and women in the latter category are those whose interests and studies have carried them far beyond the basic skills required to nail a steel or aluminum shoe on a horse's hoof. The challenge begins when we realize that if we want the best for our horse partner, it is going to be up to us to distinguish between the good, the bad and the ugly. This means we must add the ability to assess our horse's feet—the quality, shape, size (relative to the norm and also relative to each other) and health—to the mountain of information we must acquire.

Those who want to take on the challenge of creating an all-around performer need to go even further in their own education. Since you will become your horse's personal body training coach, you will need to be familiar with additional information, such as your horse's stance (at rest and while eating from the ground), as well as how he moves his feet at all gaits, with and without the influence of a rider on his back. Why? Because no one will know your horse as well as you do—or should.

Which leg a horse extends when lowering his head to the ground to graze or eat and whether he varies the leg or always extends the same one may be a clue in detecting a condition of muscular imbalance commonly referred to as "short leg syndrome." The imbalance can also be detected in the front legs by standing a horse on a flat, solid surface, such as a concrete pad or wood floor. Position the legs square to one another and at each corner of the horse, with each limb bearing weight, and keep the horse's spine in a straight line by positioning the head and neck straight. Now, observe the height of the inner points of each knee relative one to the others. If an imaginary line drawn from the inside point of one knee to the inside point of the opposite knee is not level, there is an imbalance in your horse that will affect his movement and performance abilities.

Seldom are these imbalances due to true bone length difference. Rather, they are the result of muscular changes in the torso of the horse due to moving in a crooked manner and/or hoof length or shape differences. The reason for the observed imbalance will influence how you approach returning your horse to a balanced state, but left unresolved the condition can have a negative affect on a horse's soundness over time.

If you wish to prepare the all-around athlete, you need to know your horse's strengths. You must also understand any weakness inherent in his conformation. Then, in conjunction with your specialist (farrier), you will both make the decision about what should be done to help your equine athlete excel in the discipline at which you currently have the horse pointed: which shoes will best fit the job, what might need to be done to overcome any temporary stress-related changes in the hoof, etc.

Is it necessary to become a farrier yourself? Not really, but the more you demand from your horse partner in the way of performance, the more important it will be that you make sure he is given every advantage to perform the jobs required of him without undue stress to his physical or emotional systems. Physical and mental stress can easily result from being forced to walk 10 miles while wearing a shoe with a four-inch heel on one foot, while the other foot is fitted with a running shoe.

Do You Know?

Not all hoof dressings are the same. Some dressings are designed to moisturize the hoof, helping to maintain or restore its resiliency during seasonal dry spells, while other types of hoof dressings are used to seal out excess moisture during long periods of wet weather.

Horses can lose shoes more easily when the weather changes from wet to dry, or vice versa, and their feet either dry out too quickly or are continuously exposed to wet ground or marshy conditions. Be sure to buy and apply the hoof dressing that's appropriate for both your horse's foot and the conditions he is experiencing.

Pop Quiz

Novice

1. Horses' feet need to be trimmed or reshod an average of every six to eight weeks. True or False?

2. The front feet of a healthy horse will tend to have a different shape than the back feet. True or False?

3. No horse who has to carry a rider should go without shoes. True or False?

Intermediate

1. The nails that are used to keep a shoe on your horse's foot are driven into the part of the foot known as the *bars*. True or False?

2. Turning a horse out to unlimited time on grass pasture can have a negative effect on his feet. True or False?

3. Seedy toe is an infection of the area of the hoof known as the "white line." True or False?

Advanced

1. The ideal pastern axis, when shoeing or trimming a horse, is considered to be 55 degrees. True or False?

2. A horse who exhibits navicular syndrome should be trimmed and shod long in the toe and low in the heel. True or False?

3. A hoof with an overly high moisture content tends not to hold a shoe well. True or False?

All-around horse and rider homework assignment: Attend an informational seminar or lecture offered for farriers, or spend a day observing a farrier working at an accredited school or veterinary hospital.

Why Diet Is a Four-Letter Word!

If you got a puppy or a kitten, finding the right diet for your new companion wouldn't be extremely challenging or time consuming. You can buy commercially produced dry or canned food or a specialized diet from your vet, or you could be extremely involved and research what ingredients go into making up a complete and balanced diet, and then cook up your own concoction to feed your pet. You would probably realize that feeding a puppy or a kitten is different from feeding an adult, and as the animal got older, you could adjust her diet to accommodate aging. But none of these nutritional changes would present a challenge, because the pet food industry is huge, and more than one company has figured out how to entice pet owners into parting with more of their money.

When feeding a horse, you need to consider all these different nutritional requirements as well. But unless you run sled dogs or do some serious hunting with your dogs, you're not likely to find yourself in the category of most horse owners: figuring out what foods are needed according to their horse's type of work, housing and the weather. To further complicate matters, unless you fall into the small percentage of horse owners who can keep their horse(s) at home, at least some of what makes up your horse's daily diet is not under your control. The foods are selected by the owner or manager of the facility where your horse is housed. Moreover, unless your boarding facility buys in quantity, there is going to be a constant turnover in hay, the horse's main food source, which means there is the potential for a constant variation in such vital nutrients as protein and carbohydrates, as well as negative elements such as dust, mold, weeds and foreign objects.

Want to get a headache? Visit a large tack shop and consider all of the many additives and supplements for your horse that are offered by the various manufacturers. There are regular vitamin supplements, special conditioners for the coat and the feet, fly control feed additives, mood regulators, feed additives for joint mobility and prolonged soundness—the list is endless. How is one to decide?

Let's start with a question. Do you know your basics about feeding the animal called a horse? You should know that hay is the horse's primary source of nourishment and, no matter what type, should be clean, dust free, weed free and sweet smelling. You also need to know that different types of hay meet different nutritional requirements, and that brings us back to the foal versus mature horse versus pensioner and working horse versus couch potato, and we won't even go into pregnancy—but *you* will need to if you breed your horse.

You should know that water must be supplied in quantity and should always be clean and fresh. Horses rely on taste and smell to assess the suitability of food substances, and can easily become disturbed by changes in water, especially when being transferred from place to place. Regularly adding a few tablespoons of apple cider vinegar to drinking water disguises subtle taste changes and will encourage the finicky

Do You Know?

Horses, like people, can be allergic to specific foods.

Under certain circumstances, various common food items can cause serious, life-threatening illnesses in the horse, including founder and colic.

Dusty or moldy feed can contribute to a condition known as heaves, which can cost your horse performance potential by reducing his ability to breathe.

Alfalfa hay, because it tends to have a high protein content, is not considered good hay for performance horses, especially if it is fed as their exclusive roughage. But it *is* good for pregnant and lactating mares.

When exposed to dampness, corn, a popular grain feed in some parts of the country, can become contaminated with a mold that is poisonous to horses. The affected kernels appear pink or reddish-brown. When in doubt, discard any feed that smells bad or shows signs of mold.

Oleander leaves and flowers, wilted red maple leaves, and Sudan grass are poisonous to horses.

Horses who have never been exposed to automatic waterers are sometimes frightened by the hissing sound of the water entering the bowl, and may refuse to drink out of it as a result.

It only takes about 24 hours without water to set the stage for impaction colic.

horse to continue to maintain a healthy state of hydration during travel or when stabled in strange surroundings.

You should know that salt is a requirement, and when provided in block form it should be checked regularly to see if your horse is using it (some horses won't take salt from a salt block). You should know that some types of feed (sugars, corn, oats) affect the mood of some horses. You should also know that horses, especially performance horses, are subject to ulcers that can rob the horse of his ability to thrive, cause behavioral problems and reduce his ability to perform. While the cause of ulcers in horses is still under investigation by medical researchers, it is known that ignorance of the rules of what, how and when to feed your horse can contribute to them.

Pop Quiz
Novice

1. Water should be withheld before a grain feeding so stomach juices don't become diluted. True or False?

2. The best feeding schedule for stabled horses is four times a day. True or False?

3. It is best for horses to be fed from the ground, even if the ground is sandy. True or False?

Intermediate
1. It is best to give a horse very cold water to drink immediately following hard exercise, to bring his internal temperature down as quickly as possible. True or False?

2. It is important to know where the hay you feed has come from, so you know if it is lacking in essential minerals such as iodine and selenium. True or False?

3. A horse's rations should be fed by volume, not weight. True or False?

Advanced

1. Calcium and phosphorus are two minerals of great importance in the horse's diet. True or False?

2. Stalled horses should get exposure to sun whenever possible because they synthesize vitamin D in their skin in response to ultraviolet light. True or False?

3. Lack of salt can cause decreased appetite and weight loss. True or False?

All-around rider course book recommendation: *Horse Owner's Veterinary Handbook,* Second Edition, by James Giffin, MD, and Tom Gore, DVM, Howell Book House.

Home Is Where the Barn Is

How much thought do you have to give to a horse's housing? You either board them or you keep them at home, end of story. Not quite. To make a choice about the best accommodations for your equine partner, you need to get to know the horse. Let's look at some of the issues that a good all-around horse guardian should be aware of. You can start with the knowledge that horses are herd animals and, as such, usually prefer company to isolation. When deprived of the company of their own kind, some will develop aberrant behavioral patterns, which can range from aggressive personalities to stable vices such as weaving.

In addition, horses have preferences in all manner of things, and that includes who they like and don't like as neighbors. If you want your horse to have a relaxing home environment, you need to know that his next-door neighbor isn't the barn bully—a horse who is constantly threatening your animal. It is also important that feeding buckets, hay mangers and other places where daily food rations are deposited are not close to one another (for example, the stall on the right has the manger in its front left-hand corner, while the stall on the left has the manger in its front right-hand corner). This is especially true if the solid portion of the divisional walls only goes part way to the ceiling, enabling a horse to see his neighbor(s) while eating.

Aggressive horses can bully timid horses with nothing more than body language. If your horse is housed next to an aggressive horse, he is liable to become anxious and experience a personality change, especially if he has a timid or sensitive nature. If his next-door neighbor weaves, cribs or windsucks, your horse can easily learn to copy the behavior. And once that behavior is set, it is almost impossible to correct and can lead to serious physical soundness issues.

A good barn manager will separate horses whose personalities clash. Determining such an issue doesn't require the assistance of a clairvoyant. Simply stand at some distance and watch the body language exchanged between any two horses over several minutes to several hours. In addition, broken boards, bent rails and scarred stall walls (from kicking) tell important tales of discontent and/or conflict.

All horses enjoy the freedom to run and play, at least occasionally, and while most horses adapt more easily than might be thought to being confined part of each day to what (given how they were designed to be in their "wild" or natural state) must feel like "jail cells," some horses can *not* tolerate being in a stall or small paddock without becoming excessively agitated, pawing and/or constantly moving about the area (referred to as *stall walking*). Placing such a horse in a very large paddock (half an acre at least) or pasture, in sight of or in the company of other horses, may be the only way to provide him with an environment in which he will not self-destruct, but thrive.

A stall that shares a wall with an indoor arena where a lot of activity takes place can easily produce a high level of stress in some equine occupants. Since the stalled horse cannot see what is causing the sounds he can hear, his feeling of danger is heightened. Since he has no way of escaping his enclosure and the proximity of the unknown danger, he may become alarmed and agitated any time he hears horses and riders working on the other side of the stall wall.

A good barn smells fresh and clean. A strong ammonia odor is a sure sign of a management problem. The barn or pasture environment where horses are kept (their home) needs to offer some comfort, appropriate food in appropriate amounts fed at regular times, shelter from the elements and a choice of whether to be in or out, if at all possible. If it's an enclosed space, it must have good ventilation without being drafty, lots of light (preferably natural whenever possible) and offer safety, as well.

It is unusual today for small, enclosed equine spaces to have only dirt flooring, but if that is the case where your horse lives, the floor may need regular maintenance to be kept level. Failing to tend to what may at first seem like a minor item can result in your horse constantly being forced to stand with his weight resting unevenly on legs and hooves. Over a period of time, this can cause excessive wear on joints, tendons and ligaments. It's an easy thing to miss, because bedding frequently covers the floor of most stalls, preventing a quick examination. Rubber mats over dirt will not prevent a floor from acquiring high and low spots as the horse moves around his stall over time.

Concrete or other hard surfaces alone are not the solution, as these do not offer any cushion to a horse's legs. If a floor is made from a hard, unyielding material, it should be covered with stall mats to provide adequate cushioning to the horse's limbs.

Ceilings and doorways need to be high enough to ensure that horses don't injure their heads if they rear. Electrical equipment needs to be well out of reach, and light fixtures should be recessed *and* protected with some type of barrier to prevent inquisitive equine lips from remedying an afternoon's boredom by removing lightbulbs. Ditto for watering systems, whether floats or faucets. A bored horse is one of God's most creative critters.

Do You Know?

The shavings or sawdust from black walnut trees are poisonous to horses, and using them as bedding can cause laminitis.

You should be able to expect the following from your boarding facility:

- The stable isolates new arrivals for a period of time to protect current residents from communicable diseases.

- The stable requires a current negative Coggins test and proof of up-to-date vaccinations before a new horse is allowed to move in.

- Horses are fed clean, weed-free and mold-free hay at least twice a day.

- No smoking is allowed in or near the barns, and signs are posted to indicate that.

- Horses are always fed at the same time each day.

- All equine foodstuffs are stored so that they are protected from weather damage, mold contamination and/or damage by rodents.

- Stalls are cleaned once a day.

- Aisles are kept clean and neat.

- Fire extinguishers are located in obvious places, and are checked regularly to ensure they are working.

- The names of the horse, owner and veterinarian, with accompanying emergency telephone numbers, are posted on each stall or paddock.

- Flammable materials such as hay and bedding are stored in a separate building from the horses.

- Stalls are provided with sufficient bedding to enable horses to lie down without abrasions to fetlock joints and/or hocks.

- Stalls smell fresh and have no ammonia odor.

- The horses' feeders and automatic waterers or water buckets are kept clean and free of mold, slime, decomposing feed and/or foreign articles.

- The facility gives you a five-day grace period before charging a late fee on board.

- The facility has an all-weather arena large enough to accommodate its boarders and clients safely and comfortably.

- Stable help/stall cleaners at the barn are knowledgeable horse handlers and like horses.

- Stable grounds are kept neat and clean and have no poisonous shrubs or plants.

- A halter and lead rope is available for each horse in the immediate area of his stall.

- The facility posts the rules in an easy-to-read location and enforces them.

- All dogs must be on a leash at all times, or dogs are not allowed.

- Mangers or feeding areas are free of sharp edges and are in good repair.

- There are no protruding nails, wood splinters, exposed wires or other dangerous items in the horse's stall.

- Aisles, stalls, tack rooms, arena and turn-out areas are well lit.

- There is a safe area for loading and unloading horses from trailers.

- If lessons are given regularly, boarders may either ride in the arena during lessons or have an arena of their own in which they may work.

- The managers are friendly and courteous.

- The horses are in good condition and happy.

- Necessary repairs get done quickly.

- The stable has a fire escape plan and a veterinarian on call.

An upscale boarding facility should offer these additional comforts, conveniences and services:

- Three roughage feeds a day.

- Private, lockable tack storage.

- Someone on the premises 24 hours a day.

- Stalls are either cleaned once and picked once daily, or they are cleaned twice a day.

- Turn out areas and/or pastures are regularly picked up or harrowed to spread manure.

- There are regular, seasonal on-site vaccination and dental clinics.

- There is a safe, clean place with good footing and good light to bathe a horse, clean and treat wounds, and so on.

- There is a sheltered, designated, safe area, away from distracting activity where a farrier or veterinarian can work.

- The stable has a resident riding instructor.

- The stable has at least one resident trainer.

- The stable allows outside or guest instructors to give lessons.

- The stable allows outside trainers to work with a horse at the owner's request.

- The facility has different arenas for different activities.

- The stable has an area where horses can be safely turned out to work off excess energy without tying up the general working area or arena.

- The stable offers top-quality hay.

- The stable offers a choice and/or a variety of hays.

- The stable offers blanketing and turn-out services.

- Strangers are not allowed to wander around the barns or feed the horses without the owner's permission.

- There is a boarder's lounge and a bulletin board.

- There are clean, well-stocked bathroom facilities.

- The footing in arenas is good, deep enough and worked regularly.

- There are salt block holders in the stalls.

- The stable offers trailer parking.

- Management will adjust the horse's stall assignment to accommodate the horse's mental and emotional needs and the needs of his neighbors.

- The facility owner/manager is a knowledgeable horseman/woman and obviously cares about the horses under their supervision.

- Safe areas with grounded outlets are provided for grooming and clipping.

- Stalls are roomy, bright and airy.

- Stalled horses are not cut off from visual contact with other horses.

Pop Quiz
Novice

1. Barbed wire is not a good fencing material for areas that house horses. True or False?

2. Horses who must be confined to a stall do not do well in an area less than 16 feet square. True or False?

3. Stalls only need to be cleaned and rebedded once every other day if the horse can move freely in and out to a paddock. True or False?

Intermediate

1. The dust and fumes from lime are detrimental to horses and it should not be used in any facility where horses are housed. True or False?

2. Open stable doors and gates fully before walking a horse in or out of an area, to prevent injury. True or False?

3. Crossties are the best way to secure horses for grooming in a stable, especially if they are young and not used to being handled. True or False?

Advanced

1. Cobwebs in barns constitute one of the biggest fire hazards. True or False?

2. Shavings, rather than straw, is the best bedding for horses. True or False?

3. Good stable hands are important to a horse's physical well-being, but will have little or no impact on the horse's emotional well-being. True or False?

All-around rider homework assignment: Visit three or four different stabling facilities in your area. Be a detective with your eyes, ears and nose to determine if the facility is providing a safe, enjoyable, quality-of-life environment for both its human and equine customers. Take notes, making a list of the things you liked and the things you didn't find appealing or attractive. Notice the attitude of the horses who are housed on the premises.

Tack and Equipment

It is impossible to own or ride a horse without also needing to handle the equipment that accompanies the sport. Acquainting yourself with the various items of tack needed to ride and train horses is essential to both good performance and good care skills, and aiming for the goal of all-around performer means you'll have even more stuff with which to familiarize yourself.

The most common items—halter, bridle, saddle with a cinch or girth and saddle pad—seem simple enough to learn about, at least on the surface. But a quick perusal of a major equestrian catalog demonstrates the extremely wide range of selections. The Dover Saddlery catalog, for example, which features equipment primarily for the hunter/jumper and dressage specialties, has illustrations of 45 different girths, 12 types of stirrups, 20 types of stirrup leathers, more than 60 different saddle pads, more than 80 saddles and 167 bits! These overwhelming numbers are reduced a bit if you isolate a discipline; for instance, if you limit your search to a dressage saddle, you can reduce the number of choices from 80 to 28. Each discipline has at least a few pieces of specialty equipment and, of course, a saddle type.

So how does one go about selecting from 28 saddles and 167 bits? Remember the recommendation to observe various types of equine competition? Part of what you want to look for while you're at these various events is the type of equipment the competitors commonly use.

Another good place (because most are free) to begin acquainting yourself with various types of tack and equipment are tack catalogs, both general ones and those specific to a discipline. You may not understand what each and every item is for, but most come with some type of written explanation, such as "indestructible nylon-reinforced rubber feeder," or "a new concept in reins, single lacing offers a better grip," or "stretch leather over a deep seat means extra security when riding cross country." Many catalogs also include good photographs of the equipment, and today's trend is to include performance shots, so a good, observant, all-around detective can gather clues as to how the various pieces of equipment *should* look when applied to their own horse.

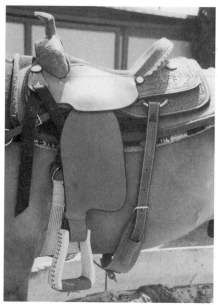

A well-made, well-balanced, all-purpose English saddle, the DSS Synergist is suitable to jumping, cross-country, dressage, pleasure and trail riding. Desirable design features include wide panels, a wide spinal channel and a level seat.

A good example of a working or pleasure Western saddle shows correct stirrup placement and a balanced, level seat area.

Knowing *what* is much easier than knowing why, when and how. That information will come through exposure and more study, but there are a few basic rules about saddles and bits that apply across all disciplines.

Saddles

There are three basic saddle types (excluding sidesaddles), and several subtypes.

1. English

   all purpose

   dressage

   endurance

   hunter

   jumper

   polo

   racing

   saddle seat

Do You Know?

When trying out a new (to you) saddle, move around, don't just sit in one spot. Can you lean right, left, twist around and reach back to touch your horse's croup, stand up, lean forward and touch his ears, all with an equal feeling of balance and freedom?

If a saddle makes you feel as though you are nailed to one spot and can't move, sitting in a chair with your feet out in front of you, losing your balance forward or forcing your hips toward the front of the saddle, the problem may be seat style or design, seat size or fit (the saddle is not sitting level on the horse's back).

2. Western

   barrel racing

   cutting

   endurance

   parade

   reining

   roping

   show/equitation

   trick riding

3. McClellan, a military cavalry saddle

   Saddle Rule #1: No matter what type of saddle you choose, you must address the suitability of the saddle to the job to be performed, to the back of the horse and to the size, weight, leg length and gender of the rider.

   If you do not pay close attention to detail in the area of saddle selection and fitting, it is a sure bet you will handicap both your performance and your horse's. While equipment that helps both athletic partners do a better job is a desirable addition to any goal, in the case of saddle selection, not having the right equipment can lead to accident, injury or unsoundness.

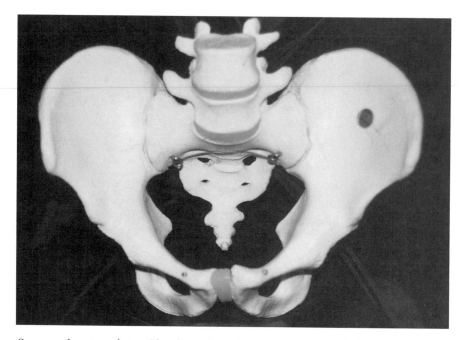

Compare these two photos. The photo above shows the "seat bones" of a woman's pelvis, and the photo below shows a man's pelvis. Notice the difference in structure and width, and the lower pubic arch (just below the spine) in the woman's pelvis. Knowledge of these details may help you understand why the shape and twist of the seat in a particular type of saddle may or may not work for you.

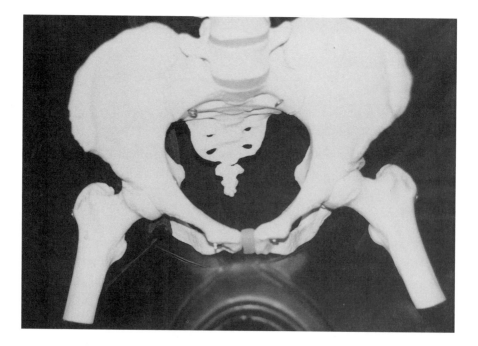

Saddle Rule #2: The majority of saddles have some type of "tree" (solid or semi-solid frame). Knowing why both the width of the tree and the angle of the bars is important to the fit factor is a *necessity!* The disciplines that require more aggressive athletic efforts from horse and rider are the ones with the least margin for error in saddle fit, and injury can and does occur when the horseman or horsewoman falls down in their responsibility in this area.

Saddle Rule #3: Horses' backs, being largely muscle, can be expected to change. The factors that most influence this change are correct preparatory training, type and amount of work, weight gain or loss, age, injury and pregnancy (in the case of mares). Just as a change of performance focus may necessitate a change of saddles, changes in the horse's back may also make it necessary to adjust or change your saddle. Keeping track of whether you and your horse are about to enter a dressage arena or run a barrel pattern is not a problem. Noticing the changes in your equine partner's back resulting from a weight gain or loss during a competitive season, or a loss of fitness during a winter layoff, is more of a challenge—but one the all-around horseman or horsewoman must meet.

Saddle Rule #4: If you have to "cut your horse in half" when tightening the cinch or girth to keep your saddle from losing its position on his back, the saddle is not a correct fit to your horse.

Sores created by a girth or cinch behind the horse's elbow, while not career ending, are painful and can sideline your horse at the most inopportune moments, so preventing them should be every horsewoman's goal. Checking your horse in this area before and after every ride will go a long way toward preventing sores from getting started or escaping your notice in the early stages.

The general rule for girth/cinch placement is three to four fingers behind the elbow of the horse. Unfit, green or fat horses are the most prone to girth galls, so good times to be extra vigilant are when you're returning a horse to work after a winter layoff, when you're first starting a young horse under saddle or when you're using a new saddle or girth/cinch.

Keeping tack clean and good grooming, which removes old dirt and sweat, especially in the area of the saddle and girth, should be standard practice.

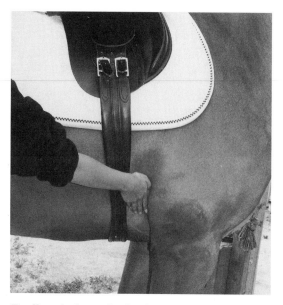

To allow the horse the freedom to move its front legs comfortably, your saddle should be designed and placed so the girth or cinch, when done up, allows the space of a hand between the front edge and the elbow of the horse.

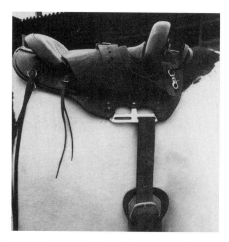

This Western saddle with latigo and cinch is set too far forward, impedes the elbow of the horse and could cause cinch sores.

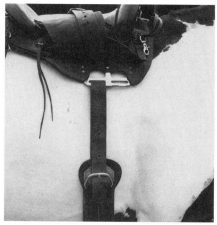

Adjusted to the rear-most position on the rigging ring, the cinch now allows the desired amount of clearance for the horse's elbow.

Bits

There are four basic types of bits (excluding hackamores). A bit type is defined not by the mouthpiece, but rather by where the bit allows or places the reins relative to the horse's mouth, which in turn governs where and how the horse experiences or "reads" pressure exerted by the rider's hand through the reins.

1. Snaffle: A snaffle bit offers a rider the greatest lateral control. Pressure is placed on the tongue, lips and/or bars of the horse's mouth. The reins are connected to the bit in a way that makes it easy for the horse to "read" the rein signal, responding by moving his nose, neck, feet and body in the direction of the pressure he experiences. The severity of the bit is governed by the type of the mouthpiece, modifying equipment such as a martingale and the rider's use of her hands. It is considered to be the mildest type of bit used in riding.

2. Curb: A curb offers a rider the most longitudinal control of the horse (that is, stopping power). It works in conjunction with a chin strap or chain in producing leverage, placing pressure on the horse's tongue, bars, chin groove and poll. The severity of the bit is governed by the type of mouthpiece, the length of the shank (specifically, the length of the shank below the mouthpiece relative to the length of the shank above the mouthpiece) and the rider's use of her hands. It is considered more severe than a snaffle.

3. Pelham: A pelham is a lever bit that also provides a rein attachment, which enables pressure from one rein to bypass the lever system, when desired. The bit attempts to blend both the

Two Western curb bits, showing different mouthpieces.

> ## Do You Know?
>
> If the roof of your horse's mouth has little or no arc to its structure (a shallow pallet), you may need to select a bit with a double-jointed mouthpiece to keep him comfortable and happy; a bit with a single joint is likely to jab the roof of the mouth whenever pressure is applied simultaneously on both reins.
>
> Horses with small muzzles often have small mouths and shallow pallets. A thick, hollow-mouthed snaffle, considered by many to be the mildest type of bit you can use, can be uncomfortable in a small mouth and may cause biting problems.

lateral and longitudinal control of a snaffle and a curb, and is best utilized by using two reins.

4. Gag: A gag is a bit that is designed to cause the mouthpiece to move up toward the soft pallet in a horse's mouth, exerting a lifting influence on the horse's head.

Pop Quiz
Novice

1. A cavesson is commonly found on English bridles. True or False?

2. To measure correct fit on an English bridle, two fingers should fit under the brow band without pulling the crown piece against the horse's ears. True or False?

3. To get an approximation of the correct stirrup length before mounting the horse, you can measure it against the length of your arm. True or False?

Intermediate

1. Rein stops are only needed with a standing martingale. True or False?

2. A bosal and a mechanical hackamore apply the same pressure points to the horse's skull. True or False?

3. The fender is a part of an English saddle. True or False?

Advanced

1. A balding girth can frequently cause chafing. True or False?

2. Girth straps, or billets, on English saddles are normally attached to the tree webs. True or False?

3. A center-fire rigging is the most common on Western saddles today. True or False?

All-around rider course book recommendation: *The Essential Book of Horse Tack and Equipment,* by Susan McBane, David & Charles.

Identifying Rider Performance Levels

Consider Yourself a Beginner Rider If:

You have never ridden before.

You have never been properly introduced to a horse and learned about his nature and what makes him tick.

You cannot properly tack a horse up (put on the saddle, bridle and other related gear of your specialty).

You do not know how to groom and handle a horse sagely and properly.

You do not know basic stable and arena etiquette.

Your riding experience has been limited to horses on rental strings.

You Qualify as a Novice Rider When:

You can catch, lead, groom and tack up your horse correctly and safely without assistance.

You know and perform basic safety procedures, such as checking your girth before and after you mount, without being reminded.

You can mount safely and correctly from a mounting block.

You can dismount correctly and safely.

You can perform an emergency dismount from a halt and a walk.

You can adjust your own stirrups and know how to determine their proper length.

You can ride in longitudinal balance at a walk, jog and posting trot, maintaining enough control of your horse so as not to interfere with other horses or riders in the arena.

You recognize and can pick up your posting diagonals.

You can halt your horse without undue force on the reins from the walk, the jog and the posting trot.

You can ride a correctly shaped circle.

You know and can steer your horse successfully through simple school figures (serpentines, diagonal change of rein, half circle and reverse, rollbacks) in walk and trot.

You Can Call Yourself an Intermediate Rider When:

You ride longitudinally and laterally centered at walk, jog, rising trot, canter or lope on both leads.

You are aware of your seat bones, where they are placed on the saddle and how much of your torso weight is distributed on each at any given moment.

You know how to care for your horse both before and after you ride, including knowing what tack the horse needs, how to apply and adjust it correctly and how to care for it.

You can ride a sitting trot or jog without stirrups and without bouncing.

You can name and identify the parts of a horse, the parts of a saddle (one discipline) and the parts of a bridle (one discipline).

You can ride in a group of riders and maintain control of your horse, both in an arena and on the trail.

You can perform an emergency dismount correctly and safely from a trot.

You can identify the type of bit your horse wears and know how and why it works.

You can correctly apply leg protection devices on the horse.

You can "feel" your horse through your hands and seat and can ride in a way that allows the horse freedom of movement, while still offering him guidance and support.

You are aware of your horse's mental attitude and body language as you ride.

You can ride in the saddles of two different disciplines comfortably, fine-tuning your position according to the discipline without sacrificing balance or security.

You Have Reached the Advanced Level When:

You can ride at all gaits in comfort and control, even on a green (unschooled) horse, both in an arena and on the trail.

You can ride a buck, shy or rear without losing your seat.

You can ride a horse through a sliding stop, spin and rollback.

You can ride a straight line at all gaits.

You can collect and extend a horse in all gaits.

You can ride over a course of three-foot jumps in good form and without using your horse's mouth or mane for balance.

You know how to fit a saddle and bridle, and select the appropriate bit for the horse and the work you want to do with him.

You can successfully prepare your horse for a six-hour trail ride and handle normally occurring obstacles such as crossing water, crossing under and over bridges, steep descents and climbs and narrow trails.

You use good safety practices at all times in the barn and when mounted.

You ride in a harmonious manner with your horse, improving his balance, understanding and obedience, and strengthening his physical condition each time you ride.

You Are a Horseman or Horsewoman When:

You respect the horse as an individual.

You consider the horse's perspective.

You put the welfare of the horse above your own desires or goals.

You realize you can spend your life learning about horses and still not know all there is to know.

Chapter 3

Setting Realistic Goals

*G*oals are usually chosen in one of three ways:

1. After a fair amount of thought

2. On the spur of the moment

3. Out of necessity

Each time you set a goal (whether intentional or through the uncon-scious process of daydreaming), you begin a process of refocusing your resources, including time, energy and money. Assuming you are not one of the few people who have an unlimited amount of all these items, choosing your equestrian goal(s) becomes a matter of some importance.

Goals: Learning Tools and Signposts of Progress

Goals lead us from one action to the next, from day to day, from year to year and from one discipline to another. For example, when you ride, the moment-to-moment goal of maintaining your balance and security gov-erns your choice of the groups of muscles you use in your body. The same goal of balance in the horse governs the cues or aids you give, according to what you feel in him and relative to your immediate task goal. Without any goals, you would be a passenger, much like most rental string riders who use the horse primarily as warm, fuzzy transportation for sightseeing.

The next step in the goal-setting process would be to complete the day's ride or schooling session with your horse in better physical condition (more supple, stronger and so forth) and with a better understanding of what is expected of him within your partnership. A goal for the week might be to have a horse who is stronger, while remaining content and happy in his work. A goal for the month would build on your hourly and weekly goals, refining his responses through repetitive patterns and expanding his performance skills (for example, from work at a walk and trot to work at a canter; from work on the flat to work over poles or cavaletti) as you gradually strengthen his body and educate his mind. Your yearly goal might be to continue to build on this foundation, adding exposure as an additional element—moving the horse to the next level of education and confidence by adding new sights, sounds and pressure performance situations to his learning experience. These might include work on the trail, work over obstacles, riding in competition and so forth.

Determining what you want out of your equestrian experiences and partnerships is important. For instance, if you fail to realize that your most important goal is the relaxed, shared companionship you enjoy when you are with your horse, you could well become involved in competition simply because "everyone else does it." Then, despite winning, you might feel frustrated, as if you aren't getting anywhere in your riding, because you are not accomplishing your true goal (since show environments seldom provide a relaxing setting where you and your horse can simply enjoy each other's company).

To achieve steady progress in your learning curve, it will be necessary not only to clearly identify your goals at the beginning of your journey with horses, but to examine them at regular intervals along the way, matching your original ideas, goals and dreams with the current realities of your life, while asking yourself the question "Am I having fun yet?" Taking the time to revisit your goals often (at least twice a year, and more often if you begin to feel burned out) is an important learning tool. Invite a trusted friend or mentor to go over them with you, especially if you should begin to feel as if you have become stuck and are making little or no progress toward what you think you want to accomplish.

Ms. X was a bright, funny, dedicated rider in her mid-40s who thought her most important equestrian goal was to compete in dressage at the Grand Prix level some day. She could be classified, at best, as a low intermediate rider, but she had the determination to improve and the financial resources to seek both a good mount and a qualified coach. The horse she selected was a 16.3-hand, heavy-boned, big-bodied warmblood with a huge stride at walk and trot. Her choice was a good one, because the horse she selected, having the disposition of a Labrador Retriever, didn't take her lack of skill or her equitation errors personally. He retained his low-key, friendly demeanor throughout their association, offering her his affection and friendship. The flaw that short-circuited Ms. X reaching her goal was her failure to take into account the fact that she only stood five feet, two inches tall. Her body also had accumulated physical issues that caused her pain when she put herself through the intense training regimen that her goals demanded. Her horse's laid-back attitude, while a strong positive in some respects, didn't help his performance when it came time for the more demanding collection of upper level work, which he found difficult and unappealing.

Here was a woman who had seemingly done all the right things. She selected a horse with big, judge-pleasing movement, she attended clinics to improve her understanding of the discipline's requirements, hired professionals to work with both her and the horse to improve their skills and much more. She even tried to address some of her physical issues with therapists, all in the quest of her goal. As an instructor and fellow horsewoman, I admired her gumption. As a rider whose body has also experienced its share of pain from injuries inflicted by a number of accidents in which horses landed on top of me, I winced inwardly as I watched her spine take a beating as she determinedly worked at a sitting trot, without reins or stirrups, during a longe lesson. Classical texts will tell you that such teaching methods (longeing a rider without stirrups and reins) produce good results, but the texts don't include the qualifiers, such as the fact that a horse used for a longe lesson should be balanced and elastic through the back or all you get is stiffer and tighter while your kidneys and spine are pounded into pulp; that the older you get, the less happily your back and spine respond to repeated concussion; and finally, that the Marquis de Sade was the one who invented that particular teaching technique.

Ms. X badly needed to revisit her goals, because despite bringing all her considerable resources to bear, she was failing to make any significant headway and was becoming increasingly frustrated with herself. When she finally did so, she was torn between acknowledging the limiting factors she was becoming increasingly aware of, and her desire to succeed once she had set her mind on a particular goal. She was also reluctant to give up the friendship that had grown between her and her horse.

Being successful at long-range goals means knowing how to quickly rebalance yourself if a short-term goal fails.

By examining her goals more closely, however, she was able to see that she actually had more than one goal. She enjoyed the company of a friendly, outgoing horse who responded to her, and she wanted to experience riding at the level of art. After redefining her riding goals, she acquired a smaller (16 hands) naturally round, Lusitano gelding with an infectious personality, whose training and type suited the baroque style of dressage, and she continues to explore the discipline that most calls to her heart. Back on the track to success, she is once again enjoying the journey. Competition has taken a back seat for the moment, but it is still very much within her reach should she decide it is still a desirable goal.

If you are a dreamer, you will find it easier to isolate and focus on long-term goals. If you are an organizer, you may spend more time thinking about, prioritizing and accomplishing the necessary daily, weekly and monthly short-term goals. In any equestrian endeavor, however, it is necessary to develop both short-term and long-term goals. Long-term goals lead you toward your dreams, stimulating and motivating you with a sense of expectation and adventure. They can influence your choice of horses and the order in which skills are learned and polished. Short-term goals get the work done. They promote daily improvement. A lack of goals can contribute to boredom, disappointment and depression, because it is impossible to feel good about accomplishments when you do not recognize them as such.

To help you understand the important part goal-setting plays in the overall picture of success, make a list of your personal goals. Then make another list of the goals you have for your horse. Break each list into short-term and long-term goals. Now make a list of your physical and emotional characteristics and your current skills. Do the same for your horse. Compare the lists. How closely do they match? If your main goal is to ride a Grand Prix jumper course and one of your horse's physical characteristics is that he measures 39 inches at the withers (a Mini), you already have an insurmountable obstacle built into the equation.

To avoid traveling toward a goal or dream that is impossible to attain, you will need to examine your goals and extract the things that mean the most to you, and maybe even the reasons behind those priorities. Is the anticipated adrenaline rush from the feel of a powerful horse leaving the ground and soaring over an oxer the hook that reels your imagination into the dream of being a Grand Prix rider? Or are you fascinated by the kind of bond between two different species that would prompt a horse to attempt to jump an obstacle of such size and width—something most horses would never do on their own? If you find your truth in the first statement, you may not be happy with the horse you have if he imposes limitations on you and your goals. If however, you discover that the second statement is the real reason behind your goal, it might be possible for you to succeed without a change in your present equine partner. You only need to revise the size of a Grand Prix fence according to the height of your equine athlete and then be content to participate in the action of the event from the end of a lead line or longe line—a less physically

Minis can get off the ground, as this playful little horse demonstrates, but dreaming of jumping five-foot fences on this guy wouldn't be a reasonable goal.

connected position than in the saddle to be sure, but not one that would diminish your appreciation of the efforts of your equine pal.

Repeated failure is a sign that your conscious or stated goals may not match your life imperatives (self-directives that can lock you out of the success you want for yourself and your horse). For example, a self-directive that states, "My friends won't like me if I beat them too many times" can sabotage the best-laid plans, bringing your hopes and dreams crashing down around your head. Making the lists I have recommended, and then checking them twice, will help you discover whether you are stuck in just such a holding pattern. And this will enable you to work through it, with some focus and time.

Paying attention to and clearly defining the short-term goals on your road to becoming a good all-around rider means learning to successfully identify the stepping-stones to your goals. When you have identified each step, it is much easier to appreciate when a step or skill is mastered or missing. When you are fully aware of and appreciate your small successes, if your long-term goal is delayed or derailed, your feelings of failure will be proportional to the facts—a mild disappointment. Better that than the crushing, suffocating depression that can rob you of all of the enjoyment of time spent with your horse for weeks and months at a time, and has been know to drive some riders away from the equestrian field all together.

All-around rider study exercise: Answer the following questions.

1. What do you want? What do you see (dream about) happening with you and your horse?

2. What do you expect accomplishing that goal will provide for you that you don't have now?

3. Is the goal stated in a positive way?

4. What has kept you from achieving that goal so far?

5. How do you plan to overcome those obstacles?

6. How and when will you reward yourself and/or your horse for making progress?

7. What do you expect the consequences to be if you fail?

8. Can you afford to pay that price? If not, how can you risk the attempt?

Choosing Goals That Flout the Odds

The very fabric of the nation we live in is woven with the idea that if you can dream it, you can do it. Cycling champion Lance Armstrong beat cancer and came back from death's door to win the most prestigious bicycle race in the world, the Tour de France, not once but five times. Tiger Woods, whom David Owen describes in his book *The Chosen One* as a "breakthrough athlete in America's most tradition bound and racially insensitive sport," changed not only the face of golf but the lives of thousands of children with his example of hard work, determination and good sportsmanship. The real-life examples set by these men leave no doubt of the meaning of the Bible verse that encourages people to push beyond their perceived limitations with the simple statement "If you had but the faith of a mustard seed." In the equestrian world, stories abound of those who made the seemingly impossible happen.

Two Who Beat the "It's the Expensive Horse Who Wins" Myth

Pieraz, an Arabian gelding purchased by Valerie Kanavy for $500 cash, became, through his owner's vision and dedication, a two-time endurance World Champion, winning the gold medal for his country in 1994 and 1996.

Farther back in history, a gray plow horse who was literally bought off a truck on his way to the slaughterhouse by international jumping rider Harry de Leyer would eventually become known as Snowman to his millions of show jumping fans, and win Horse of the Year at Madison Square Garden in 1958 and 1959—demonstrating how one person's vision changed, if not the world, then at least the world of one horse.

Two Who Defied Breed Performance Stereotypes

A mustang filly who was almost trampled to death during a roundup and was put up for adoption by the Bureau of Land Management was purchased by a compassionate young woman with an interest in trail riding. Besting hundreds of Arabians (the breed with the best track record in

Two-time World Champion endurance gold medalist Valerie Kanavy and Cash, her World Champion endurance horse.

endurance), Mustang Lady and Naomi Tyler not only won the A.E.R.C. National Middleweight Championship Title, but placed second in the famous, grueling, 100-mile one-day race over the Sierra Nevada Mountains, known as the Tevis Cup. The prelude to both of those remarkable accomplishments in 1990 was also a postscript: After being selected to compete in the Pan Am Endurance Championships, the pair helped their team win a bronze medal in 1989 and again in 1991!

At the 1960 Grand National Horse Show and Rodeo at the Cow Palace in San Francisco, the men on the runaway favorite breed to win the Working Cow Horse Championship, the Quarter Horse, never saw her coming. A tall, lanky, long-legged woman astride a little bay mare stole the title right out from under their collective noses. The mare was Ronteza, an Arabian whom Sheila Varian had bred and trained. The event created quite a stir, because not only was Ronteza the first Arabian ever to win the title, but Sheila Varian was the first woman to capture the title as well!

Two Riders Who Refused to Believe the "Big Is Better Than Little" Myth

Succeeding at accomplishing her goals while having to overcome some serious stereotyping from much of the rest of her equestrian contemporaries, three-day event rider Maryann Tauskey qualified herself and her horse, the diminutive 15.1-hand Marcus Aurelius, for a spot on the 1976 U.S. Equestrian Team, then won a gold medal.

Lendon Gray likewise refused to bow to the dressage world's preference for big horses. She competed with the 14.2-hand Seldom Seen at the National Grand Prix Championship in Kansas City, making the crowd-pleasing little horse a poster child for the sound training philosophy that teaches that good dressage is good dressage, regardless of the size of the horse. In the process, the pair became the standard-bearers for thousands of riders with an interest in the discipline but no desire to trade in their present horse for an SUV-size model in order to succeed in front of a judge.

Most horses who are structurally well balanced (and a few who aren't), of average size (between 13 hands and 16 hands), reasonably athletic and possessed of a good mind and temperament are capable of doing well in a multitude of performance specialties. With the right preparation and rider, they can succeed locally, regionally, state wide, even nationally within a breed specialty if not always in open or international competition.

The All-Around Horse Who Almost Wasn't!

The story of a 15-hand horse named The Kopper Kat is a case in point. The Kopper Kat was the result of an unplanned breeding on a Quarter Horse ranch somewhere in Oregon, around 1960. The ranch pasture-bred its mares, letting them foal in a natural setting. Other than bringing the young stock in occasionally for worming, shots and to trim hooves, the horses were left pretty much to themselves until they turned three years old, when they were rounded up, driven to holding pens at the home ranch, then gentled and started.

But in 1963, a smart, quick chestnut colt with a blaze on his face, chrome to his knees and hocks and a flaxen mane and tail had other ideas. Escaping the ranch hands that year, the colt spent another winter living the life of a wild horse before he was finally penned as a stout four-year-old. Just how he made his way to California is unclear, but he arrived an as unbroken gelding. After repeated unsuccessful attempts to ride the colt, his new owner, a member of the Shriners Mounted Drill Team, enlisted the help of his weekend drill team buddies in his attempts to break the flashy horse. But the determined colt, his muscles strong from years of running wild in the hills, was having none of it. The more aggressive his captors became, the more committed he was to dislodging them from his back as soon as they climbed aboard. Snubbing his head up to a roping horse proved only a temporary solution. Finally, in desperation, his owner sent him to the barn of a well-known trainer.

One month later, the trainer reported what had to be view as a qualified success: he was able to sit on the colt's back without being bucked off as long as the colt's feet were ensnared with a device known as a running W—a contraption of ropes and pulleys that could be worked by a man on the ground to throw a horse to his knees when he tried to buck. After another month the trainer returned the chestnut to his owner, telling him the colt was too smart for his own good. He would behave himself only when rigged with the running W; otherwise he would toss any man who put his foot in the stirrup to step up. His last comment was a recommendation to sell him to the rodeo string. Not a man used to being thwarted, his owner turned him out to pasture at his East Bay ranch while he considered what he wanted to do with his unruly horse.

That chestnut gelding was about to become the focal point of my equine goal setting. A visit between friends on a Sunday afternoon found the Shriner and the Sheriff's Posse rider swapping horse stories. I had reschooled the latter's Posse horse as a hunter for his daughter and she had done well with the horse at local shows. Apparently that was enough to make the man my champion, laying down his money in a bet with his Shriner friend that this young horsewoman could be successful where a half dozen cowboys had failed.

Shortly thereafter I received a phone call asking whether I wanted to train the colt. Within a week I drove out to the ranch to have a look-see. The chestnut I saw locked in a stall was a solid-bodied, athletic-appearing, well-balanced horse with a panicked look in his big, intelligent eyes. His broad forehead suggested he had brains, a somewhat short neck was nonetheless set well into a very well sloped shoulder. He had a tremendous hip, short, strong, straight cannons and well-shaped, good-size feet. All in all, he was a very nice horse.

When I agreed to take him in training however, both "gentlemen" conveniently forgot to provide me with any of the horse's history, simply letting me believe he was a raw, unstarted colt. My first goal, then, became to gain his confidence. By my third visit, he had allowed me to groom, longe and saddle him, all without any resistance. Had I been older and more experienced, that alone would probably have sent up a warning flag. But I accepted the colt's compliance, knowing that not all horses offer a fight the first time they are saddled and ridden. In fact, any good trainer makes every effort to ensure a horse isn't frightened into bucking with his rider on the first ride, wanting to keep the experience a pleasant one and set the tone for the partnership to come.

Finally, having gone as far as I thought necessary with ground work, it was time to climb aboard. I tacked the colt up with my English saddle and asked a ranch hand to toss me up on him. Less than a third of my weight had come down onto his back when the gelding exploded, leaping into the air. Only partially in the saddle and not expecting behavior of that sort, I was thrown in a great long arc, landing in the middle of the plowed field in such a way that I severely sprained one of my ankles. The ranch hand caught the snorting colt, who had immediately stopped his acrobatics when he was sure I was well and truly launched. I hobbled painfully to my car and drove home to put ice on my ankle.

Any experienced trainer would have read the signs and realized that the horse had been spoiled, carefully learning the skill of depositing his would-be riders in unceremonious ways on the ground. I, on the other hand, housebound while my ankle healed enough to enable me to put weight on my foot again, daydreamed about his beautiful copper coat, his intelligent eyes and the feeling of his raw power as he uncoiled beneath me, leaping toward the sun.

By the third day of my confinement the horse had gotten under my skin, and I phoned his owner offering to buy him. When the man agreed, I was so excited I couldn't wait for my ankle to feel good enough to take my rig and pick him up, so I arranged to have a horse transporter bring him to a local barn. When I was able to walk again and ready to ride, I used a Western saddle, thinking it might tip the odds of staying on in my favor. This time he waited until I had all of my weight settled in the saddle before he bucked. I quickly "blew" my stirrups and once again found myself sailing through the air. This pattern was becoming a discouraging one. Picking myself up from the ground yet again, I realized my goals for this horse had been reduced to the eight-second increment of a bronc rider, and I wasn't meeting them. Twice more I tried and twice more got dumped, but in the mean time I also named him. He was now The Kopper Kat.

I may never have succeeded had it not been for the advice of an old vaquero who had watched our drama unfold. As I led the horse to his stall, frustrated by my lack of progress and wondering where to go from here, the old man took me aside and pointed out some facts. The horse had a pattern when he bucked: three powerful jumps in a straight line with his nose between his fetlocks, then, if he hadn't succeeded in tossing me, he'd raise his head and launch us skyward as though he were trying to jump the sun, only to break himself in two and rush madly earthward again. The whiplash force of his spine doubling up on itself like that inevitably sent me sailing. The old man tipped his hat back, smiling at me with his crooked teeth, and continued by telling me I wasn't strong enough to pull a horse's head up when he had it stuck between his front legs, but also that Kopper, in order to make his leap from the ground after his third buck, brought his own head up. He said if I was quick enough and used all my strength and *both* of my hands to pull on the rein on one side, I might be able to pull the horse's head around to my knee and prevent him from making the spine-jarring leap that inevitably unseated me.

Young, dumb and determined not to let this horse get the best of me, I set out to follow the old man's advice. His instructions included my wearing spurs, for after I had doubled and spun Kopper first one way and then immediately in the other direction until he was dizzy, I was to straighten him out and spur him into a gallop. Once he was in a run, the vaquero continued, I was to use my spurs to make sure he continues to gallop until the horse was ready to let me sit on top of him for a bit, if I'd agree to let him slow down just a bit.

Somehow I was able to get the job done just exactly as the old vaquero had advised. Moreover, it worked! Kopper only made a half-hearted try after that first successful, hair-raising ride, never again offering any serious attempt to unseat me. During this time, one of the thoughts I had used to console myself was the observation of a respected horseman I remembered, who had said, "If a horse can buck, he can jump." Shortly thereafter, Kopper demonstrated the accuracy of that statement. Arriving one day just after the evening's feed of hay had been put in the horse's mangers, I interrupted Kopper's dinner to take him out to the big arena and turn him out for some exercise. When he effortlessly cleared the four-foot-six-inch arena gate on his way home to the barn and his dinner, my new goals for him crystallized on the spot. If he insisted on living so much of his life with all his feet off the ground, I would turn him into a jumper!

For the next two years, I focused my efforts on that goal. Early in his schooling, I quickly learned he wasn't like most other jumpers. When Kopper jumped, he wouldn't extend his body in the same graceful arc of the Thoroughbreds. Instead, Kopper jumped in squares and rectangles. He kept his small, muscular frame in a bunch as he approached his fences, and when it seemed to me that we were close enough to the fence for him to knock it down with his nose, he would leap straight up into the air as though he had springs glued to his shoes. He was very careful to aim himself well above the top rail of any jump, because he never liked to tuck his knees any tighter than was absolutely necessary and he often didn't bother to retract the landing gear by folding his feet into his belly. Pronging up to his fences and straight into the air like a stag, he would then somehow magically move forward through space, sometimes over huge oxers set at maximum allowable spreads, unfold his legs and land in a steep, descending angle.

His unorthodox style quickly won him a fan club. No one, including me, could ever quite figure out how, once he got himself in the air, he propelled himself to the other side of some of the huge jumps we eventually negotiated in competition.

Schooling him at home in an attempt to educate him in the finer aspects of his discipline proved futile, until we attended a jumping clinic conducted by Gene Lewis, a successful West Coast competitor and clinician, who was known for his unorthodox training system. Gene had begun to train very successful jumping horses using a classical system for jumpers known as *grids*. These consisted of closely related poles (cavaletti) and post and rail uprights and oxers, commonly used to teach a horse how to stay in balance and maintain rhythm during an approach to a fence, while compressing his body to achieve a powerful uncoiling action from his hind end at the base of each obstacle.

The difference between Gene's grids and a classical grid was three feet; a classical grid is set under the assumption that a horse takes a 12-foot stride at canter, while Gene's grids assumed and taught a 9-foot canter stride. That three-foot difference was the key to helping my 15-hand horse learn to do what he did naturally, only better. Soon we had moved out of the preliminary division and were negotiating fences as high as five feet in jump-offs with horses who had a height advantage of nearly six to eight inches over the Kat.

Short-term goals dominated my thinking that first year, leading Kopper and me from one week and show to the next, in almost random fashion. Gradually I began to appreciate the extent of the talent in the little horse and started to make bigger plans. The first long-term goal I deliberately selected for my horse, however, was not to be met in a show arena.

It was midway into the second summer I owned the Kat. I had been riding horses all morning, and was ready to take a break. I headed to the mailbox and found the newest issue of my *Western Horseman* magazine. Carrying it into the house with me, I browsed through its pages as I munched on a quickly thrown together sandwich. As I turned a page, an article caught my eye. It described an event that challenged a single horse and rider to traverse 100 miles of rugged mountain trails in 24 hours. The thought stopped me cold. I had never even considered such an undertaking might be possible. Oh, I had read about pony express riders and the cavalry, but those horses traveled about 35 miles a day.

As I read through the article, I learned there was an annual event called the Tevis Cup. Held each year in California in July or August, during the full moon, it was officially known at the time as the Western States 100 Mile One-Day Ride. Riders and their horses broke from a starting line on the main street of the mountain town of Tahoe. Riding all day and into the night, they followed wilderness trails traveled by silver miners and trappers, through the Sierra Nevadas to a finish line in the gold mining town of Auburn. By the time the horse and rider teams reached their destination (if they did), they had ascended a total of 19,000 feet and descended more than 22,000 feet, with only three one-hour rest periods. Those who were successful (less than 50 percent most years) were

The author competing on The Kopper Kat at the Oakland National Horse Show in 1966.

With a change of saddle and rider outfit, The Kopper Kat could win ribbons in Western trail classes.

A special Tevis buckle, presented to a handful of riders who have finished the famous race 20 times.

awarded a special sterling silver belt buckle. The article finished with the claim that the ride was one of the greatest tests of horsemanship in the world.

It took my random musing about a month to evolve into an actual goal, which is about the time it took me to transform that article from an interesting tidbit into two burning questions: Was I a good enough rider to complete such a feat? And was I a good enough horsewoman to prepare a horse to successfully meet such a grueling test? There was only one way to answer both questions: Just do it!

This was my first true experience of planning a long-term equestrian goal on my own (12 months is long-term when you're only 21). I had to design and write 52 weekly training schedules that would result in turning a successful show jumper into a successful endurance horse. How many miles on the trail each week? How much gymnastic (dressage) schooling to keep him balanced and supple? Did I want to stop showing in jumping events all together until the ride (no)? I had to figure out how to count backward from the ride date, in six-week increments, to schedule his shoeing dates . . . the list was endless.

Days ran into weeks and weeks turned into months. The plan I made seemed to be working well and both the horse and I were meeting our goals regularly. The first monkey wrench I encountered was on the day I went to tack up and noticed five lumps just under his hide in the area of the saddle. A call to the vet left me with the news that my horse had warbles. The lumps were subdermal larvae of flies that mostly bothered cattle. They migrate to the tissue of the back from the stomach, where they secrete an enzyme to make a breathing hole through the skin, and within four to six weeks emerge through the holes and drop to the ground! The other elucidating fact I learned was that if you just happen to crush several of the larvae simultaneously (for instance, by putting a saddle over them and sitting in it), you can send a horse into toxic shock. Well, goals are only that—goals. You need to be flexible to be successful, so I started to get flexible.

I couldn't halt my conditioning program for six weeks (or more) without risking arriving at my target date (the ride) with a horse who was not as fit as he would need to be. In addition, my vet informed me that sometimes the larvae don't emerge from horses the way they do from cows, but became entombed under the skin. I also couldn't risk the possibility that having a saddle on top of those lumps might irritate my horse's back, causing the ride vets to disqualify him at some point in the long, grueling test. After weighing all my options, I decided to have the larvae surgically removed. Then I borrowed a friend's horse and ponied Kopper, which meant he would continue to get his conditioning miles, just not with any weight on his back. He healed nicely.

By this time, I was experiencing success on two fronts. My goals for getting him ready for the Tevis Cup were being met (he was very fit and feeling great), and we were continuing to win more and more of our jumping competitions against horses up to two hands taller than he was, with riders much more experienced than I was. That success led to my second experience of planning a goal further away then the end of a week or a month. I decided my flashy, unorthodox jumping horse might have a shot at making the State of California Jumping Team. Eliminations were to be held at the prestigious Pebble Beach Equestrian Center in Monterey, and those horses and riders who made the team would compete in team events for the rest of 1966 and into 1967 at big circuit shows, against teams from other Western states.

I proceeded with both those goals in mind (but only one with important dates on paper) and still ended up being surprised by the fact that right smack dab in the middle of the planned 10-day trip to Auburn to preride the portion of the trails Kopper and I would be negotiating after dark, he and I were also expected, as members of the jumping team, to be at one of the year's biggest events back in the San Francisco Bay area (a drive for me of about three hours). This only proves that the saying "a person of two minds" has a literal as well as a figurative meaning.

Catching the error in my planning before actually leaving for Auburn, I made another quick adjustment to my Tevis goal plan. I would trailer Kopper up to Auburn, stay to ride the trail for a few days, hotfoot it back to the Bay area on the Wednesday before the show, compete with him, including the Team Jumping Class on Sunday, and hotfoot it back to Auburn. If I gave him two days of rest, I still had two days to train over the trail before I had to haul him to Tahoe on Friday to check in at the starting line for the ride. Done and done.

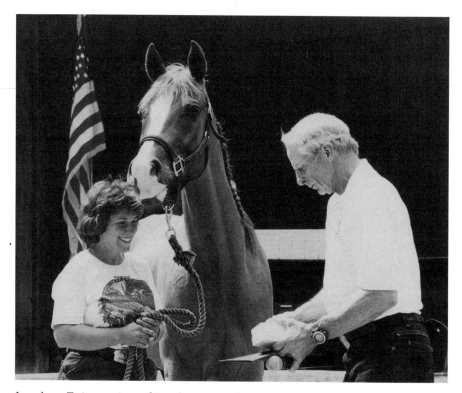

I used my Tevis experience thirty-four years after earning my own buckle, to help prepare client Judy Reens and her horse Benjih to win the prestigious event.

We trained, we traveled, he jumped (better than he ever had before). The team won the silver, Kopper tied for first place in the high jump at a height of five feet nine inches against a Canadian team horse who stood all of 17 hands, *and* he took a ribbon in a Western Trail Horse class!

We started the Tevis, and 18 hours later my little chestnut jumper trotted his hooves over the finish line in Auburn, winning me my coveted silver buckle by finishing 20th out of 89 starters.

We competed together as a successful team for seven more years, during which time I expanded our repertoire, showing him in eventing at the preliminary level, as a hackamore reining horse, a Western pleasure horse and a trail horse. He won ribbons for me in all of his events. When I "retired" him at age 14, he became a foxhunter, galloping after hounds until his death at 32 years of age. He even played a role for a short time as a rehab horse. He was a true example of an all-around horse.

Have You Won or Lost Before You Start?

The ability to focus the mind is as important to the successful competitor as the ability to physically perform the various mechanics of his or her sport. Scientific studies abound that have shown the effectiveness of positive visualization and mental practice. Are you aware of what pictures you hold in your mind before, during and after an event or competition?

We use visualization each time we plan or dream about something. From there, we translate our plan into action, perhaps by writing it down and elaborating on it as we go, or simply by beginning to move toward a realization of the plan by doing something physical. Whether we write or act, we are moving toward a goal we have set, even if that goal is nothing more than to explore the possibilities of our idea(s).

Your mind will feel most comfortable with what is familiar, and cannot tell the difference between a vividly imagined experience and a real one. Mentally imagining success is the first step to achieving that success. In other words, learning to succeed can be practiced! On the other hand, unconscious self-sabotage could easily be triggered by your mind's discomfort at being in unfamiliar territory—that is, the winner's circle.

When you fear something, you've created an image of the thing or event in your mind. It is also possible simply to fear the unknown. Fear of the unknown is like a magician's trick: it requires misdirection of attention. We cannot fear what we cannot conceptualize, so before we can fear the unknown there must be a picture on our mental computer screen of what the "unknown" consists of. As soon as we realize this, we can escape our fear of the unknown, because we can remember that it is not the unknown, but rather a "false known" that we fear, and it is we, ourselves, who are producing and directing the script of that "false known."

Once we've allowed a negative event to dominate our mental computer screen (fearing our horse will loose a shoe, bring a fence down in the jump-off or fail to spin or slide well), we have a tendency to drive toward that negative event. Some people will first focus on a negative, then take elaborate precautions to avoid that situation. While this method of staying out of the ditch does work, it requires twice the energy. First, you imagine the event, then you must think about how to prevent the imagined possibility. I learned that you can usually keep your car on the road more easily and with less effort by simply focusing on the direction you want to travel, rather than investing in and installing multiple cumbersome, costly and weighty electronic devices that will take control of the vehicle *if* you ever steer the car too close to the shoulder.

Competitors with a negative vision, sometimes referred to as worry-warts, can also accomplish their goals. But they frequently fall victim to unexpected disasters and delays along the route. Their success rate is erratic. Their misfortunes, when they occur (and they frequently do), are often more disruptive and/or devastating than those that befall other riders, and their down time is considerably longer.

These are the negative planners: riders who get trapped into worrying about all the things they fear will or could go wrong. Rather than act to minimize their concerns, they simply continue to move toward their ultimate goal, hoping they won't encounter the nightmare. And sometimes they don't, in which case they feel not blessed but cursed, because to their way of thinking if they didn't meet a "bear" (negative event) on the trail today, the odds are just that much greater they will encounter one tomorrow.

Brave or hardy souls, as we like to think of them (sometimes also thought of as foolhardy), will simply see the challenge or goal and immediately spring into action, beginning to move toward it and never considering the inherent risks (yes, riding horses *is* risky). While these people are easy to admire and do end up in the winner's circle, it is not the best path for most of us and does not produce the most consistent performers, since if some unexpected negative event does occur, this kind of competitor can easily be derailed. They are denied the success of their ultimate goal by becoming entangled in and overwhelmed by the events of the moment with which they are forced to deal, and they have no clear trail markers or mental map to lead them forward, once the emergency has been dealt with.

The smart mental athlete will envision an event as they want it to occur, then spend some time thinking of things that might prevent the event from unfolding as they project. Selecting the most likely of these potential wrong turns, they will spend a reasonable amount of time thinking or envisioning, not the actual disaster, but rather what they might do to avoid the problem or salvage the event, *if* anything goes wrong. This person is a consistent competitor, and is also the competitor who will most likely climb the ladder of success in any discipline.

Which type of competitor are you? Which type would you like to be? If you find yourself in the wrong category and want to change, start by changing things in your mind. Write down the concerns or fears that seem to keep dragging you down, draining your energy. Then take a hard look at them. Are they realistic? If the answer is yes, don't spend your energy obsessing over them; rather, write down a plan of action that will help you circumvent the imagined disaster and another plan to minimize its impact *if* it occurs. Then put those plans away in a storage compartment of your brain, take out a clean sheet of paper and write a script for success, just as you would like it to happen. Now move into action, checking your positive script from time to time to be sure you are on the right track.

Chapter 4

First Foot in the Stirrup

*T*he definition of an all-around rider could easily be expressed in simple terms as a truly good horseman or horsewoman. The rider who is *classically* trained can ride a variety of horses (breeds, sizes, temperaments and training levels) in different types of saddles (hunt, dressage, stock, endurance, polo, etc.), successfully performing a diverse number of jobs (hack, jump, work cattle, ride trail, run barrels, race, etc.). To understand the foundation needed to become such a rider, you must understand that the phrase "classically trained" is not used here to refer to riders who were trained in Europe or even in the United States in a dressage system. Rather, the phrase is used to describe a sequential system of skills acquisition and refinement whose requisites are:

1. A solid and secure seat that is maintained primarily through balance, using the core trunk muscles to stabilize and/or move the human pelvis.

2. The ability of the rider to mentally and physically access, with pinpoint clarity, the major joints of his or her body (which is the human shock-absorbing system), especially the hip, knee and ankle joints, and use them to help maintain correct skeletal alignment without introducing undue, counterproductive tension in unnecessary muscle groups. This is a constant, ongoing process in all forms of good riding.

3. The ability to isolate the various muscles groups that are respon-
    sible for producing the desired biomechanical action in the rider's
    fingers, hands, arms and legs in a way that enables those limbs to
    be used independently as a signaling or communication system,
    without disturbing the communication center—the rider's seat.

4. The ability to read or feel and identify both the horse's intent and
    his physical actions.

5. Understanding the biomechanics of the various movements a
    horse is capable of performing, including all the normal gaits of
    walk, trot and canter or gallop, as well as backing, jumping, buck-
    ing, rearing, spinning and sliding.

6. Knowing the exercises that, when directed by the rider/handler
    and done by the horse, strengthen all of the equine motion sys-
    tems, equalizing the two sides of the horse's body in its capacity
    to bend, stretch, push and support; and promoting the specialized
    biomechanics for such athletic actions as jumping, sliding, spin-
    ning, quick lateral movements (cutting horse, pole bending, etc.)
    and slow suspended movements (piaffe, passage, etc.).

An American System Has Emerged

The adult rider in the United States today who wants to improve or
expand their equestrian skills has a distinct advantage, because in the
last half of the 20th century two innovative and remarkably effective
learning systems emerged: Centered Riding and TTeam (Tellington-
Touch Equine Awareness Method).

Centered Riding, pioneered by Sally Swift (author of the book by the
same name and *Centered Riding 2, Further Exploration*) is based on the
work of F. M. Alexander, and stresses the mind-body connection in promoting the development of a balanced, flexible, fluid, coordinated body,
free of the unnecessary muscular tensions that cause fatigue, pain and
limited movement. The system also offers the added benefit of improving the rider's security in the saddle. Since a rider's body is her primary
means of communication with her horse, it stands to reason that such a
system would enhance our ability to communicate clearly with the horse
when mounted. Clear communication is the prize all riders seek, since
the rider's ability to communicate clearly with her horse is directly

It is necessary to be proficient in the basics of general equitation before trying to specialize or assuming the stylized position of a specific discipline, for the same reasons that it is necessary to master the basics taught in kindergarten, grade school and high school before tackling the specialized courses and more complex thinking required to successfully attain a Bachelor of Arts, Master's or Doctorate degree.

reflected in the horse's ability to understand and his willingness to perform. More over, that enhanced understanding and willingness leads directly to greater joy in the relationship for *both* participants.

The ground or unmounted exercises advocated in Centered Riding have an impressive success rate in adults, whose cognitive system is given a chance to create or change a desired action or skill before the body is pressed into the layered, multidimensional, complicated, coordinated actions required in good riding. Frequently, these exercises mimic body patterns used when the rider is mounted, heightening an adult's familiarity and comfort levels with the muscle patterns that are most likely to produce a secure, comfortable, effective, efficient position on the horse. This pre-ride patterning of "muscle memory" enables quicker and more accurate processing of the brain's imperatives for security and balance when the rider *is* mounted. As a result, the rider immediately feels more secure. As the rider is able to relax into that feeling of security, the normally heightened physical and mental tension that comes with riding for most adults (whether conscious or not), and that is a barrier to reading the horse and answering with clear signals, is greatly reduced.

Clear communication is also a focus of the method of educating horses developed by Linda Tellington-Jones, known as TTeam. TTeam exercises, based on Feldenkrais exercises, are initiated and/or guided by the handler/rider mainly from the ground. They are designed to improve the horse's balance, coordination and understanding. Originally designed by Linda primarily to affect/influence horses, TTeam exercises also benefit riders because it is impossible to participate in them without experiencing a heightened awareness of your own balance and movement and how that affects a horse's ability to perform—*even when the handler is separated from the horse and standing on the ground!*

BECKY SILER

A young Western rider competing in a bareback equitation class on his cantering Appaloosa pony shows lovely classical form. It doesn't get any better than this.

When a rider mounts up after working with her horse in the TTeam exercises, she has both a deepened sense of connection with the horse and an expanded visual schematic of the animal's biomechanical movement patterns and potential. These visual images are a valuable contribution to the basic cognitive program that dictates rider decisions about critical issues, such as where and when to apply the aids—a crucial piece in the overall picture of equestrian success.

The photo above is an excellent example of an elegant, softly erect body and classically correct alignment (ear, shoulder, hip and ankle). His eyes are forward and up, his shoulders are square but relaxed, his hand is correctly placed relative to his horse's withers, while his arm shows the slight bend in the elbow that is required for suppleness through the arm and a good feel of his horse's mouth. His pelvis is balanced directly up over his seat bones, while his thigh and knee drop down the pony's side without any visible tension or grip. His knee is slightly flexed, putting his calf on his pony's side and his foot under his torso. Finally, his toe is carried above the height of his heel, giving stretch and strength to the muscles along the back of his calf.

The natural aids are:

- Seat
- Hands
- Weight
- Voice
- Legs

Children, who are innately more flexible than adults, with less tension in their bodies and usually less mental tension as well, are best taught in the time-tested progressive educational system known as Pony Club. Today the United States has its own Pony Club manuals. Written and illustrated by Susan Harris, a Centered Riding level IV instructor and professional illustrator, the series is based upon the British prototype.

Like adults, different children learn in different ways. Some respond best to auditory learning, some to visual and some to kinesthetic learning. However, in general children's learning seems to be stimulated by motion, while many adults experience the best results when the mind has time to digest and understand a goal before being pressed to produce a series of actions or movement patterns in the body.

Good Equitation Defined

Good equitation is *always* the position that best enables the horse to do his job in *the most efficient manner*. All good riders have the following four elements:

1. **A correctly aligned skeleton,** expressed in the rider's use of her joints and an absence of unnecessary tension in the muscular system

2. **Correct use of the respiratory system;** shallow breathing or holding the breath create tension in the body

3. **Independent use of the aids** (hands, legs, seat and weight), enabling clear communication with the horse

4. **A clear understanding** of cause and effect of the dynamics of riding

Achieving and maintaining balance and independent use of the aids under all circumstances requires effort and time, but the rewards are worth the investment. And no matter what the age of the rider or the learning system selected, the goals of good equitation are universal:

- Control (safety)

- Comfort (of both horse and rider)

- Performance

The rider's ability to sit balanced and tension-free on her horse directly affects:

- The horse's long-term soundness

- The horse's short-term balance

- The horse's ability to use or develop his inherent athletic capabilities

- The horse's mental state

An unbalanced rider must use muscle tension to keep herself seated on her horse. That tension communicates itself to the horse as a series of resistances. Many riders are unaware of the tensions which create the log-jams in their body and produce a negative effect on their horse. Tension:

- Reduces the ability of your joints to function as shock absorbers

- Is experienced by the horse as an impediment to free forward movement

- Produces tension in the horse's body

- Makes the horse expend unnecessary energy to push through his own muscular tension to move and perform

Tension can be caused by excitement, discomfort (physical pain or a poor saddle fit), an incorrect or inefficient frame in the horse, or a tense, gripping or unbalanced rider. Tension in any area of the horse or rider's body has a domino effect. When the dominoes fall, they cause increased wear and tear on the horse's joints because the horse must expend more effort to bend those joints when performing. Anything that inhibits the horse's ability to support his weight with his hindquarters will tend to cause the horse to travel on his forehand. This, along with tense muscles, causes debilitating changes in the horse over time, prematurely wearing or damaging the tendons and ligaments, causing ring bone,

Our biggest barrier to good riding is our distorted kinesthetic sense. This phrase describes what happens when your brain tells you that you are doing something, but you really aren't. This woman thinks she is standing the way she is picturing herself in her mind's eye, while her mirror shows her she is actually standing with her knees locked and her back in an arched or hollowed posture.

BETHANY CASKEY

navicular and arthritic changes, creating problems with irregular hoof size, causing sore backs and asymmetrical muscling and creating behavioral problems.

The All-Around Rider and the Balanced Seat

There are a variety of riding styles. Usually referred to as "seats," they include hunt seat, stock seat, dressage seat, forward seat, saddle seat, and the military seat, etc. Each style of "seat" or type of riding has developed around a specific job or discipline. If you are a novice or an amateur, all those different names can sound confusing and make the topic of good riding seem very complex. The all-around rider will look to the source; the seat best suited to adaptation, commonly called the balanced seat. A balanced basic/neutral position, the seat is defined by a relaxed, upright torso with the weight evenly distributed on the rider's seat bones, buttocks and inner thigh muscles, (which must not pinch or grip the horse). The rider's legs must "hang" around the horse's barrel, with knees pointing more downward, toward the ground, than forward toward the horse's nose. The length of the rider's thigh bone relative to the length of the stirrup will determine the degree of angle in the hip, knee and ankle joints (with short stirrups the joints are flexed to a greater degree, while with long stirrups the joints are more open.

The rider's calf should rest lightly against the horse's ribcage directly under her torso or hip. This calf position offers the rider increased lateral security and a strong controlling and guidance system. The depth and width of the horse's barrel relative to the rider's length of leg will determine exactly *where* the rider's calf will fall on her horse's side. In the case of a very long-legged rider on a short or narrow horse, the rider may find her feet below the belly of the horse—in which case she needs to give her leg aids with the top of the calf muscle. A short-legged rider, on the other hand, can easily connect with her horse throughout nearly the entire length of her inner leg, down to and sometimes including the ankle bone (a five-foot-two woman on a 17.2-hand Warmblood is a good example), enabling her to deliver her aids to the horse's side from a somewhat lower point on her leg.

The length of a rider's leg relative to the horse she rides will determine the length of the spur neck, if spurs are used, and may also influence the placement of the spur on the boot. Short riders on large horses would do

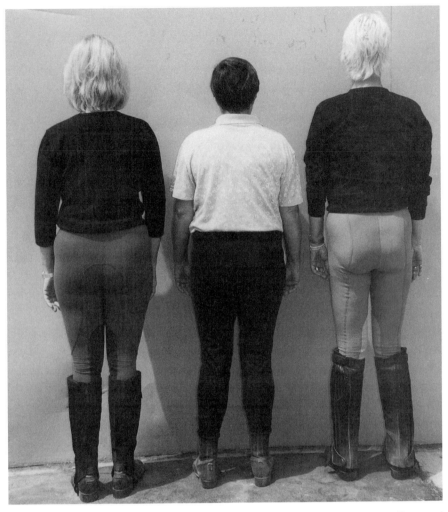

Your body type can influence the challenges you face as you learn to master all-around riding skills. From left to right, these women are 5-foot-5, 5-foot-2 and 5-foot-7. However, the torso length of the first and third woman is nearly the same, while the middle woman's leg length and torso length are evenly proportioned.

well with a short-necked spur, set at a normal position on the heel or even lower, toward the bottom of the boot. A tall man or woman with long legs, riding a small or narrow horse, may need a long-necked spur that, when set on the boot at the top of the rider's heel, will enable her to touch the horse's side with her spur without lifting her heel and dropping the toe— an undesirable, unstable position.

The strongest body for riding is one with a short, compact torso and long legs. The body type that appears most attractive on a horse—a tall, slender torso and long legs— may often come with the handicap of weak back muscles that will need to be strengthened. Riders with a tall, thin upper body and short legs face the greatest challenge, but can learn to make up with quick reflexes what their longer-legged, more substantially built counterparts manage with muscle.

A rider's knees should be free of tension, acting like springs at all gaits and in all positions. The knee is an important part of the lower shock-absorbing system; the need for flexibility in this joint is the major reason why the accomplished all-around equestrian does not ride with her foot wedged against the stirrup. The other reason is the simple law of gravity that doesn't change when a rider mounts her horse: To be in balance when standing, the foot must be under the torso; to be in balance when riding, the foot must also be under the torso. The rider's ankle must also be relaxed, to enable her foot to remain under her body, allowing her foot to rest *laterally level* on the stirrup with the heel and slightly lower than the toe.

The light yet deep seat, so sought after by horsemen and horsewomen around the world, is achieved when the rider allows the energy of the horse to pass up through her body without resistance. The internal energy, or toning, that dictates the rider's posture while riding, is directed in equal parts upward, lifting the rib cage and lengthening the spine (preventing the rider from collapsing or becoming heavy in the saddle) and downward through the rider's legs and feet, grounding the rider and helping to create the desired deep, secure seat.

The Forward Seat

When posting to the trot, galloping, riding up or down hills or jumping, the torso of the rider should be brought into a slightly more forward position by closing the hip joint (not by rounding the spine). This is the forward seat, also known as the half seat. If the rider wants to adopt a more extreme forward position, for instance when galloping or jumping, she folds toward the horse's neck from the hip, at the same time allowing her hips to slide a little to the rear of the saddle, This continues to keep the torso mass centered over the base of support, that is, the lower leg and foot. The rider's back must remain flat and unarched. As the rider moves her shoulders forward, weight is transferred from the buttocks to the inner thighs and stirrups, freeing the horse's loins and hindquarters.

To achieve and maintain this position easily, the rider should shorten her stirrups from two to four holes. The shortened stirrup length increases the degree of flexion and the shock-absorbing capacity of the rider's ankle, knee and hip joints, preparing them to handle the increased forward and upward thrust of the horse at faster gaits and/or over extreme topography. During this torso shift, the rider's calves remain steady on the horse's sides in the area of the girth or cinch, and do not swing like a clock pendulum.

The Defensive Seat

There are times it may be wise for a rider to adopt what is known as a defensive seat. This position is most commonly observed in the cowboy, the huntsman, the steeplechase jockey and the polo player. In the position, the rider sits as deeply as possible with the pelvis, keeping the shoulders one or two degrees behind the hip, and the lower leg (usually positioned directly under hip and shoulder) now deliberately placed a little bit more forward toward the horse's elbow, in anticipation of actions such as jumping a broad fence with a drop landing, bucking, sudden stops, sideways leaping, spook gymnastics and spins—especially the ones where the horse drops a shoulder before turning (quickly and usually unexpectedly). The position can only improve the rider's security if the ankle remains elastic and the heel is lowered as the foot is brought forward, to provide a slight bracing action with the leg and foot. Overstiffening either the knee or ankle will have a reverse effect: the horse's energy traveling up the rider's leg through the stiffened joints jars the rider's seat loose from the saddle.

Riding Hills, Sliding Stops and Drop Jumps

The all-around rider will want to spend time working outside the arena to hone their skills. Riding hills, sliding stops and drop jumps have a common biomechanical denominator: the hip joint. If the rider is free of tension and her skeleton is correctly aligned when working over undulating terrain, she will experience motion in her hip joint similar to what she would feel if she were walking or jogging up and down hills on her own feet. Riders who are stiff, lean back, use exaggerated body sway when going down a hill or stand up over the horse's withers, putting their weight on their stirrups, when climbing a hill, interfere with the horse's ability to move his limbs freely. This can result in a shortened stride, unnecessary weighting of the forehand, use of inefficient muscle groups, stumbling and tendon damage.

To ride down hills effectively and securely, the rider needs to adjust her leg slightly forward from the "at the girth" position, bringing the torso forward to balance her upper body directly over her foot. Positioned this way, the rider's knees can spring upward alternately. This subtle, alternate, upward springing action in the knees enables them to act as shock absorbers, helping stabilize the mass of her torso over the horse's undulating body. In addition, this rider position and free joint function, enables the horse to lift and round his back, giving him the freedom for clean articulation of the legs, better engagement of the foot underneath the belly, a better downhill stride and better balance. In viewing the old training films used to teach the riders of the U.S. Cavalry how to ride their horses safely off the edge of a bluff and down long, steep sliding descents, the position advocated is clearly that of the forward or light seat.

The all-around rider will quickly come to realize that those same biomechanical skills, practiced and refined while trail riding, successfully apply to the job of riding the reiner's sliding stops. A horse who must sit down behind and slide with his hind legs while continuing to canter with his front legs benefits from a rider who can absorb the shock of the stop with her knee joints, while remaining light and vertical in the saddle. When mastered, this rider position will facilitate the horse "getting into the ground" with his hind end. Posture that places the rider's legs stiffly out in front of her center of gravity may look dramatic to an audience, but doesn't help the equine athlete in the execution of his job.

Think About It!

The laws of gravity and balance relative to the accelerating and decelerating forces introduced by speed and undulating terrain don't change from discipline to discipline, the way the style of a rider's clothes or saddle do.

A Western rider demonstrating a chair seat.

Corrected leg placement, allowing a balanced position.

A rider demonstrating a chair seat in an English saddle.

The leg placement has been corrected and the leg placed under the torso to form a straight line from the shoulder through the hip to the ankle.

Riding up a hill teaches a rider to lighten the weight over the horse's hindquarters and loins by folding her torso forward from the *hip joint* (not by rounding the spine), *without* placing all her weight in the stirrups (to do so would bring the rider's entire weight to bear on the part of the saddle where the stirrups are hung, making it difficult for the horse to free up his back and effectively use his hindquarters as a pushing mechanism). The same torso position and hip joint flexion need to be mastered to ride a good hunter round. The international jumping seat, more upright to the base of a fence (to access the strong driving power of the rider's pelvis), requires a rider to use more muscles to move herself into the folded or jumping position as the horse leaves the ground, but involves exactly the same biomechanical actions in the rider's hip joints as those of a rider whose horse is scrambling up a steep cliff.

The ability of the rider to move her torso fluidly from a forward jumping position to a more open descent position, with foot placement determined by the degree of security required by the pull of gravity and the speed and degree of the descent, are precisely the set of biomechanical skills that must be mastered by the successful event rider to negotiate drop fences, especially those where the horse lands in water.

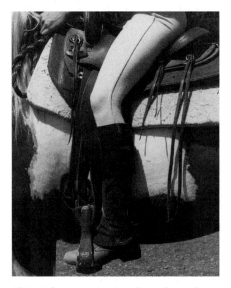

This rider's stirrup is adjusted too long, and her toe must be lowered to make contact with the stirrup, tightening her ankle joint.

With the stirrup this short, the length of the rider's thigh bone forces her seat against the cantle of the saddle, putting her behind the horse's balance point.

Understanding the Role of the Riding Instructor

While accurately assessing your starting point will facilitate your learn-ing process, it is also important to know the various levels through which you will progress and what you may expect to encounter at each of those levels. Even if you are an equestrian prodigy, you still need to progress in a systematic way or risk gaps in your riding skills and your under-standing of horses. A rider who wants to specialize in one discipline may be able to force her body into a trendy posture style, especially if it doesn't involve riding anything more challenging than a circle or two in an arena, a low course of fences or a quick run down and spin. If you have a horse who will cover or compensate for your mistakes, you can even bring home awards. But if you want to be an *all-around* rider, you must well and truly learn to *ride*, not just pose!

The all-around rider needs to be able to adjust her position to a vari-ety of activities, if not a variety of horses. She can be equally at home riding a 3-foot-6-inch course of fences in a hunter seat saddle, jumping a ditch on a cross-country course, riding a dressage test in a dressage saddle where she not only has to sit a trot well, but also use her back and seat to shape her horse's body and energy, bringing out the best in her horse's movement by balancing his body and empowering his stride. That same rider can climb aboard a stock saddle and put in a credible performance at speed around a barrel pattern, put her horse through a smooth reining routine, including spins, rollbacks and sliding stops, work a cow down the fence or out of a herd, or ride 100 miles in 24 hours over terrain reserved for eagles and mountain climbers!

The challenge of becoming an all-around rider is well worth taking on, with self-confidence, grace and self-esteem the rewards at its end. The final vote on your success belongs to your horse—his soundness, his fitness, his happiness and his performance will be your report card. The eyes of every other true horseman will be your jury.

As important as your choice of mount, is your choice of the person or persons who will guide you as you acquire skills, search for knowledge and select worthwhile goals—your coach-mentors. Selecting a qualified candidate, then, is an important goal. The following information can play an important role in your screening process.

Test a teaching relationship by taking a few lessons or auditing a clinic before you make a commitment. Saying no and stepping back is not a sign of weakness or lack of talent. It also doesn't necessarily reflect negatively on an instructor. People learn in different ways. A teacher whose methods bring the best out of a child in kindergarten probably won't be the one who can challenge that person when they are ready to write their Master's thesis, nor necessarily the teacher best suited to help a student with learning disabilities. If a boot doesn't fit and you hike 10 miles, you will be rewarded with painful blisters. If a boot doesn't fit and you hike 100 miles in it, refusing to acknowledge your discomfort and pain because you're stubborn or don't want to display weakness or be seen as incapable, you could do serious, long-term damage to your muscular and skeletal systems. And arriving at the end of the journey may not produce the gratifying experience you had anticipated, especially if you lose touch with yourself during the trip.

Know Yourself—The Level I Rider (Kindergarten)

In the first stages of riding, the goal of the instructor is to teach you control of your body. The more adept you are at self-control, both physical and mental, the easier it will be to control your horse and the more enjoyable the riding experience for both of you. When a well-schooled longe horse is available, work on the longe line produces the fastest progress. Mounted exercises to improve your balance, relaxation, coordination and strength will be introduced by a good instructor during this period, and practiced by the student rider while both on and off the longe line. A good instructor's tool kit will include strengthening and suppling exercises for each part of the rider's body.

Before change must come awareness. A good instructor helps students create accurate mental pictures (of their goal(s) as well as their present state) by:

1. Making the student aware of what she is currently doing with her body

2. Creating a clear picture for the student of the biomechanical functions and interactions of the joints, muscles, and skeleton of her body (a fine example of this can be found in the book *Centered Riding* by Sally Swift)

3. Helping the student construct an accurate mental picture of the goal being pursued (physical demonstration by the instructor is particularly useful here)

When you have mastered enough self awareness and control to sit upon your horse without severely interfering with the horse's movement or being in jeopardy of falling off, it is time to ride off the longe.

In level I, you must expect your control of your horse to be confined to *quantity* of movement, with limited directional control, so a confined space, such as an arena, ensures the greatest degree of safety. Since you are still in the early stages of learning to control your body when mounted (especially if no longe work has been done), you will probably resort to the reins as your primary means to control the horse. A good instructor knows students must pass through this natural stage of learning and will avoid pressuring the student mentally by over-emphasizing the discomfort the student's ineptitude may cause her horse. Instead, the instructor will choose exercises for you that will minimize the need for strong or precise rein actions.

Nontraditional exercises, such as stretching, Centered Riding and TTeam, are a great adjunct to more traditional work, especially for novice adult riders, who will gain confidence as they become more familiar with the horse and the biomechanics of their own body.

During this and other phases of instruction, the goals are:

1. Security

2. Learning how not to abuse the horse

3. Effective use of the aids

4. Unity

The best way to teach these goals consists of (in order):

1. Clear explanation (audio)

2. Demonstration (visual)

3. Perform and practice (kinesthetic)

4. Critique (further clarification of the map or mental images from which the student is operating)

The Level II Rider (Grade School)

In level II your instructor should focus on teaching you the influencing aids (seat, back, legs and hands), while continuing to drill you in exercises that help to improve your security. You must learn *how* and *where* the aids are applied to be most effective, and *when* to apply them. School figures are the proven way of accomplishing this task. The more innovative and clever your instructor is at selecting and combining basic gymnastic exercises such as circles, serpentines, straight lines, transitions, etc., the more interesting the work will be for both you and your horse. With heightened interest comes heightened awareness and increased desire to perform.

Without acquiring a moderately secure seat and tension-free position during level I, if you are pressured to ride the more demanding work of school figures, your skills will improve, but only slowly. You can expect to be unable to produce the required aid as needed or on your instructor's command, and also be inconsistent in the placement, pressure and/or timing of your aid. The horse's behavior and response, then, will also be inconsistent. Lacking the expected, desired feedback from your horse (confirming the correctness of your aid choice and execution), it is easy to become frustrated and resort to increased force or become bored with your lessons. If, on the other hand, you have really mastered the work of level I, level II will come relatively easily for you when you're mounted on modestly challenging horses.

Work outside the arena should be introduced in level II, and used to confirm and enhance the skills you have already learned.

As you continually succeed in influencing and improving your horse's performance, your self-confidence, enthusiasm and interest in riding will grow. An instructor or clinician may get a student's attention using showmanship, but knowledge is required to build a student's trust, respect, and skills.

The Level III Rider (High School)

In equestrian high school an instructor's job title and functions change from teacher to coach-mentor, and the student takes her place as the primary trainer of the horse. From this point on, the coach, the rider and the horse function as equal members of team.

The coach's job is to:

1. Help the rider select appropriate goals for herself and her horse

2. Help the rider select the system best suited to develop her horse physically and mentally toward the chosen goal(s)

3. Help the rider design her horse's training program

4. Oversee or track its correct and continuing application

As the rider, your job is to:

1. Do the daily work of suppling, strengthening and conditioning your equine partner

2. Make any necessary "at the moment" decisions about changes to the training program or exercise being ridden

3. Share with your coach what you have observed and/or felt in the horse and, if not working with a coach every day, report your assessment of the progress you and your horse are making toward your selected goal(s) at periodic intervals

4. Clarify with your coach any questions you may have or confusion you experience about things that may occur as you ride and train your horse

By level III (if not sooner), you should have selected a specific discipline, and work during a lesson or coaching session will include discipline-specific exercises and pattern practice for horse and rider. For example, a dressage rider would focus her work around the various movements required for competitive tests at various levels, a jumping rider's work would include gymnastic grid work and work over courses, a reiner would work on exercises to perfect spins and stops and so on. At level III, the *quality* of all work is the primary focus.

More Thoughts on Instructors

In seeking out a school or teacher, knowing your level of experience becomes important if for no other reason than to be able to accurately evaluate the teaching resources that may be available to you. Even if you have your own horse and he is suitable to your learning needs, you will expand your skills much more rapidly if there is more than one suitable horse on which to learn. Ask any good horsewoman and they will tell you that every horse has his own lessons to teach.

If you are an inexperienced rider and present yourself to an instructor, clinician or coach on a green horse, safety will demand that you be taught some form of control over your horse in the shortest possible time. Since it is impossible for an instructor to teach anything except survival to a student who is mounted on a horse that is out of control, the instructor's job in such a case must be focused on limiting the potential damage to all involved: horse, rider and any others in the class. A good coach or instructor will make it clear to the rider, that what they're learning in such a situation is only the crudest type of riding. Instruction in the important topic of rider balance and independent use of the aids (level I) will be delayed.

In a group lesson on a green horse barely under control, your attention will be so divided that you can expect to experience difficulty focusing on or carrying out even simple commands given by your instructor, and you may quickly find yourself feeling overloaded. If an instructor pushes too much information at you in a desire to help you, your thought process may simply shut down, slowing your progress even further.

It is important that both you and your instructor realize that during these early stages of learning (particularly in the scenario I've just described), you and your horse will probably acquire some bad habits, and your progress may periodically be interrupted as the consequences of those habits are encountered. If you or your instructor fails to recognize when you are stuck on one of those consequences (that is, old patterns that prevent you and your horse from moving your skills forward), you may become frustrated or bored, feel you are standing still or worse, going backward or even blame your horse. Likewise, any time you become stuck in your learning, you and your coach must look for the hole(s) in your basic skills.

Safety First—Always!

Flying, like riding, has a certain amount of built-in danger. As the "pilot" of your horse, you should do a pre-ride check, running through the following list each and every time you mount up. Arrogance (thinking the odds won't catch up with you or assuming you know it all) or ignorance are the two greatest blocks to learning. They are also the two greatest precursors to injury, both of horses and of riders.

The Rider's Safety Checklist

1. Protective head gear, correctly fitted and secured

2. Clothing appropriate to the job

3. Boots with a heel and/or safety stirrups

4. No loose jewelry or baggy clothes

5. No gum (it can cause choking if it's accidentally swallowed in a fall) chewing while mounted

6. Emotionally suited to be mounted at this time

Safety Check of Your Horse

1. Sound

2. Emotionally suited to his job and his rider

3. Physically suited to his job

4. Physically suited to his rider

5. Correctly shod for the work being done

6. Tacked up correctly for the job, his training level and the rider's skill level

Safety Check of Your Equipment

1. All hardware on the bridle

2. Leather and hardware that secure the bit to the headstall and reins

3. Condition of leather in bridle and saddle

4. Condition of stirrup leathers or fenders

5. Stitching on billets or condition of latigo strap

6. Stitching on stirrup leathers

7. Safety catch on stirrup bars of English saddle in unlocked position

8. Condition of saddle tree

9. Condition of girth or cinch

10. Tightness of girth

11. Width of stirrup iron is suited to the rider's foot and footwear

12. Fit of bridle and saddle are suited to horse and rider

13. Condition of buckles, stitching and leather of auxiliary tack

14. Proper application of bandages or boots, if used

15. Suitability of saddle and bridle to job

A Western saddle correctly sized for the young rider who is using it.

Designing a 60-Minute Education Session

Recognizing and acknowledging your present level of competence, learning how to screen your teachers, selecting your horse partner and setting reachable goals are all ways of taking responsibility for your own success. Another is to understand the elements of a well-constructed schooling period or lesson. While you need not adhere *exactly* to the following format each time you ride or receive instruction, if you wander off the path too frequently, don't be surprised when your arrival at your destination is delayed.

The Lesson Format
Warm-up, 10 minutes
Goal: Horse and rider are relaxed, mentally present, ready to work.

Specific warm-up exercises will depend upon the stage of the rider's development, the stage of the horse's development and the work to be done later in the lesson. During the warm-up the rider should work on both reins, including brief times at all three gaits, when appropriate. Basic rider position checks (equal weight on seat bones, seat bones in the proper place on the saddle, legs well stretched down, feet under torso, etc.) and loosening exercises are used during the warm-up phase.

Review, 15 minutes
Goal: To refine the understanding and application of the aids. To strengthen and improve suppleness and refine response time in the horse.

Rider and horse execute exercises they have already learned, becoming familiar with each gymnastic pattern, its underlying concepts, its mechanical execution (the sequence and application of the aids) and the feel of improved movement and carriage in the horse. An instructor's input here should be designed to help educate the rider about the importance of selecting productive exercises aimed at improving her horse's performance, while encouraging the rider to choose the *order* of exercises and asking for an explanation of why the rider chose that *particular* exercise and why she placed it where she did in the work sequence.

New Material, 20 minutes
Goal: To expand the athletic capabilities of horse and rider. To increase strength, balance and endurance. To polish execution and improve focus.

An instructor will not add totally new material every lesson; it may take the average horse and rider weeks (if not months) of physical and mental practice to begin to grasp and execute each of the basic steps of riding. However, new *exercises* that stress the use of previously learned skills will be introduced frequently to make sure neither the horse nor the rider become bored with the work. When the student is ready to move to the next level of riding and new material is introduced, an instructor should:

1. Demonstrate the new material.

2. Explain the exercise.

3. Explain its purpose, the correct aids, possible evasions and corrective action.

4. Have the rider execute the exercise.

5. Offer feedback about the work.

Absorbing and practicing one new concept or exercise per week is a good goal. The best results are accomplished when a horse and rider are allowed time to learn an exercise thoroughly. Rushing into new exercises or advanced patterns short-circuits successful learning. A good instructor will have a great variety of exercises for each stage of learning that will enable riders and their horses to improve their skills while ensuring the lessons stay fresh for both.

Cool Down, 10 minutes

Goal: To return the horse's muscles to a state of nonperformance relaxation.

When exercises, weather or other factors have caused the horse to become heated, time must be allowed at the end of the work period to return the horse to a normal condition. This is especially important if the work is physically demanding. Without proper attention to cooling down the horse's muscles, he may become stiff and sore, which teaches him to anticipate future work sessions with resentment.

Wrap Up, 5 minutes

Goal: To clarify the rider's understanding of the exercises practiced and the results obtained that day.

An instructor should give a concise recap of the lesson and the goals accomplished or attempted, or ask the rider to do so. Any questions the rider may have about the material covered or the execution of the exercises should be encouraged and answered. Your instructor may also give you a homework assignment.

If you are riding this session on your own, without an instructor present, at the end of the session enter a few notes in the horse's training log book. List the exercises you did or attempted to do, including details such as size of circles, what gaits were they ridden in and so on. Note how the horse responded (for example, "performed well to the right, leaned on the inside rein to the left"), and any corrections you applied to either yourself or the horse that seemed to improve the work (for example, "horse leaning on inside rein going counterclockwise, rode some shoulder-fore exercises and his carriage to the left improved and he became lighter on the inside rein" or "horse rushing fences, dropped height and worked over cavaletti, then a simple grid, returned to working lines and he maintained his tempo between fences much better.").

Chapter 5

Developing Skills

*T*here are 10 basic lessons the all-around rider must master. In order of importance, they are:

1. How to align (balance) the skeleton with a minimum of tension, using efficient and appropriate muscle groups.

2. How to locate his or her center of gravity and selectively, influence its location.

3. How to make an accurate mental map of the location and normal range of motion of the body's shock absorbers, the joints.

4. How to articulate the body, using the joints.

5. How to recognize and become attuned to the two planes of balance in the rider and the horse.

6. How motion changes the picture of balance for both horse and rider.

7. How a rider's weight, tension level, breathing patterns and center of gravity affect a horse's balance and movement.

8. How the innate design of the horse's structure affects his balance.

9. How to control, coordinate and balance the body on the kinetic surface of a horse's back.

10. How to isolate, activate, coordinate or neutralize his or her body, both as a whole unit and in selective parts, to influence, enhance and strengthen the horse.

The Impact of the Kinesthetic Sense on Learning to Ride in Balance

One of the most valuable insights offered to riders by the Centered Riding method is that it is possible to improve your mounted skills while on the ground. This is a very new and controversial idea in the equestrian disciplines and many find it hard to believe. Yet not only is it true, it is also easy to demonstrate.

Since good riding is about harmony of motion, it is also about balance; before the human body can begin to refine motion, balance must be refined. The baby who struggles to stand succeeds in balancing his torso over his feet, usually with the assistance of an object against which he steadies himself the first few times. That first step from all fours to two legs is an immense one, which some scientists claim divides us from the animal world. But when that same child initially tries to put himself in motion, boom—down he goes on his diaper. Balance in motion is a different skill than balance in stillness, and riding is all about motion. But before we can attempt to do anything more than hang on to our horse with the muscles in our legs and arms, we need to regain the knowledge we discovered as babies: how to stand up and balance ourselves efficiently, without excess tension.

In this first lesson, then, you will make yourself aware of how you currently use your body when you are not in motion. Position yourself in front of a mirror, then turn sideways so you have to look directly across one shoulder to see yourself. Standing on a level surface, with your feet comfortably placed under your hips, look straight ahead and perform the action of standing up straight. Now, before you look across your shoulder into the mirror again, check the following: Notice where most of the weight is located in your feet, evaluating them from toe to heel. It is common to find most of your weight is toward your heels. Place one hand behind your back and feel the area of your lower back, just below your waist; notice if it feels hollow or curved under your hand. Now notice that your mind is telling you that when you hold your body in this position, you are standing up straight. Now turn your head and look at yourself in the mirror.

If your weight is on your heels or, less commonly, on your toes and your back is hollow or arched, you are not standing in *natural* balance, but rather are in a *compensating stack*. The compensation is usually required because you have locked your knee joints. Locking the knee has a ripple effect, causing each major body block above it to shift to keep the entire body from crashing to the ground. Sometimes the shifts are subtle, but they are never accomplished without adding tension to the body, because when each section shifts, more muscles are called upon to take up the job of helping to keep you erect.

This compensating stack generally works, except for one small problem: You want to ride and you want to ride well, which means your body

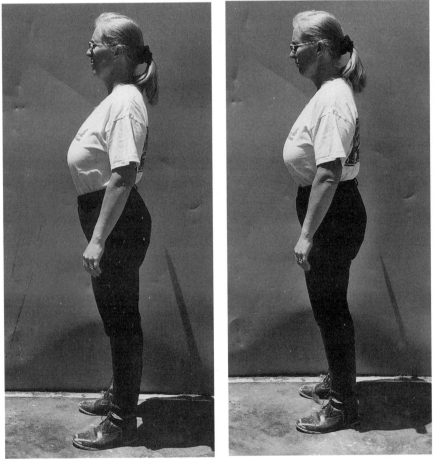

Standing in a compensating stack, with the knees locked, the weight on the heels and the back arched.

Standing straight in natural balance.

Tension turns your seat into a bouncing tennis ball.

BETHANY CASKEY

must be able to follow the horse's movement. Excess tension is your enemy, providing temporary security at the cost of freedom of movement for both the rider and the horse. When your body becomes tense, the joints have more difficulty functioning. Think about what would happen if you put a block of wood on a horse's back next to a soft cloth. When you move the horse around, which do you think would stay on the longest, and why? While you can't be limp like a rag (since you must use your body not only to follow the horse's movements, but to control and shape them as well), there is no doubt that the stiffer you are, the more the horse wants to bounce you, like a tennis ball, off the court of his back when he moves.

Rediscovering the freedom of a child's body involves learning how to deliberately choose to release tension from various muscle groups and realign your skeleton efficiently. Starting with your knees, you'll release the lock by tightening the quadriceps muscles (the muscles at the fronts of the thighs) and then relaxing them. As you do this, you will feel your knees unlock or flex slightly.

Proceed up to your hip joint. Feel for the precise spot where the top of your leg bone (the ball of your hip joint) actually joins your pelvis (the socket of your hip joint; see the photo below)—not just where you *think* it is located. This is an important detail! If your mental map of your hip is skewed or fuzzy, when your brain tells your leg to move (for instance, when you want your horse to go from a walk to a trot), you will activate 10 times more muscles in the area of the hip as you need to. But if the leg moves, what's the problem? All the unnecessary muscles are loaded with tension and that tension is working against both you and your horse, making your jobs harder, robbing you of security and robbing you both of fluidity and comfort. That's the problem!

Finding the exact spot on your body where the ball of your hip joint actually joins your pelvis (the socket of your hip joint) is critically important to finding the correct basic position on the horse and being able to easily modify that position to accommodate your style of riding to the different activities you may want to try with your horse.

Think of it this way: You're a colonel (the nerves) in charge of a squad of soldiers (the muscles) and your commander (the brain) gives you an order to move an important piece of equipment. But you don't know precisely where that equipment is located, so you have to send in a lot of soldiers to ensure you get the job done quickly. If you knew the precise location of the equipment, you could just send two men instead of tying up 200. That is exactly what happens in your body when your mental picture of the physical schematics of how you function is not clear.

After you have found your hip joint, keep your knees slightly unlocked and notice that you can fold or close your hip joint and bring your torso forward with your back flat (that is, without curving or arching it).

Now, knowing the exact location of the joint, your goal is to move your torso forward *only from the hip joint* (you shouldn't sway from your feet). Stop moving your torso forward when your shoulders are directly over your feet. This may make you feel as though you are leaning forward at

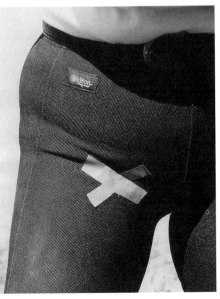

Bringing the torso forward by using the hip joint.

Bringing the torso forward by rounding the spine makes the hip joint tighten and stress the back.

first. When you experience this distorted kinesthetic sense, check to see what the reality of gravity tells you by noticing again where your weight rests in your feet (between the heel and toe), then turn your head and look in the mirror. Disregard, for the moment, any tendency you might have to appear slightly round-shouldered; just look for the plumb line that now drops from your ear through the middle of your torso and your hip joint to your ankle. Your back should appear flat (not arched or rounded), your knees should be *very slightly* flexed, and your body will be directly over your feet (refer back to the photos on page 95).

When you first find a balanced position, use the mirror to confirm that you are truly upright—since your kinesthetic sense, which has become distorted through years of inaccurate input, may try to fool you into thinking or feeling you are actually learning forward—then learn to trust the feel of the equal distribution of weight in your feet.

The experience of distorted kinesthetic sense can happen both longitudinally and laterally. If you accept and input inaccurate labels, such as "straight," into your sensory system, when in reality you are using a lot of tension to balance your body, your system not only accepts the misalignment as normal, but will eventually fight any attempt to correct the distortion by giving you inaccurate sensory feedback!

Ever take a riding lesson where your instructor had to tell you either to sit up, lean back or lean forward over and over again, and no matter how hard you tried, you couldn't seem to do it or hold the right position? If so, your inability was probably controlled, not by a lack of effort or anatomical issues, but by your distorted kinesthetic sense. Your brain was insisting that you were already where your instructor wanted you to be (so why in the world couldn't he see that?). When your brain is feeding you that type of misinformation, you tend to simply tune out an instructor and stop trying to correct your position.

As you practice this exercise, after unlocking your knees and moving or floating your torso forward until the weight in your feet feels evenly distributed over the whole foot, resist the temptation to follow the misinformation your brain may be feeding you and just study your reflection in the mirror. Now deliberately and *slowly* allow your body to move back into your old position, watching yourself closely in the mirror as you do. Notice just what you are doing with your body as you return to your old *known* and *therefore comfortable* position. Chances are you'll see yourself lock your knees and pull your shoulders back, pushing your pelvis forward as you do, which will throw most of your weight back onto your heels. After watching yourself move into this out-of-balance or compensating stack posture, which has been normal up to now, release your knees again, then move up to the next joint (the hip) and unlock it by touching the area (on the front of your pelvis) with a finger and floating your torso forward, until once again you feel the weight of your body is balanced equally over your feet, from heel to toe.

If your back is very hollow and tense, you may have to work at releasing the tension there, until your back appears flat, before your balance will settle in the middle of your feet when your shoulders are directly over your ankles. Repeat the exercise several times at first, then once a day for a week, then a couple of times a week for three more weeks. By the end of that time, your brain will have accepted the new, efficient position, and if you force yourself back into your old stance, you will notice you no longer feel comfortable. You may also notice your back feels more relaxed in the new, adjusted position, especially when you have to stand in one place for any length of time.

If you have trouble finding your balance when you *float* (use this word to picture your torso as a helium-filled balloon that is anchored to your legs at your hip joints, but moves easily and always wants to rise toward the sky) or allowing your shoulders to move forward, add the grounding influence of a kangaroo's tail. As you allow your imaginary tail to rest on the ground behind you, the heavy tail tends to pull your pelvis (to which it is attached) into a vertical position (rather than allowing the top of the pelvis to tip forward, as it does when there is tension in the lower back). Realize that now you no longer have to balance on your two legs, but rather, imagine balancing on the much more stable tripod formed by your legs and your imaginary kangaroo tail. This is also one of the ways in which you can learn to change the center of gravity in your body from the front, behind your belt buckle, to in the back of your body, against your spine. Once in the saddle, that action will help you plug your seat bones into the back of the horse, making a clear connection along which information can travel both ways.

Each time you repeat the stacking exercise, breathe in, feel the changes, notice areas of diminishing tension in your body and, if necessary, verify the change. Confirm what you feel by looking in the mirror. Working back and forth between the two extremes—the known and the new—will help you more quickly adapt your mental map and find the place where your back feels most comfortable and where you feel balanced and grounded over your feet.

When you have practiced your standing position for a few days, widen your stance and bend your

This rider is demonstrating an arched back posture. Notice her seat bones are pointed backward.

Think of your kangaroo tail to help remind your body how to allow your pelvis to find a vertical alignment, rather than tipping forward or backward as you settle into your saddle.

BETHANY CASKEY

knees, as though you had just mounted your horse, and start again. Keep going back and forth between what you feel in your body and what you see in the mirror. Remember, to allow your horse complete freedom to move, your body must be in balance over your feet. If it is not, gravity is dragging you back and down when your horse goes forward or accelerates.

After becoming accustomed to your new body map by practicing it on the ground, it will be time to do the same work on your horse, where you will also float your torso directly up over your seat bones so your feet can stay directly under you, acting as a broad base of support under your torso. Check your back with your hand when sitting in the saddle, to make sure it is still relaxed and feels flat, not arched or rounded.

When exploring the alignment of your skeleton in the saddle, notice what the various changes of position (leaning forward or leaning backward) do to change the tension levels in the muscles of different areas of your body, including your back, abdomen, chest, seat, thighs and legs. When you realize that a good balanced position results in less tension in specific areas of your body (for instance, the muscles of your lower back, groin and inner thigh), you can use these areas for spot checks as you ride to confirm the correctness of your position when there are no mirrors to look into or an instructor to tell you when you are properly positioned.

The books *Centered Riding* and *Centered Riding 2, Further Explorations* by Sally Swift, *Connected Riding* by Peggy Cummings, *BodySense* by Sally Tottle, *Ride With Your Mind Essentials* by Mary Wanless, *The Less-Than-Perfect Rider* by Lesley Bayley and Caroline Davis, and *An Anatomy of Riding* by H. Schusdziarra, MD, and V. Schusdziarra, MD, delve deeply into the subject of rider balance. These books promote biomechanical freedom, using drawings and illustrations to help the reader/rider create accurate mental images of the goals to be achieved.

Lateral Balance

Do you remember the nursery rhyme that goes "Humpty Dumpty sat on a wall, Humpty Dumpty had a great fall? All the king's horses and all the king's men couldn't put Humpty together again!" Being an egg (or at least egg shaped), H.D. had nothing to secure his position on that wall except his balance. Riders, for the most part, have it easier. Your legs, which hang down on either side of the horse's body, tend to stabilize your torso, preventing you from sharing H.D.'s fate even when you are unevenly balanced on a horse's back. Since gripping with the legs keeps you from feeling you are in danger of falling, you may not notice an unbalanced lateral position. Besides, if you are not in danger of being dislodged because of your uncentered position, it's not really a problem.

If you think that, just talk to anyone whose work involves transporting heavy loads: a longshoreman, a trucker, a sailor, a pilot, a hiker with a backpack. Each of them will tell you the potential disasters that can be caused by an unbalanced load. It can sink a ship, cause a driver to loose control of his truck, crash a plane and injure a hiker. So let's revisit our question: If you sit a little off center on your horse's back, is it a big deal? The answer is yes! Rider imbalance contributes to multiple problems in horses, including sore backs, muscle fatigue, cramping, lameness, uneven muscular development, tendon and ligament injuries, saddle fit problems and, most importantly, it can and does rob your horse of his athletic potential. The more you want to help your horse become good at more than a single job, the more important it is for you to understand and practice riding in balance on *both* planes.

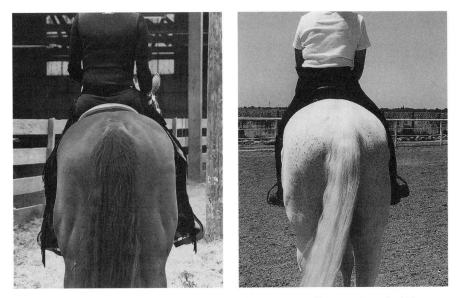

Study the photos of these two riders. Both are sitting off-centered to the left.

Three of the most common causes of lateral imbalance are:

1. **Curling.** This term refers to riders who have a collapsed or contracted side when mounted. The rider's shoulder is closer to her hip on one side of her body, causing what appears to be a C curve in the torso or spine. The posture is important to recognize and eradicate, because the rider in this position cannot place both of her seat bones equally into the saddle; the seat bone opposite the curled or compressed side lifts off the saddle, since the pelvis is not level. A rider then unconsciously struggles to level her seat as she rides by reaching down with the leg on the same side as the floating seat bone. This action eventually pulls the rider's saddle off center. It can also account for the constant feeling that one stirrup is shorter than the other—an extremely annoying sensation that many riders try to solve by adjusting their stirrups unevenly.

   If you find that you curl your body to one side when you ride, there is a simple Centered Riding exercise that can help. While sitting in the saddle, lift your hand and arm on your contracted side into the air and stretch your rib cage up. Breathe into that side of your body, and as you do, reach down with your leg on the same side. Position your hand so your palm points inward, not forward or backward. Hold the position for a few strides and

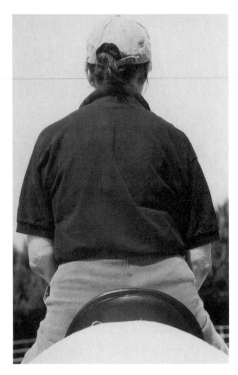

Here you see a collapsed right side. The rider's right shoulder is lower than her left, there is a pronounced wrinkle in her shirt just over the area of her collapsed rib cage, and the collapse in her body has sent her seat to the left so you can see more of her buttocks and thigh on the left side of the cantle than you can on the right side.

notice any changes in your body. Remember, the distorted kinesthetic sense may try to tell you that you are wrong. But wait and notice the tension pattern in your body and the pressure in your seat bones. Is it more even? Did the feeling of always losing one stirrup stop for a few strides? Are your back, shoulders and neck more relaxed? How about your horse? Now lower your arm and continue to ride with an awareness of the feeling in your seat. When you begin to lose your feeling of balance, repeat the exercise. Do it as often as you think necessary, until your body and brain begin to accept the new position as normal.

Just like the wicked queen's mirror in the story of Snow White, a mirror doesn't lie, so you can use it to check yourself to see if you have a habitual curl in your body. Standing with your feet comfortably spaced, face the mirror and look at yourself. Do the angles of your shoulders appear to be the same, or is one as steep as a ski slope while the other appears almost level? A sure sign of a strong contracted pattern is that if you raise your arm on your short side (the side with the lowest shoulder), your head will want to tip toward the raised arm. You'll have to watch yourself in the mirror to believe it, because your brain will try to tell you you're only centering yourself. But in fact, as you look, you'll see the bridge of your nose is no longer lined up with your breastbone, and when you force yourself to level your head and bring your nose back to the middle where it belongs, your brain will scream at you that you are out of balance. Remember, the old patterns want to dominate and your brain will work against you for about one month before it will be willing to accept the new, balanced pattern as correct.

Now try to see if the top of your pelvis is level. If it is not, your pelvis may be rotated and you may need to consult a chiropractor and have your spine realigned before you will be able to sit evenly balanced on both seat bones when you are in the saddle. Change takes time. Maxwell Maltz, MD, a famous plastic surgeon, says in his book *Psycho-Cybernetics* that it takes 28 days to change a body pattern, so don't become discouraged.

It's best to have an instructor's feedback during this time, but videotapes made of you while you ride will also enable you to assess your progress if an instructor is not available. Even a friend who doesn't ride can help you, if you point out your patterns to them. It is next to impossible for a rider to feel straightness in her horse if she cannot make even contact with the saddle with both seat bones.

2. **A hooked leg.** This occurs when the rider twists one leg to use it against or under the horse's belly for an increased feeling of security. The toe of the hooked leg turns out and sometimes the heel is pulled up as well, while the rider's other leg hangs down the opposite side of the horse's barrel in a relaxed, correct manner. If your body is positioned this way, you may also expect the muscles and ligaments around the hip joint and the groin on the side of your hooked leg to be significantly tighter than those of your other leg. The more time you have spent riding in this particular position, the more difference you can expect between your two sides in the area of your hips. This tightness may make it difficult for you to lengthen your hooked leg, even after you understand the mechanics of what you are doing and know you don't want to ride in that position.

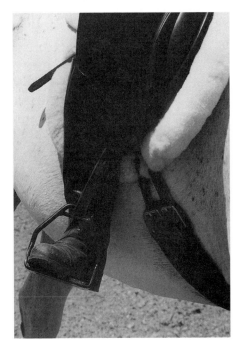

A hooked leg.

The actively contracting muscles on the hooked leg side tighten the hip joint and act as cables, contracting that side of the body, which, in turn, pushes your seat toward the opposite side of the saddle, causing you to become laterally unbalanced on the horse's back and eventually making the saddle crooked on his back as well. To correct this problem, lift the hooked leg away from the saddle from the hip, rotate the thigh inward, pulling the heel outward and away from the horse's side, then relax your leg, letting it fall back against the horse, but with the *inner side* of your calf in contact with the horse's barrel, rather than the muscles at the back of your calf.

A hooked leg can also cause a diagonal imbalance in your seat, bringing one seat bone further forward, while forcing the other seat bone toward the cantle. This can make it difficult for a rider to find and rise with the correct diagonal at trot, and can also cause the horse to refuse to take a canter lead in one direction.

3. **Not sitting in the middle of the saddle.** When you're dealing with lateral balance issues, it pays to do a quick spot check to see if your back muscles might be stronger and better developed on one side than the other, which can also contribute to a rider sitting crookedly. Try positioning yourself on your hands and knees on the floor. Keep your head in line with your spine (look at the floor during the exercise), your back flat and your spine straight. Now lift and extend one leg and the opposite arm. Hold the position for two minutes, or until you become shaky, then switch, lifting and extending the other leg and its opposite arm. You will quickly feel a difference if you are contracted or unevenly developed in the musculature of your back.

Try this exercise to discover if your back muscles are stronger and better developed on one side than the other.

Before leaving the issue of lateral balance, I must mention the saddle. A crooked saddle tree will cause a rider to sit crookedly. Trees can become twisted or warped a number of ways. Even a brand new saddle can have a twisted tree. Heat and humidity can warp trees, as can storing a saddle in a position that does not correctly support the tree. Finally, a crooked rider and/or an unevenly muscled horse can tweak a tree over time and repeated use. A saddle with a twisted or warped tree must be replaced. However, if you replace the saddle without addressing your own unbalanced position and/or the horse's uneven muscling problem, eventually a new saddle may also become distorted.

The Significant Role of Joints as Shock Absorbers

The rider positions for speed work, jumping and ascending and descending a hill all require the use of the joints. Your joints must be unlocked and elastic so you can fold your body into the compressed frame required for these jobs. To fold from the hips, the shoulders must be brought forward, which means the hips must be allowed to move rearward in the saddle or the rider ends up feeling as though she is precariously balanced on a diving board, about to take a nosedive over her horse's front end.

For example, to ride downhill efficiently, a rider moves with her horse, allowing the horse's energy to come up from the stirrups through her flexible joints—especially the knee and ankle joints, which, acting as shock absorbers, accept the roll of the horse's barrel and shoulders without resistance. This unlocked, tension-free position allows the horse complete freedom of movement, giving him the ability to access his full range of motion, as well as the full shock-absorbing capacity of his own joints, which he needs to defend himself against gravity and contact with the ground.

Conversely, if the rider is positioned in a way that interferes with the horse's necessary biomechanics even a little, tension is created. As a result of this limiting tightness and tension in his muscles, the horse is handicapped, exhibiting a shortened stride, which forces him more to carry his weight on his forehand. This poor-quality movement can aversely affect the horse's biomechanical systems, and sometimes his emotional state as well.

This same pattern can be observed in the rider approaching a fence who, unable to allow her body to flow with her horse on the approach to the jump, throws herself stiffly forward onto her horse's neck as he leaves the ground. The sudden shift of balance hinders the horse's efforts, sometimes causing the horse either to hit the top rail or refuse the jump.

While a rider's correct upper body angle (forward, not backward) is of great importance in the equation of balanced riding and a horse's subsequent efficient movement, it is not the only factor. To maintain this efficient position, the rider needs to address several items. Her foot must contact the stirrup in a way that enables her toes to rest higher than her heels, giving the ankle and knee joints the ability to flex with every stride. Her knees must be able to compress slightly in an alternating manner with each stride the horse takes (this is invisible to someone watching, but feels to the rider as though she had springs in her joints). Like shock absorbers, the knees and ankles of the rider assimilate the upward traveling energy of the foot strike as each of her horse's legs contacts the ground. This is particularly true at the moment a horse touches down from his flight over a jump.

The stirrup must be short enough to make a platform for the foot to rest upon lightly when the ankle, knee and hip joints are flexed. The more flexed the joints, the greater shock absorbing capacity they provide, hence the generally shorter stirrup length for jumping and racing and the longer length for Western riding or hacking on flat ground.

Tips for Riding on Uneven Ground

For some, riding through fields and on trails is as normal as breathing and they don't give it a second thought. But if you've spent most of your riding time in an arena, venturing out onto varying topography can be a big deal and somewhat intimidating at first. The good news is that the biomechanics of riding over uneven ground can be learned and practiced in the arena, and are basically the same as learning to jump or riding over cavalletti in two point (half seat).

The three most common mistakes made by riders attempting to negotiate uneven terrain are:

1. Leaning back with the torso

2. Stiffening the joints

3. Standing in the stirrups

Leaning Back

Leaning back is inefficient because it forces the rider's weight to the rear, interfering with the horse's ability to round his loins and engage his hind legs. It can also strain the horse's stifle joints and hocks.

For your horse to carry his own weight and yours on his hindquarters, freeing his front feet to reach out (so he can lengthen his stride, climb a hill or slide down a steep bank), fold his cannons and lift his knees (so he can jump) or unfold and land lightly (ensuring long-term soundness), the horse must be encouraged to place his hind feet well under his body. A horse carrying at least half of his weight on his rear limbs is both easier to control and safer to ride. He can easily correct a stumble, quickly lift a foot off a sharp stone to avoid a stone bruise, or reposition a foot that has landed in a hole to avoid a fall or a strained tendon. If you throw your weight backward, toward the rear of your horse, you load the loin muscles of the horse and hamper the bio-mechanics the horse must execute to flex his hip, stifle, hock and pastern, while engaging his hind legs to carry himself efficiently and athletically.

Stiffening the Joints

The second mistake commonly made by riders is stiffening the joints of their ankles and knees. Stiffness prevents the rider from absorbing and dissipating the energy generated by the horse's motion. The energy is then amplified by the rider's tension and returned to the horse as jarring impact, causing tension in the horse, especially in the muscles of his back. Without a freely swinging back, the horse's shoulder and hip are less free to allow the horse's legs to move, and again, we have a situation where the horse can't balance and defend himself because he can't freely use his own limbs.

The same position rules apply to a rider jumping a fence well, and riding a horse at high speeds. In all instances, the rider's joints must both open and compress to accept the movement of the horse as his energy passes through her. Holding a two-point position while trotting downhill is a good test of rider position (that is, balance) and free movement of the joints. Cantering descents magnify the test even more, but must be undertaken with care on moderate slopes, as they invite loss of balance in the horse unless he is sufficiently strengthened and trained. And if the footing is hard or wet, this type of work can cause injury.

Standing in the Stirrups

When a rider stands in her stirrups, all of her body weight and much of her energy is directed downward, through her feet, onto the stirrups. The stirrups displace this pressure up the stirrup leathers into the saddle tree, focusing most of the rider's weight onto a restricted area of the horse's back, just behind his shoulder blades. Pressure in this area pinches the muscles the horse uses to move his forelimbs, making the job of climbing more difficult.

Since the horse is unable to freely and comfortably stretch his front legs when this happens, he shortens his stride. With his back muscles impeded, the horse will raise his head to climb—a biomechanical action that further shortens and contracts the back and stiffens the horse's entire body, reducing the ability of his hindquarters (his most efficient power source) to push him up an incline. The horse then grabs at the ground with his front legs, *pulling* rather than *pushing* himself up the hill, overusing and taxing the muscles of his neck, chest and forearms, and the flexor and extensor tendons of his front legs as he attempts to do a job with second-string muscle groups. The pattern is most evident when a horse who is mentally and physically unprepared is put to a really steep incline; this can cause a horse to panic and attempt to rush up the hill by lunging up the incline.

An optimal rider body position to help a horse climb uses the hip, knee and ankle joints. The rider closes her torso over her horse's neck by flexing at the hip joint. This will lift her buttocks slightly out of the saddle, redistributing the weight from her seat onto her inner thigh muscles (no gripping!), causing a smaller amount of weight to descend to the stirrup. Her weight, being centered over her feet, does not overload the horse's front end or his hind end. If the terrain becomes extremely steep, the rider can grab a handful of mane to help maintain her upper body position and increase her calf pressure slightly to keep her legs and feet from swinging back, bumping into the horse's stifles.

The horn placement on a Western saddle will force a rider to transfer more weight to the stirrups to lift her seat further out of the saddle so her torso can be brought forward without the horn impaling the rider's ribcage.

To enable the rider to bring her body forward on an ascent, the horse must lengthen his top line as he climbs, lowering his head and neck. A horse whose back is hollow, forcing his head up, would make it very difficult if not impossible for a rider to put herself in an efficient posture. The situation can quickly become a catch-22: The horse can't work efficiently unless his rider is correctly positioned, and the rider can't position herself well if her horse is using his body in the wrong biomechanical posture.

Horses can use inefficient patterns to perform a required job for many years, even performing it fairly successfully, but sooner or later incorrect

In this sequence of photos, we see an example of the maximal athletic effort asked of an event horse on cross-country at Rolex, one of the highest level three-day events in the United States. The horse, who is jumping out of water, must touch down on the top of the narrow middle element, before dropping off the other side into water again.

The rider, erect rather than forward, is balanced with her horse. Her defensive riding position could interfere with the horse's ability to lift himself out of the water, but definitely adds to the rider's ability to stay aboard if her horse should slip or misstep during the sequence of huge jumping efforts demanded by this multiphase obstacle.

By looking at the horse's use of his body, however, we can see that his back is rounded and the rider's position did not interfere with her horse's mechanics or his ability to do his work.

Compare this horse's topline to the horse in the previous three photos. Here, the rider has been left behind the motion over the same jump, and the horse is struggling with the rider's awkward balance point.

biomechanics that reduce optimal performance and alter load distribution will increase the horse's risk of injury and accelerate degeneration. Caring riders take their part in the team effort very seriously by improving their own mechanics as well as training the horse to correctly use his body when carrying a rider.

For an illuminating look at the similarities of correct rider biomechanics in both jumping and cross-country riding, I recommend watching Horsemanship Volume 3 of the *U.S. Army Training Films—Cavalry Collection* from Vintage Video (P.O. Box 551, Greencastle, PA, 17225, www.vintagevideo.com).

The Secret of Lateral Balance on a Bending Line

When a rider fails to keep her center of gravity balanced over the horse's center of gravity when they're riding on a curve, the horse must use his body as a counterbalance for the rider, tensing his muscles to do so. This forces the horse to work harder, but more importantly, the horse's body is stiffened by the tension, reducing his ability to bend his joints or to keep himself level through the turn. In other words, a laterally uncentered rider will cause her horse to lean when traveling through an arc.

While horses naturally tend to lean rather than bend through an arc, a balanced horse who is supple and strong will contract his muscles to the inside of the bend, while allowing the ones on the outside to stretch, thus keeping himself level while traveling through an arc, rather than leaning in like a motorcycle. This levelness improves:

- Safety—less chance of slipping or stumbling

- Control—a horse in balance is easier to steer

- Comfort—the rider doesn't end up feeling like she is about to be flung to the ground

- Soundness—landing stress is better absorbed by the hoof when it lands level on its lateral plane, rather than on the inside or outside edge

While these factors all improve when you're laterally balanced riding through a turn, speed is lost. This is why you see extreme examples of leaning in the tight turns required in competitive barrel racing. By studying this discipline, you can learn the following important dynamic for staying in balance with a horse on a turn: The faster the speed and the greater the degree of inward lean in the horse's body, the more the horse's center of gravity moves inward toward the center of the arc. Any rider who wants to allow her horse the maximum amount of freedom to use his body, both for speed and to stay upright in such a precarious position, knows she must practice the principals of balance as she would on the ground. She must keep her inside hip over the foot that is on the inside of the turn, and her torso level. Everyone

This barrel racer, correctly balanced in this speed turn, keeps her inside hip over her inside foot. Balanced with gravity and centrifugal force as well as her horse's center of gravity in this way, she is allowing her horse maximum biomechanical freedom to use himself to his utmost in this extremely demanding sport.

learned this as babies; it's a simple law. No one walks around a corner with their hips flung to the outside and their shoulders leaning in, but lots and lots of riders ride that way through a turn!

To give you a feeling for what I'm talking about here, try the following exercise. Get a partner to play the role of the horse. Stand side by side and hook arms, then take a short walk together. Tell your "horse" partner to turn away from you. Allow yourself to be pulled through the turn with your linked arm, but keep your weight to the outside of the turn, perhaps even leaning a little away from the direction of the turn with your upper body. Insist your "horse" work as hard as necessary to complete the turn as quickly as possible. Now walk straight ahead again. Then ask your "horse" to turn away from you again (if your "horse" is on your right side, that means you would be turning to the right). This time, stay centered with your "horse" during the turn by keeping your inside (right) shoulder in contact with your "horse's" left shoulder throughout the turn. Now stop and talk over what you just experienced. Was the second turn easier for your "horse" to execute? Did it feel smoother?

Was the "horse" able to make a much tighter turn the second time? If you've done the exercise correctly, the answer to all these questions will be a resounding yes.

Now do the exercise again, with you playing the role of the horse and your partner acting as first the unbalanced, then the balanced rider.

Now that you know how much difference correct positioning and balance make to being able to execute a turn effortlessly, let's consider the biomechanics that will help you get into that optimum position when you're mounted.

If you face a mirror during this exercise and observe what you see as well as what you're feeling, you will learn with your eyes, your brain and your body. Begin the exercise by bend your knees and pretending you're sitting on your saddle. Hold your hands the same way you would if you had your reins, then move your body as though you are turning your horse to the right (but don't move your feet as you turn your shoulders). With your body in the turned position, see if you can lift your left foot an inch or two off the ground. You should be able to do this easily, keeping your foot up for several seconds without crashing to the floor. If you are like most riders, you will find you have to shift more of your weight from your left foot to your right foot before you can lighten your left foot enough to be able to lift it up. Now here's the revelation: The amount of weight you had to shift to your right foot in order to free your left foot is the amount of weight you were carrying off center during that turn!

To align yourself with your horse during turns, try the following. Before you begin a turn, look in the direction of the turn with your eyes, then flex and drop or lower your knee towards the ground slightly on the side toward which you are turning. Now turn your chest toward your direction of travel by swiveling *at the waist,* so both your chest and head face the turn. Pretend your collarbones are airplane wings. Keep your wings level as you go around bending lines. If you bank your turns by dropping your inside wing (or shoulder), you will unbalance yourself and your horse.

Practice these combinations of biomechanical exercises on the ground to develop your feel, then practice the same exercises in the saddle by riding your horse through a marked slalom course in an arena or through trees on a winding trail.

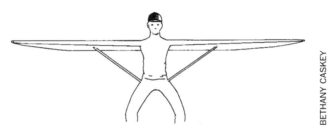

BETHANY CASKEY

To help remain balanced when riding turns, think of your collar-bones as airplane wings.

BETHANY CASKEY

This rider is riding through the turn in a balanced fashion, with his wings level.

BETHANY CASKEY

While this rider, banking his wings in the turn, is pulling the horse's weight onto the horse's inside shoulder.

Exercises to Improve the Rider's Seat, Position and Independent Use of the Aids

Every good athlete knows the importance of warming up their muscles. Simple stretching exercises are an important part of getting ready to ride. An excellent reference book for good stretching exercises is *Bob Anderson's Stretching*. Remember to take into account your age and flexibility before jumping into any exercise program, and never push your body into pain. Honor the feedback you get from yourself, and remember that if you stretch gently each day, taking yourself to the edge of your comfort level, the next day you will be able to stretch farther than the day before. Pilates and yoga are excellent cross training for riders.

The classical approach to rider training and strengthening involves a situation where the rider is allowed to concentrate on finding and

This position, with the back straight and the pelvis upright, stretches the iliopsoas and quadriceps muscles as the hip is moved forward and asked to open. Repeat on both sides.

This stretch addresses the groin, hamstring and front of the hip, as the hip is asked to close. Repeat on both sides. If you are less flexible, use a lower support for the raised leg. If the foot on the ground is turned at a right angle to the raised leg, the exercise will also stretch the muscles on the inside of the thigh of the leg on the ground. Always do any stretching with care and in moderation!

maintaining their basic position while on a longe line, often without the use of stirrups or reins. The instructor controls the horse and gives the rider suggestions for improving her position. Mounted exercises help create an independent seat by strengthening the back, making the torso more supple and promoting independent use of the rider's hands and legs. Done on or off a longe line, safety should always be paramount, which means a calm horse, under control.

The following illustrations show only a few of the many mounted exercises used to help riders find a better and stronger seat. Smart riders add them regularly to their warm-up period. To get the greatest result, perform the exercises slowly and precisely, with your focus on your body, and keep breathing deeply and regularly; don't hold your breath.

Airplane Wings

Affects: Torso and waist

Use: Makes the waist more supple

Develops the rider's independent control of the torso and legs

How to do: Lift your arms straight out from your shoulders as though they were airplane wings, then rotate slowly at the waist pointing your chest right, then front, then left, then front again, then repeat. Try to keep your lower leg in place against the horse's side as you rotate through the various positions.

BETHANY CASKEY

Toe Touches—Same Side

Affects: Torso, back and hips

Use: Develops flexibility in rider's waist and hip joints, strengthens the back

Improves balance

How to do: Fold your torso forward over horse's shoulder and reach down with your hand to touch your toes on the same side, without losing your balance.

Toe Touches—Opposite Side

Affects: Upper body

Use: Develops flexibility in rider's waist and hip joints

Improves balance

How to do: Swivel your shoulders, fold at hip joint and reach down to touch the toe opposite the hand you are using. When touching the opposite toe with your hand, you must release the muscles in the middle of your back in order to rotate your shoulders in reaching across the saddle, folding at the hip joint to touch the opposite foot.

BETHANY CASKEY

Knee Lifts

Affects: Flexibility in the hip joint, balance

Use: Improves rider confidence and balance

Improves hip flexibility

How to do: Float your torso forward and up, expand the muscles in the lower back, exhale and draw your knees up until they are touching (when possible) over the top of the saddle. Then release the legs and let them fall freely back to the sides of the saddle. This exercise can be done at a halt and a walk ONLY.

BETHANY CASKEY

Backward Windmills

Affects: Upper body, shoulders, neck, waist

Use: Balance

Independent hands

Releases tension from the shoulders

Helps prevent slouching or rounding of the shoulder

How to do: Start the exercise by placing one arm at the 12 o'clock position and the other arm at the 6 o'clock position. Then slowly rotate both arms backward, as if you are doing the backstroke. Keep the arms opposite each other as you do the circles.

Climbing a Rope

Affects: Upper body, midback, chest, shoulders, head

Use: Opens the chest

Relaxes tight shoulders

Helps correct rounded shoulders

Lifts the head and rib cage

How to do: Grasp an imaginary rope in front of your saddle and climb the rope, hand over hand, until your arms are fully extended above your head. Repeat several times. Can be done at halt, walk and/or a sitting trot.

BETHANY CASKEY

Toe Circles

Affects: Ankle flexibility

Use: Releases tension

Makes the ankle joint more supple

How to do: Imagine there's a pencil at the tip of your toes and try to draw a perfect circle by rotating your ankle. Draw 8 to 10 circles clockwise and then do them counterclockwise. Do the exercise one foot at a time so you can notice how each ankle feels during the exercise. Do at halt and/or walk.

Backward Bicycle

Affects: Hip joint, pelvis and lower back

Use: Loosens the hip joint

Releases the lower back

Helps the rider find the necessary two-sided motion in the pelvis to enable the her to sit deeply and perform a good sitting trot

How to do: Imagine the horse is a bicycle and use your legs and feet to peddle the bike in reverse. Do 20 to 30 repetitions. This exercise can be done at a walk and a slow trot or jog. Be sure your foot is making a complete circle and not just being lifted up and down in a straight line or simply being swung like a pendulum from the knee down.

Scissor Kicks

Affects: Groin and hip area

Use: Loosens the muscles and ligaments around the hip joints

Stretches the quadriceps muscles

How to do: Lock your knee joint and swing your legs from the hip only, in opposite directions at the same time. Perform this exercise only at a halt or walk.

BETHANY CASKEY

PERFECT PRACTICE MAKES PERFECT

First, stay centered.

Second, learn to control your seat (pelvis) with your "core" muscles and the muscles of your back.

Third, develop independent use of your reins and leg aids.

Fourth, learn the language of the aids so you can speak in intelligible sentences to your horse.

Fifth, study how horses move and learn to picture what your horse is doing in your mind's eye. Then, when you are in the saddle, feel him with and through your body and connect your remembered mental pictures with the feelings you receive through your legs, seat and torso.

Sixth, practice timing until it becomes a sixth sense.

A Learning Outline

You'll need to tackle the steps of your education in an organized, progressive way to maintain learning continuity and progression. Like a map that leads us toward our destination, the learning outline guides our journey through the topics of equestrian knowledge. Ask a young horse for too much too early, and you will ruin him. Bring him along slowly and systematically through the acquisition of skills, introducing each task when both his body and his mind have been correctly prepared, and he will not only succeed, he will excel—perhaps beyond your wildest dreams. If it is so for the horse, do you not see that it is so for the rider as well?

1. Prepare yourself for successful execution of your physical goals.

- Sharpen your mental images of your goals by attending lectures and demonstrations, participating in unmounted exercise programs such as Pilates and yoga, and watching other riders either schooling or at shows in the discipline you want to master.

- Study books on human and equine biomechanics and the causes and effects of riding.

- Select a coach who works well with you at your current level of experience.

2. Study the horse to know him, and know your equipment.

- Safe handling techniques (approaching, haltering, leading, tying, etc.) are as important as correct position in the saddle.

- Understanding the horse's point of view (he is a herd animal and a prey animal, his flight or fight response, etc.) helps you make good choices regarding riding and performance.

- Understand how to properly groom your horse (the tools, the sequence, the reasons for each step, how to groom safely, etc.), and use grooming as a time to observe your horse closely and connect with him emotionally.

- A good rider knows her equipment, what it does and why, knows how to apply it and adjust it correctly and safely and make the horse comfortable in it.

3. Important first lessons in the saddle.

- Learn correct and safe mounting and dismounting.

- Learn correct body posture and tension release work.

- Learn basic rein control for steering and stopping.

- Connect with the feel of the horse (the Centered Riding exercises at the beginning of this chapter are among the quickest and easiest ways to accomplish this step in rider awareness).

- Learn an emergency (vaulting) dismount.

4. Work for an independent, balanced seat.

- Hands-on manipulation of your body from a qualified instructor, will give you a feel for what is correct as you position your seat in the saddle.

- Learn correct leg placement and position and which muscles to use in order to maintain it.

- Ride on the longe line with and without stirrups.

- Perform precise mounted exercises.

- Learn the efficient biomechanics of a correct posting trot, including how to select and change your posting diagonals by feel.

- Expand your basic position to include work in the half-seat (the two-point position). This work will lay the foundation for more advanced work in disciplines that require galloping, jumping and work over uneven ground, such as trail riding.

5. Learn the correct use of your aids.

- Learn correct placement and activating muscle groups for using the hands and legs for guiding and controlling the horse.

- Learn to ride the school figures (circles, serpentines, diagonals, reverses, etc.) correctly and precisely.

- Learn the biomechanics of the half-halt and practice it by riding transitions between and within the gaits.

- Add the canter.

- Learn the correct position of the hands and the direction of applied pressure for the five rein effects, and how and why they influence the horse's lateral and longitudinal balance.

The Half-Halt

The half-halt is probably one of a rider's most important tools, yet it is also the one most often misunderstood by the largest number of equestrians. The half-halt is a biomechanical action of the rider's body that sends a signal to the horse to do one of four things:

1. Rebalance himself mentally and/or physically

2. Slow or collect his gait

3. Make a downward transition between gaits

4. Bring himself to a full halt

To apply a half-halt to the horse, you use your pelvis controlled by your core muscles to deliver any of the above four messages to the horse through his back and the reins The basic mechanics of the pelvis are the same in each instance; the difference lies in how much pressure is exerted by your seat bones on the horse's back and how long the pressure is applied.

Your core and back muscles are the primary controlling mechanism for the pelvis during the half-halt. Your upper arms remain in quiet contact with your torso, neither pulling back nor releasing the hand forward. Your seat, which normally follows the swing of the horse's back, becomes momentarily heavy and the seat bones, controlled by the back, cease their assenting, following action. By becoming still (momentarily resisting the rise of the horse's back), they convey to the horse your request for the horse to use the large muscles of his hindquarters to slow his progression or rebalance himself.

Your leg is applied a fraction of a second before your back acts, to encourage your horse to step more deeply under his body with his hind feet. This, in turn, causes the horse's shoulders and neck to rise and the horse to become lighter on his forehand. Your hands echo the seat's slowing action by remaining closed on the reins, allowing the horse to

A horse is like a seesaw: When one end goes down, the other end goes up. Point A is a forehand heavy horse. Point B is a horse in self-carriage. Point C is a collected horse. The half-halt is a tool for changing the balance of the seesaw.

BETHANY CASKEY

experience pressure from the bit if he is not instantly responsive to the signals he is receiving through his back from the rider's seat.

The mechanical action becomes muddied if a rider:

- Tenses or pinches with her knees during the application of her aids

- Pushes against her stirrups with her feet during the half-halt

- Brings her shoulders significantly behind her hips, in which case the pelvis becomes a driving force rather than a retarding signal to the horse

As soon as the horse shows any indication of compliance, the posture of the half-halt is released and the horse's energy is allowed to again flow unimpeded through his back. The entire sequence is then repeated to achieve a cumulative effect whose whole is greater than its parts.

The Centered Riding exercise known as *buttress* offers some of the best rider biomechanical education in the half-halt. This is taught by reenacting of the physical priorities of the rider when applying a half-halt in the saddle, through exercises practiced on the ground. The groundwork prepares the rider's nervous system both to understand and to respond correctly when the half-halt is attempted on the horse.

6. Strengthen your legs and back, and refine your timing of the aids.

- Learn two-point work with and without stirrups.

- Learn how to post without stirrups.

- Learn advanced rider exercises for control of each part of the body.

- Canter on a longe line without stirrups or reins.

- Learn how to do a sitting trot on a longe line without stirrups or reins.

- Learn how to make the transitions between and within the gaits without stirrups.

7. Learn to feel and control your horse's tempo and balance.

- Ride curved lines.

- Repeatedly lengthen and shorten the horse's stride.

- Work on transitions between the gaits.
- Learn, understand and ride lateral work (that is, leg yield and shoulder-in).

8. Work on uneven ground (it's time to leave the playpen).

- Learn to control the horse outside an arena.
- Work at all gaits on uneven ground.
- Learn to safely gallop cross-country.
- Learn the rules of the road of courteous trail riding.

9. Advance your skills by riding multiple tests.

- Familiarize yourself with cavalletti and master riding through them.
- Ride grids (gymnastic jumping lines).
- Ride jumps in related lines.
- Learn and practice riding the courses and patterns of various disciplines (hunter course, dressage test, trail course, reining patterns, cross-country course, gymkhana patterns, etc.).

10. You've done your homework, so what's left? Competition.

- Learn to control your focus.
- Make your nerves work for you.
- Learn how to analyze the course or job.
- Understand that strategy plays a part in any winning game.
- Videotape yourself riding.
- Review your performance.
- Make a plan to strengthen your weak areas.

- Try again.

- Learn to accept and enjoy your successes.

- Learn how to turn failures into stepping-stones to better performance.

Penmanship and Riding

Penmanship, which many of us learned in our early school years, is a series of exercises designed to train the mind and the muscles of the fingers, hand and arm to produce (eventually through habit) the figures that constitute our written communication system in a way that increases our chance of being understood. Writing may therefore be considered a form of body language. And learning to speak clearly to your horse with your body language is at the heart of any successful partnership with the animal.

The exercises in penmanship class consisted of drawing each letter on ruled paper, being careful to get the relationships of each line and curve right to create the letter of the alphabet you wanted. When you were able to clearly reproduce each letter of the alphabet in this way, you strung various letters together to form simple words, then words together to form sentences, then finally, multiple thoughts were put together as a complex way of expressing yourself.

Learning to communicate with your horse through the aids is like penmanship. You need to start with being able to reproduce, precisely, each "letter" of the body language system you want to use with the horse. Then you need to learn how to string those aids together in cohesive statements that will be noticed and understood by your horse. By the end of an hour's ride or training session, you will either have carried on an intelligible conversation with your horse that brings you closer to your harmonious partnership and active athlete goals, or you will have ended your time together in a stalemate or worse, with both of you frustrated by the experience.

Remember the ruled lines on penmanship paper? They served as visual aids that governed a physical destination. The classical lines and figures of the equestrian arena serve the same purpose: They develop the correct musculature and correct responses in your horse, *if you make your execution accurate* as you ride each training exercise. Like ruled paper, they help you articulate your alphabet to the horse. When strung together, the clear, well-timed articulation of this communication system between horse and rider (also known as the aids) creates a conversation that will enable the horse to grasp the goals you have for the partnership and help you prepare his body for the many tasks that lie ahead.

The School Figures

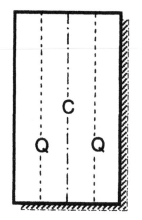

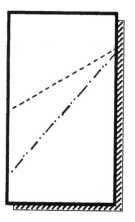

The riding lines in an arena include not only the track and the second track, (approximately four feet from the wall), but also the center line and the quarter lines shown here.

The diagonal line is most normally used to change rein or the direction of travel in the arena. Shown are the correct departure and arrival spots for both the short and long diagonal. A diagonal can be ridden from the long side immediately following the second corner of the short side, from any direction.

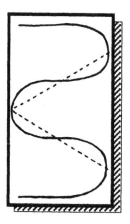

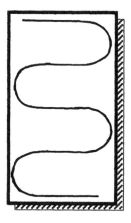

A serpentine of three loops, across the width of the arena. The solid line represents the correctly ridden figure. The broken line is what not to do.

A serpentine of four loops. When practicing serpentines, try to make each loop the same size.

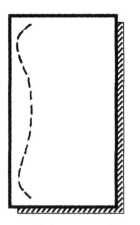

A single loop serpentine on the long side of the arena. The depth of the loop determines the difficulty of the exercise for both rider and horse.

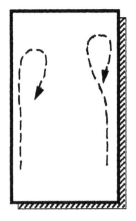

A half circle and reverse and a half circle in reverse. Again, the degree of difficulty is determined by the size of the arc and whether or not tempo and bend are maintained throughout the figure. Riding a turn with the half circle in reverse can help a horse who tends to be quick in his gait to slow his pace in anticipation of approaching or turning into the fence.

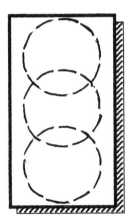

The most common location of 20-meter circles in a large arena. When ridden correctly, circles teach balance and help stabilize a horse's tempo.

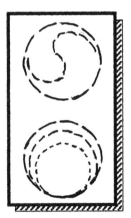

This diagram shows a change of rein through a large circle (also called an S change of rein), and a 20-meter circle, a 15-meter circle and a 10-meter circle.

Chapter 6

Getting Agreement

*I*n considering how to best build the team of an all-around horse and rider, our focus so far has largely been on the rider's role in the equestrian partnership. It is not the purpose of this chapter or this book to tell you which of the many systems of training horses that are popular on today's equestrian scene will be the best choice for you and your horse. Instead, my goal in the following pages is to make sure you are aware of some basic concepts that may affect your choice of training methods, and to make the interaction between you and your horse easier and more enjoyable for both of you.

We'll start with some basic concepts about the horse that every rider needs to understand.

1. Horses are every bit as individual as humans in their likes and dislikes, but are most often motivated by their basic needs. These include companionship, food, water, sex, exercise and play. The order or importance of these needs can vary with age and with the individual personality of the horse involved.

2. The horse is a herd animal, and as such is used to following a leader and living in a community with an established hierarchy. Most horses feel threatened if a leader is not present or if they are isolated or denied the company of others.

3. When interacting with people, horses are not likely to make allowances for a human's appalling lack of (horse) manners or social skills, because of the "different species" distinction. Upon first meeting a human, a horse is likely to be thinking, "Funny-looking horse, and just where do you fit into the social order of my herd?"

4. Understanding the social rules of horse behavior is important because the horse to human weight-size ratio favors the horse in the extreme. That means if your two bodies try to occupy the same space at the same time, the human is most likely to come up on the short end of the stick and it won't be the horse's fault. And nine times out of ten, it won't be personal either.

5. Horses respond best to positive reinforcement. However, they can and do easily differentiate between reward and bribery, and they also can and do recognize a *job*. Not only that, but they also know when they've done a job *well*, as most long-time horse owners can tell you. They can also be downright smug at times.

6. The horse naturally carries much of his weight on his forehand or front legs, so the focus of at least a part of your horse's training will be to prepare him for, and then influence him to carry, his weight and the weight of his rider evenly distributed over *all* four of his legs when he is under saddle. You may even want to reverse his natural tendency so thoroughly that he'll end up carrying or supporting all of his weight on his rear limbs in extreme movements such a sliding stop, a levade or when he leaves the ground to launch you both over a big obstacle on cross-country.

Establishing Your Leadership

The first step in training a horse is to establish your leadership status. If you've attended any of the multiple, nationwide horse expositions, such as Western States Horse Expo, or, Equine Affair, you have seen or heard what I will call the round pen system of training horses. Round penning is about establishing leadership in your herd of two (you and your horse). Of course, you can use a round pen simply to exercise your horse, but running a horse around a circular pen will not necessarily establish a connection with the horse or establish you in the position of herd leader. In fact, it is possible to abuse a horse mentally and physically by running him around in a pen. So if you intend to use the round pen as a tool for establishing your leadership, you need to understand some basics:

- The dominant horse, or leader, controls the movement(s) of the submissive horse(s).

- Horses are consistent and seek consistency in their leader and companions.

- Horses relate to body language, and you're using it whether you know it or not.

- Movement or pressure from behind the horse drives him forward.

- Movement or pressure in front of the horse's shoulder blocks, slows, stops or turns the horse.

- Horses need to be taught to move away from physical pressure, but will move away from mental pressure or discomfort on their own.

- Horses will move toward comfort.

- Horses are basically lazy, preferring to hang out with each other, eat and play.

- Horses are infallible barometers of congruency.

- All horses are right or left "handed" (sided), just like people.

- Being successful is not just about getting the horse to do what you want him to do; it is about getting the horse to think it was his idea in the first place.

Different horses will have different needs. Like humans in various stages of life, each horse will have been exposed to certain situations before you come in contact with him (unless you have bred and handled him from the time he was a foal). These experiences will have left an impression on your horse, making him easy to be around, or not, or possibly even difficult or dangerous. Before you can begin to choose the type of training that might best suit the needs of you and your horse, you will want to know if your horse will agree to consistently perform these three actions:

1. **Go** when you say so

2. **Stop** when you ask

3. **Respect** your space

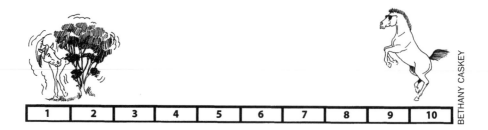

BETHANY CASKEY

You should assess the horse's physical condition as well as his mental state, and you will want to get to know his personality (which can change over time and with different experiences, just as humans do).

A helpful tool for mentally assessing a horse before you have to handle him, is to assign the horse a score on a leadership scale of 1 to 10. One represents the most timid personality you can imagine; the filly who shows the whites of her eyes when you try to approach and will shake if you look at her cross-eyed isn't about to lead anyone anywhere. Ten represents a very self-assured, confident personality, the type of personality one might expect in the leader of a herd.

While you want to occupy a higher place on the leadership scale than the horse you are going to interact with, you need to know that the lower the "leadership" number of the horse you want to work with, the less you will need to be above him to be the leader of your herd of two—especially if trust and friendship are your ultimate goal. For instance, if you are dealing with a horse who is a one, you want to present yourself as only a one and a half. If you are a boisterous, strong personality, an extrovert who displays a lot of energy through wide hand and arm gestures when you speak, or a pressure-cooker type who smothers anger under the facade of a calm exterior, you may find you have to tone down your personal presentation to be able to make a connection with a horse whose leadership number is in the lower range. In that way, he can assimilate the information you want to teach him, rather than focus on trying to escape you because you intimidate him.

On the other hand, if your horse is above a five, you will need to represent yourself as at least two points on the scale above your horse. For example, if your horse is a six and you only express yourself at a seven level of confidence and command, pretty soon your horse will begin to realize that with just a little more effort on his part, he can puff himself up to a seven and challenge you for the role of leader. Why would he want to do that? Because it is in his nature.

The dominant horse's responsibilities are to protect the herd against possible danger, and the species against annihilation. He gets the first water, the best food and the greatest respect for his personal space. While a horse lower on the scale may have to wait to drink or eat and give way when a horse who is higher on the scale moves into *his* personal space, he is also the one whom the big horse protects from predators. A horse who is lower on the scale experiences himself as such and wants to be protected. He needs the proximity of a big horse to feel safe from potential danger.

It is important to know that most timid horses are not comfortable when forced to occupy a big horse position in a herd. But, since instinct demands that a hierarchy exist in any herd (keep remembering, you and your horse constitute a herd), if you are unwilling to take the role of herd leader (or if your behavior is inconsistent with a leader), your horse will be *forced* into taking up the position. If a little horse is forced into a leadership position by his owner/handler/rider, the horse may become increasingly nervous to the point of becoming neurotic. Think of it from the horse's point of view. Here he is, trapped in captivity, sure there's a predator out there somewhere waiting to eat him (and maybe you, as well), and he has no big horse to protect him. In his position, you'd be a nervous wreck too! In our attempts to put right transgressions against the horse in history, today's politically correct approach to horses is "let's be partners." That position is fine, as long as you realize that within any partnership your horse still *needs to be a horse*, and know (and be able to honor) the herd hierarchy, before he can feel comfortable in his own skin.

When you understand the relationship of the personality scale to herd dynamics, it is easy to see and understand the underlying principals of it in the round pen system of training. When you use your authority and body language to control a horse's movement in the round pen, you are establishing your position as herd leader. If you are also consistent and clear in your requests, the horse you are working with will soon accept you as his leader, take directions from you willingly and even begin to look to you for comfort.

Understanding the privileges and responsibilities of leadership can also help you to understand why it is important for your safety that you function as your herd's leader. Remember, the lead horse's personal space gets the most respect. If your horse becomes frightened and tries to flee the scene, and you occupy a lower position than him in the herd, he has every right to move into your space as he attempts to leave, even if that means he runs over you in the process. If that happens, try to remember it was *you* who was in the wrong according to *his* social rules. Since he thought of you as subordinate, he expected you to carry out your responsibilities—that is, read his body language when you are in close proximity to him and move out of his way at the *slightest* (think ear twitch) indication he may intend to move in your direction. The system actually makes sense if you consider that *the stronger horse is the one capable of successfully protecting the herd*. If he is slowed down in his flight from danger by a weaker horse who is *not* capable of protecting the herd and falls victim to a predator, the entire herd is at risk. Nature tends to be very wise in these matters, and understood in this light, the personality scale has no overtones of privilege relative to a human sense of entitlement. Rather, it is engendered by nature's unerring sense of survival of the fittest.

It is your responsibility to establish your leadership role with your horse. If you do not, you cannot then be angry when your horse does something that is natural to him, even though his actions may cause you pain or injury.

Assessing Your Horse

Whether you're selecting a horse or selecting a system of training techniques that best fits your horse's needs, you must take into consideration your own personality, your horse handling skills and the level of your mounted skills relative to your horse's education. You will also want to have an idea of where you intend to be headed as a team—dressage, Western pleasure, jumper, trail horse, cow horse, reiner, etc.

Why is assessing your horse's abilities relative to a specific discipline important if you are looking to make him into an all-around horse? Even the most learned Renaissance scholars start by trying to master only a few topics at a time, adding to their depth of knowledge over years of study. Your all-around horse must receive a good, basic education before proceeding to any specialized training, and you will want to start his specialized training in an area that is appealing to him. For example, with a high-energy horse, you might want to allow him to experience jumping or cattle work before asking him to assume the sedate personality of a pleasure horse or a dressage horse.

No matter which specialty you school in, you will return regularly to *basic* work. You'll also want to avoid the pitfalls of being seduced into using the trend of the year training gimmick, and the siren song of the winners circle, which can catch you in the net of *drilling* your horse, rather than educating him, and exact a high price in his physical soundness or cause him to burn out mentally.

Determining Your Horse's Basic Level of Education, Balance and Sensitivity

Before beginning to work a horse under saddle, it is a very good idea to make sure your horse has had some basic education in ground work. Like school placement tests, your horse's ability to learn and perform the exercises that follow will give you clues to where he may be lacking in knowledge. They are also an outline for what you should teach your horse before you climb into the saddle and put yourself at risk aboard an animal whose very name is used to measure the power of racing cars and jet engines. Remember, the original comes with the very real possibility of being unresponsive to his pilot because he has an opinion of his own.

Test 1. The Command to Stand/Whoa

Give the "whoa" command to your horse, then walk out to the end of the lead rope and move around the horse as far as the lead line will allow in each direction. The horse must remain stationary.

To teach the *whoa* lesson, start by giving the command, then patiently replace your horse in the exact same spot each time he moves his feet, repeating the command. When you're first teaching any lesson, try to eliminate any distractions so your horse can focus his attention 100 percent on you. Calmness, patience and persistence are necessary for you to succeed in teaching a horse almost any lesson.

> Advanced exercise: Drop the lead rope completely and walk around the horse in a full circle.

> Graduate exercise: Give the command *whoa* while you're in a group of other horses, then have their handlers lead them out of the arena while your horse continues to stand.

Test 2. Leading Exercise

Position yourself at the shoulder of the horse, begin to move and the horse should follow you in any direction, slowing his stride or speeding up in harmony with your gait, without you having to pull on his lead rope in order to get him to stay with you.

Advanced exercise: Move at a pace fast enough to require the horse to trot to keep himself shoulder to shoulder with you.

Graduate exercise: Add *distractions* (such as new or scary objects) in the arena and ask your horse to follow you over or around them, again without your having to tighten the lead rope to restrain his movement or getting after him in any way in order to encourage him stay up with you.

Test 3. Giving the Head to Pressure

The horse will lower his head until his nose is touching ground when you lightly touch him on the top of his head just over his poll, between or just behind his ears.

Advanced exercise: Maintain the lowered head position for two minutes without the horse attempting to lift his head while there is an exciting activity going on close to the two of you.

Graduate exercise: Lower the horse's head into the same position with a touch on his neck in the area of his withers.

Test 4. Giving the Hindquarters to Pressure

The horse will move his hindquarters away in either direction at a signal from his handler, keeping his front feet relatively still while he moves his hind end.

Advanced exercise: Teach the horse to move his hindquarters while you stand at his shoulder and only point at his hindquarter with your finger, and cluck to him.

Graduate exercise: Be able to move and stop the horse's hindquarters in any combination of steps, in either direction, by applying or withdrawing the finger pointing cue.

Test 5. Giving the Forehand to Pressure

The horse will move his forehand away in either direction at a signal from his handler, keeping his hind feet relatively still while he moves his front end.

Advanced exercise: Teach the horse to move his forehand while you stand at his shoulder and only point at his forehand with your finger, and cluck to him.

Graduate exercise: Be able to move and stop the horse's forehand in any combination of steps, in either direction, by applying or withdrawing the finger pointing cue.

Test 6. Backing

Back your horse with a signal from in front of his head.

Advanced exercise: Back him in a straight line while standing in front of him and without touching his body.

Graduate exercise: Back the horse up a hill in a straight line while standing in front of his head.

Test 7. Longeing

Longe the horse at a walk, a trot and a canter in both directions without him pulling on the line or cutting in on the circle, causing the line to go slack.

Advanced exercise: Change gaits using only voice commands.

Graduate exercise: Free longe the horse in a large arena without using a whip, and do canter to halt and halt to canter transitions. Most successful trainers use some type of signaling tool to help them teach exercises four through seven. Some give it the name of a vegetable, other call it a wand. No matter what prop you use, what you *do* with it and the clarity of your *intent* are what matter most to your horse.

Test 8. *Cavalletti*

Longe the horse over cavalletti on the circle and in a straight line down the long side of the arena.

> Advanced exercise: Extend the trot over the cavalletti and slow to a walk on the other side without pulling on the line or pulling the horse off the straight line.

> Graduate exercise: Canter your horse over one set of cavalletti on a straight line, make an arc and return him to trot again over a second set of cavalletti on the opposite side of the arena. Remember to increase the space between the cavalletti to a canter stride distance before you practice this.

Thinking About Training Techniques

As you and your horse become acquainted with each other and as you begin to clearly define your goals for the team, it will be time to consider which of the many training approaches will suit you or when each different technique might be most appropriate.

Training techniques that seem similar can produce very different results. For instance, round pen work and longeing do not teach a horse the same lessons. Either of these methods can be used simply for exercise, but the body language that establishes leadership in round pen work is a kindergarten subject and should be introduced before teaching your horse to longe. Attempting to teach the hierarchy lesson on a longe line could easily become dangerous because of the limiting, entangling factor of the line. Conversely, helping your horse establish tempo and bend, and learn how to "go on the bit" while running around a round pen, if not totally impossible, would certainly be a drawn-out procedure with more potential stumbling blocks than necessary. With a longe line and a snaffle bit, an experienced horsewoman can teach her horse communication through the longe rein; the *feel* of information is passed through your hand as it would be passed through a rider's hand.

Lateral suppling and collection is more easily accomplished while longeing, but work in a chambon (a piece of schooling equipment designed by the French to encourage a horse to lower his poll by lowering the entire neck, *without* forcing the horse's nose behind the vertical or into his chest) can be made clearer to a horse if there is no additional outside pressure on the bit, such as the pressure of a longe line.

An Arabian gelding wearing the French training device known as a chambon, shown being free longed in a round pen.

THREE LITTLE WORDS

Very wise trainers through history have distilled the basic rules of training into three words: calm, forward and straight. Why?

Calm. If you try to teach a lesson to a horse who is upset and anxious, the horse will have difficulty learning. Even if he does perform what is required, there is a good chance that each time he is required to repeat the behavior, he may again become agitated, because excessive tension and adrenaline were a part of the sensory input during his initial learning period.

Forward. Horses need to move. Forward motion is the easiest motion to direct and control in the horse. A horse who is denied forward motion will express his need to move by going sideways, backward or up—all alternatives that significantly increase the chance of injury to horse and rider.

Straight. Unless a horse can be made straight, his athletic potential cannot be fully accessed and he will impair his physical soundness prematurely if put to serious work.

If you want to be successful at training your horse in a variety of skills, you need to start by closely and thoroughly examining the requirements of each skill or set of tests you will want your horse to learn and perform. Breaking down the various actions of the horse when he is doing the work or patterns will help you understand what is required of the horse's body. It will also help you understand the mental predisposition that would best suit the task. A hot horse will more than likely enjoy working cattle, the action of gymkhana games or galloping and jumping, but will be less likely to tolerate the repetitive, detail-oriented, gymnastic work of dressage.

An example of performance skills that may at first appear similar are the reiner's spin and the dressage horse's pirouette. But the pirouette in dressage requires collection and a slow tempo, demanding that the horse's inside hind leg continue to keep the beat of the canter (move as though the horse were continuing forward). The reiner's spin, on the other hand, demands that the inside hind leg of the horse be planted and that the horse spin around the leg in a fast, level manner. In training the all-around horse, you need to understand the basic biomechanical differences between these two training goals to select the best training system for producing each one.

Dressage is a good *basic* training system, because it is a system designed to build the carrying abilities of the horse, as well as make him straight. Once these goals have been accomplished, you could elect to explore a system of training that focuses more on speed.

Not all horses are mentally suited to doing a variety of work, even though they may be physically well suited to do so. Study the various training techniques that are advocated by the different representatives of the individual disciplines. A well-known dressage coach named Colonel Lindgrin liked to remind students that there was "more than one road to Rome"—a true statement. However, any astute horseman also knows that not all of those roads get to Rome in the same amount of time or with the same amount of effort; further, you must remember that arriving in Rome is only part of your goal. If you arrive there with your horse about to fall apart, or badly used up because of the roughness of the route you choose, your journey may well have been wasted. Arriving at your goal is only part of your goal. Being able to get there *repeatedly*, then *successfully* continuing on to another exciting goal is the ultimate challenge for the all-around horse and rider.

The pirouette in dressage requires collection and a slow tempo, demanding that the horse's inside hind leg continue to keep the beat of the canter.

The reiner's spin demands that the inside hind leg of the horse be planted and that the horse spin around the leg in a fast, level manner.

A Simple, Sequential Training Outline

Training a horse isn't rocket science. No matter what method you choose, the information should be presented to the horse in a sequence that makes sense and enables him to learn easily and comfortably.

Control the Gas Pedal

In classical equestrian literature, this step is often referred to as "putting the horse in front of the leg." Establishing "forward" is the first and most important step in training a horse, because a horse who does not go forward will express his nature by going in another direction, such as backward or upward. When a horse learns to evade the rider's control by getting behind the bit, "running backward," bucking or rearing, he becomes a liability. He is not only a danger to his rider, he has also begun to walk a path toward self-destruction.

Horses who are confirmed in such behavior must be lucky enough to meet a trainer with sufficient skill and courage to successfully rehabilitate them. While the horse's behavior may have been justified in the beginning because of fear, discomfort or a number of other reasons, once the pattern of response is set, it can be hard to break. And horses, like

---

THE MOST COMMON MISTAKE

The most common mistake made by amateur and professional trainers alike is to give a lesson that is too complex for the horse to understand clearly. Before you learned to read, you were taught to recognize the letters of the alphabet. Then you were taught how to combine various letters into simple words. Finally, you were encouraged to use words to form simple sentences: "See Jane run. Run, Jane, run. Spot is Jane's dog. Spot likes to run with Jane."

If you approach your horse's training using a basic system that is clearly understandable to your horse, then teach him the basic rules of "conversation" piece by piece, when you ask him a question, you'll get the right answer. Horses like to please their humans, if they respect and feel comfortable with them.

humans, are creatures of habit. Horses who have acquired dangerous habits seldom lead happy lives.

Recommended exercises for teaching the forward response:

- Correct preparation through ground work

- Transitions upward *between* the gaits

- Transitions upward *within* the gaits

These exercises must be practiced and refined, with the focus of the work divided into two parts:

1. Response: Your horse must be taught to respond promptly and fully under all circumstances to the rider's aids whenever they request forward energy.

2. Frame: Improving your horse's balance and helping to prolong his soundness will depend on your ability to create a correct frame, or muscular use pattern in your horse, when he moves forward in response to your request. This frame or outline, sometimes called a rainbow frame, is exhibited by horses who are "on the bit" or "round" when they work. To help develop your mental picture of what this means in horses doing a variety of jobs, I recommend studying the drawings and illustrations in the book *Horse Gaits, Balance and Movement* by Susan Harris. To be able to produce a good working frame in any type of horse, you must be able to successfully put your horse in front of your leg, keep him straight and have him relaxed in the jaw, neck and back.

Make Sure the Brakes Work

Interestingly enough, this is the *second* most important thing a training program should teach a horse. Without brakes, the horse can be a liability to both himself and his handler/rider. A horse who bolts or flees the scene of his discomfort (either mentally or physically) is an accident waiting to happen. The horse's solid respect for the word *whoa* is one of the most important tools you can have when you're trying to get yourself and your equine partner "out of it alive."

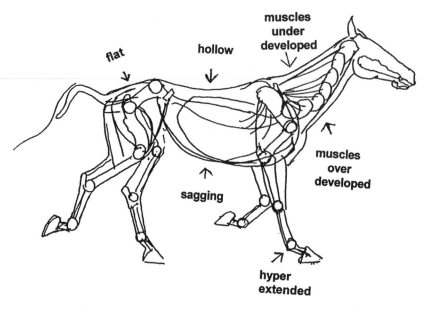

Energy falling on forehand - concussive

This horse is moving in a poor "frame," with his back hollow and his back muscles contracted.

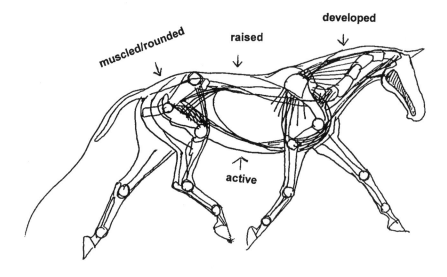

**Energy channeled up as well as forward
Movement light, stride lengthened**

This horse is moving in a rounded frame, using the most efficient groups of muscles.

Recommended exercises for teaching respect for *whoa*:

- Correct preparation through ground work

- Frequent downward transitions from all gaits to balance the horse and to teach him to compress and control his forward momentum

- Use and enforcement of the verbal *whoa* command both from the ground and in the saddle

- Use of reining pattern "roll away" maneuvers to slow a horse in motion, using only one rein at a time

- Turning the haunches around the forehand to disengage the horse's "power train"

In mastering the horse's forward motion under all circumstances, you need to sort out and progressively focus on different levels. If a horse is rushing forward, unbalanced emotionally or physically or both, the highest priority is safety. Refined control of a horse's biomechanical systems cannot be achieved until you can successfully control the horse's mind. This refined control is achieved when the rider's aids, acting in harmony, can regulate the driving power of the horse's engine and the braking system in the horse's *mind,* to get any desired speed, from very slow to very fast, without loss of control and with a soft feel between horse and rider through the reins.

Mastering the *whoa* and the *go* through the repeated practice of these and similar exercises will also enable you to get your horse to produce the desirable round working frame, which is so important to balance, strength, soundness and maximum athletic potential.

Develop Give and Lateral Suppleness in the Jaw, Poll, Neck and Rib Cage

Lateral control is a doorway into longitudinal control of the horse. But more importantly, it is the key to straightness—and straightness in the horse's body is the foundation of his ability to both collect and extend. Without cultivating both of those biomechanical dimensions of movement in the horse, it is impossible to develop a good all-around athlete.

Recommended exercises to help teach a horse to soften, release and bend his neck and body at the request of his rider:

- Using a leading rein, ask the horse to release his neck and follow his nose around to your knee without moving his feet. Do the exercise in both directions. Do not repeat this exercise ad infinitum; once your horse gives his neck comfortably in both directions, move on to other lessons.

- Release the back of the horse by riding school figures precisely and in tempo. This will also help engage the horse's hind legs under his body, improving his longitudinal balance and strengthening and making the joints of his hindquarters more supple.

- Refine directional control of the forehand and the hindquarters independently. Turning on the forehand and turning on the haunches are good exercises to accomplish this goal.

- Use the horse's understanding of the aids I've just mentioned to introduce lateral work, including leg yielding, shoulder-in and haunches-in.

Training Using Gymnastic Patterns

Gymnastic patterns have been used for centuries to prepare horses' bodies for the demands of the various jobs and sports they are called upon to perform. Today they are most commonly associated with the discipline of dressage, but reining patterns and jumping grids can easily be considered gymnastic patterns as well. A gymnastic pattern consists of three elements:

1. School figures, including circles, straight lines, curving lines and serpentines

2. Changes of gait

3. Changes of speed or stride length within a gait

Using these elements, you (or your trainer/coach/instructor) can put together a sequence of gymnastic patterns to be performed by your horse. When ridden carefully and precisely, these progressive patterns improve the horse's:

- Suppleness

- Strength

- Balance

- Focus

These same exercises can improve the rider's balance, coordinated use of the aids and focus. Arena or school figures (see the diagrams in Chapter 5) can be strung together in endless variations, ensuring your horse never becomes bored with the work.

Here are some things to consider about each element of a gymnastic pattern.

- **Straight lines:** To be truly straight, a horse's shoulders must be centered in the middle of his hips, the spine must be aligned, and the horse must be pushing with equal force from each hind leg.

- **Circles and curving lines:** The horse's spine should directly match the curve of the circle. To accomplish this, the horse must allow the muscles on the outside (of the curve) of his spinal column to stretch, while contracting the muscles along the inside of his spinal column. He must also *swing* his outside legs to cover the greater distance on the outside of the arc, while *flexing* the joints of his inside legs, making a slightly higher, rounder movement with his limbs on the inside of the arc. To do this well, the horse must be tension free, supple from poll to tail.

- **Serpentines:** Serpentines require the horse to accomplish all of the work I've just described, *and* completely change the way his body bends in rapid succession. While each of the curving figures requires a certain degree of strength, flexibility, submission and attention, the combined demands of the serpentine exercise, because they require the horse to constantly reorganize his balance, increase the difficulty of each of the individual elements. As the horse gains suppleness, strength, straightness and balance, his hind legs become "engaged" under his body, causing his forehand to lighten, making the horse better balanced, easier to control and steer, and less subject to front-end concussion.

- **Changes of gait and speed:** This can be thought of as longitudinal suppling of the horse. The ability to smoothly decelerate and accelerate, shorten or lengthen the stride, make transitions from one gait to another, and so on, depend directly on the horse's ability to flex his joints while continuing to deliver power through his body, keep his mass balanced level over his four legs or slightly toward the rear legs, and accept the aids and directions of the rider without tension or resistance.

> # Did You Know?
>
> Most horses have poor posture when ridden.
>   Poor posture undermines:
>
> - Safety
>
> - Soundness
>
> - Control
>
> - Comfort
>
> - Performance
>
> When you train a horse, you are using your aids to control speed and direction, *but you must also* direct the horse's selection of the muscle groups he uses to animate his skeleton, so you can influence his posture or carriage.
>
>   Horses are "trained" when their response to the rider's aids is consistent and habitual.
>
>   Successful training makes the desired response stronger than an emotional choice.
>
>   If you can't control the horse emotionally, you don't own the horse physically.
>
>   When you can shape (not just confine) the horse physically, you can control his emotional energy.

Some Tips for Designing a Workout Program

- When designing your horse's workout session, remember that variety keeps things interesting.

- If you're not satisfied with your horse's performance on a particular exercise after a couple of tries, work on another exercise that includes some of the simpler elements of the one you are having difficulty mastering. Then go back to the pattern that gave him trouble and try again. You might even wait until another day to try the difficult pattern again.

- Work each pattern you select in both directions, so your horse is stretched and strengthened on both sides of his body.

- You may want to spend more time on your horse's "stiff" or difficult side, but warm up in his "easy" direction before reversing and asking for work in the direction in which it is harder for him to perform.

- A 45- to 60-minute workout will include precise practice of three to six different exercises or combination of exercises.

- Design your horse's workout so you move sequentially from the easiest exercise to be ridden that day to the most difficult, but allow enough time to finish your session with a final simple exercise that you know your horse can do well. That way, if it's a "bad hair day" for you both, you can at least finish the workout on a good note by performing the first and last exercises well.

- When your horse is equally strong and supple on both sides, pat yourself on the back. You've made it over one of the biggest training and performance hurdles you will ever encounter.

Pattern Sequence One

Exercise 1

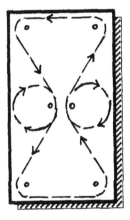

The diagram here shows a sequence where the rider and horse ride a simple, single loop serpentine on the long side of the arena. By riding through the arena corners both before and after the loop, the horse is asked to bend deeply, given a short time to straighten his body, then asked to reverse his bend (the height of the arc around the cone marks the top of the loop) to a lesser degree, and straighten a second time, before being asked to bend his body fairly deeply once more to correctly execute the next corner of the figure. The sequence repeats itself after a short trip in which the horse is straight in the body while crossing the short ends of the arena. The exercise is ridden on both reins, so both sides of the horse are asked to stretch and contract in equal amounts.

Begin the exercise in the direction of the horse's hollow side. Progress to the next level of difficulty by asking your horse to hold his bend for an entire circle (shown in this diagram) each time he arrives at the middle of the serpentine loop. The degree of difficulty of this exercise will depend upon the size of the circle. A green horse should not initially be asked to perform a circle smaller than 45 to 50 feet in diameter. To do so would tax his ability to balance himself and encourage him to evade the exercise by leaning on his shoulder, losing his tempo (hurrying or slowing down) or falling out in the hindquarters—all undesirable actions that would negate the purpose and benefit of this exercise.

Exercise 2

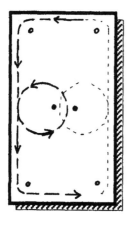

In the second pattern the work advances by riding a simple circle half the width of the arena (as shown), and either increasing or decreasing the horse's stride on the circle. If your horse is sluggish, ask for an increase of energy on the circle. If he is quick or hot, use the circle to relax him and stabilize his tempo. This pattern is also good for introducing the canter.

Sending your horse into a circle immediately after an upward transition will help diminish any temptation to accelerate and encourage him to place his inside hind leg well up underneath his body, as he bends and balances himself to execute the circle pattern. When riding a canter transition as a part of this pattern, your circle can be larger at first, reaching the track on the other side of the arena (65 to 80 feet), if necessary. Gradually reduce the size to 32 feet (the size shown) as your horse becomes better balanced and more relaxed.

Exercise 3

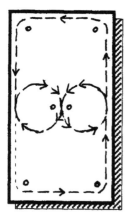

This exercise accelerates the training demands on your horse because it asks him to quickly rebalance himself on the center line, with a complete reversal of bend, as the two circles, ridden in their same respective arena locations, become immediately sequential, forming a figure-8 across the arena. The pattern can be ridden every time you reach the center of each long side, or you can ride one long side without the pattern, letting your horse have a rest and/or working on his straightness during that time. The straight lines in between the figure-8 and the arena corners give you an opportunity to *feel* for the straightness and equal-sided thrust the suppling work on the bending lines of the figure-8 has encouraged in the horse.

Exercise 4

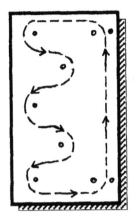

This exercise increases the demand for engagement and balance, as your horse bends his body to the smaller arc, then must quickly and smoothly reverse his bend (four times on the one long side), without losing his balance or, ideally, altering his tempo. While partial arcs are less demanding then a complete circle because they do not require the horse to hold the bend as long, the quick succession of changes makes great demands on his lateral and longitudinal balance and suppleness, and your ability to coordinate your application of aids. The long side opposite the three-loop serpentine in this exercise is ridden on the *second track (approximately 6 feet from the rail or fence)* to ensure the horse travels straight and does not lean against the wall with his shoulder.

Pattern Sequence Two

Exercise 5

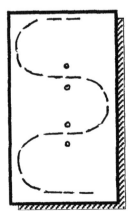

This exercise again makes use of serpentines, circles and straight lines, with the final part ridden either as a turn on the forehand or a turn on the haunches. The first exercise is a simple three-loop serpentine the width of the arena, where you ask your horse to execute a series of half circles followed by a straight line across the width of the arena. As you cross the center line, prepare your horse for the next half circle in the opposite bend. The straight lines between each bend enable you to practice straightening your horse.

Exercise 6

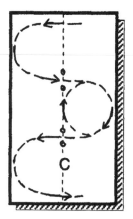

This exercise continues the theme begun in the previous exercise, but inserts a complete circle at the center of the second loop of the serpentine. This circle, which requires a greater balancing effort from your horse, further increases the suppleness of the joints and develops the carrying strength of the horse's inside hind leg.

Exercise 7

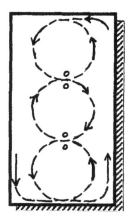

In this exercise you string three successive circles together down the center line of the arena. Each circle can be ridden one or more times before passing on to the next circle in the series. The size of each circle will determine the difficulty of the exercise, but take care to ride each circle correctly, making sure it is *round*. Each change of direction, gait and length of stride within a gait requires your horse to reorganize his balance. After completing the series, a trip straight down the long side of the arena enables you to use the increased momentum and engagement generated during the exercise to improve your horse's carriage, straightness and expression of his gait.

Exercise 8

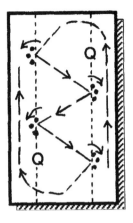

This exercise is a departure from the previous three patterns. It includes either a turn-on-the-forehand or a turn-on-the-haunches at the apex of each zigzag change of direction. These movements, performed from the halt, walk or trot, require precise control of the horse's hindquarters and forehand. The straight lines preceding these changes can be ridden in any gait. The faster the gait preceding and following the transition, the more difficult the exercise. Prompt and precise upward and downward transitions are important to getting the most benefit from this exercise.

The necessity of control and the required and desired degree of balance in the horse make an increase in pace also increase the difficulty of any exercise shown here. Most patterns are ridden first at a trot. Parts of patterns can be ridden at a walk. When this happens, the transition becomes an integral part of the gymnastic work of the pattern. For example, in exercise 3, one circle may be ridden at either a walk or a canter, while the other circle is ridden at a trot. If exercise 1 is ridden at a canter, it becomes a very technically advanced exercise requiring the horse to perform the balancing gymnastic move known as "counter-canter" during either the single loop on each long side, or the more difficult circle at the loop's center.

In exercise 5, the gait can be changed each time the horse and rider cross the center line (that is, pass through the markers). In exercise 6, the circle in the middle loop may be ridden at either a walk or a canter. Each of the circles in exercise 7 can be ridden in different gaits or alternate gaits. For example, trot on the first circle, walk or canter on the second circle in the sequence and trot again on the third circle. This means practicing not only bending, but also longitudinal balance and obedience to the aids, every time you ask your horse to change his gait. Another variation is to walk on the first and third circles and either trot or canter on the second, or canter on the first and third circles and trot on the second. The combinations are almost endless.

THE HORSE'S "ACHILLES' HEEL" IS HIS BACK

All horse's backs are not created equal. If a horse's back is weak, his performance potential under the saddle will be limited. When ridden and competed, he is likely to be subject to more soundness problems than horses who have broad, well-muscled, strong backs.

Preparing a horse's back to support the weight of a rider before starting him under saddle is worth the time it takes. Part of the reason for the longeing phase of classical training is to teach the horse to use his abdomen muscles when he moves, stretching and raising his back, developing the muscles that support the rider's weight. This will not happen simply by running a horse around on a longe line, nor by running him in circles in a round pen.

Consider the horse as if you were a structural engineer. The best place for a horse to carry weight is on top of his withers or on top of his croup, because that is where the columns of support (his legs) are located. The rider however, sits almost dead center *between* these supports, on the weakest part of the back. All horses will respond at first to the introduction of weight on their backs by contracting their back muscles, hollowing the back. As long as the muscles of the horse's back remain tight, the horse is robbed of some of his potential range of motion (stride length), and power, speed and suspension.

The greatest enemy of the horse's back is poor saddle fit. The second is poor rider balance and the third is lack of a training and fitness regimen that includes developing the strength of the horse's back as well as the rest of his muscular systems, his tendons, ligaments, bones, heart and lungs.

The muscles of the back are like any other muscles on a horse's body. They can work for only so long before they become fatigued. Smart riders and trainers take this into consideration in their training and riding. This is why it is not a good idea to spend a great deal of time at a sitting trot on a young or green horse.

The Cavalletti Gymnastic Training System

To think of cavalletti as a training tool only for hunters and jumpers is to shortchange your horse's workout program. The list of what can be done using cavalletti and the disciplines it can help is nearly endless. Ground poles, as they are sometimes called, can be used for:

- Improving balance

- Improving tempo and rhythm

- Improving articulation of all of the joints of the legs (because the work makes a horse more attentive to where he is placing his feet)

- Increasing the muscle strength of the back

- Loosening the hips and mobilizing the shoulders

- Increasing thrusting power

- Altering stride length

- Creating a better jumping bascule

When working over cavalletti, you want to keep your horse calm but also require him to move in an active manner. Any mental or physical tension in your horse hinders his ability to move well. Work over cavalletti is all about relaxed, forward movement, so your horse can learn to adjust his body quickly and invisibly to accomplish a variety of athletic maneuvers— using the most efficient muscle groups.

When incorporating cavalletti exercises into your training program, start *simply*, putting one pole on the ground and asking your horse to walk over it repeatedly until he does it quietly, as though it were no big deal. From there you can add additional poles, one at a time, until you

SOME RULES ABOUT CAVALLETTI

1. Don't scare your horse by riding him into a long line of poles the very first time you work him over cavalletti.

2. If you use poles on the ground, be sure they are secured so they will not roll if your horse steps on them.

3. Adjust the distances between the poles to your horse's stride length.

4. Use "wings," if necessary, to help you funnel your horse through the cavalletti without having to do a lot of pulling on his mouth.

5. Splint boots and possibly bell boots (for young, unbalanced horses) should be used to protect your horse's legs when working over cavalletti.

have six, allowing your horse to become comfortable with what you are asking him to do each time you add another pole, until he is negotiating all six poles quietly at a walk. Then start again, this time trotting over two poles, working up to six in a row. Finally you can add work in a canter, but again, begin with one pole and only add additional ones when your horse no longer makes any extra fuss or effort when cantering over a single pole on the ground.

When working through the various cavalletti exercises, the distances between the poles must be adjusted for the horse's gait and speed, and also for your horse's stride length; a 17-hand Thoroughbred should not be expected to have the same trotting stride as a 14.2-hand pony. The distance between poles will also be decided by what you wish to teach the horse. If you wish to collect his stride, begin with a distance the horse finds comfortable to manage and gradually shorten the distance between the poles over several weeks. If, on the other hand, if you wish to teach your horse to lengthen his stride, gradually increase the distance between the cavalletti.

When the horse is familiar and comfortable with poles on the ground, you can graduate to true cavalletti, which offer three height settings. The lower two can be practiced at a walk or a trot, and the highest is reserved for cantering work. Cavalletti poles are generally 12 feet long, but can be modified to as short as 6 feet in length.

Understanding the use of cavalletti takes time, study and experience. The definitive book for such study, *Cavalletti,* was written by two-time Olympic dressage gold medalist Reiner Klimke. (A videotape by the same name is also available.) Read the book and try some of the exercises suggested in these pages. If you really want a record of the progress your horse makes as you put him through this world-renowned training system, have a friend do a "before" video of some early work, then videotape the horse again after three months and again after six months. Videotape the same exercise and compare the tapes. This way, you not only improve your horse, but you also expand your own equestrian knowledge and experience.

As with other exercise patterns, exercises using cavalletti can be arranged in an infinite variety of ways. Here are only a few.

Exercise 1

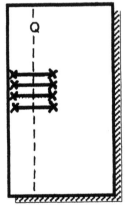

This is a basic, straightforward line of cavalletti. When set at the low height they are six to eight inches above the ground. At medium height, they are 10 to 12 inches high, and at their highest position they are 18 to 20 inches high.

Step 1: Begin simply, at a walk with all the poles at the lowest height.

Step 2: Raise every other pole to medium height.

Step 3: Raise all the cavalletti to medium height.

Step 4: Return to the lowest height and increase or decrease the distance between the poles to work on collecting or lengthening your horse's stride.

Step 5: Return to lowest height and work through the polls at trot, repeating steps 2, 3 and 4. The *average* stride for a 15- to 16-hand horse at a trot is four feet six inches to five feet six inches; at a canter it's 9 to 12 feet.

Step 6: Return to the lowest height, set the distance for a canter and work the line in the canter, repeating steps 2 and 3. Then put the cavalletti at their highest setting and work through the line quietly and calmly before continuing on to step 4.

Exercise 2

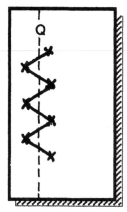

Set the zigzag line shown in the diagram. The line down the very center of the zigzag should measure four feet six inches between poles. Ride your horse through the line closer to the closed points to ask the horse to shorten and collect his stride; ride closer to the open ends to encourage your horse to lengthen his stride. This exercise requires precise steering from the rider and straightness from the horse.

Exercise 3

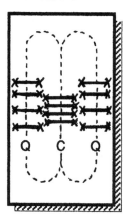

Set one line of four cavalletti on the center line and one line on each of the quarter lines. You can alter the length of the trot stride from collected on the center line to medium or working on one quarter line and extended or strong on the other quarter line. Or you can set the middle line as the working stride length and each outside line at a different distance. To advance the exercise, set the outside cavalletti at a canter distance, make a transition to a canter on the arc of the turn and canter the quarter lines, returning to the trot again at the end of the line and before turning to go down the center line again.

Exercise 4

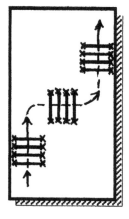

This is another exercise that works on lengthening and shortening your horse's stride, only it adds a steering question between each set of cavalletti. Use your imagination and knowledge of your horse to decide the distance between the poles in your lines of cavalletti; you might try a long distance to a short distance, then again to a long distance or short to long to short, and so on. If you keep the diameter of the curving line between the sets of cavalletti fairly tight, you will focus your horse on gathering himself between the cavalletti. If you make it more open, you will have more time to move your horse forward from your leg.

Exercise 5

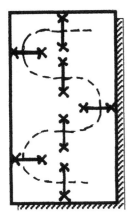

This is a three-loop serpentine with the cavalletti placed as shown. If the loops are big and open, this pattern acts primarily as a curving line balance and tempo exercise. If the loops are tight, the pattern acts as an engagement and power exercise. The exercise can be ridden at a trot or canter. When riding at a canter, ask for your lead changes in the air over the cavalletti set on the center line.

Exercise 6

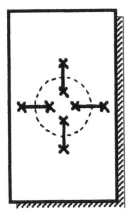

This is a 50-foot circle with cavalletti set at the four compass points. This exercise can be ridden in both directions, at all three gaits and with cavalletti set at any of the three heights.

Exercise 7

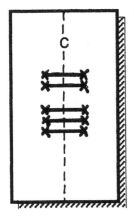

In this line, one or two cavalletti are left out somewhere in the line. The goal of the exercise is to maintain the horse's forward movement and tempo in the open spaces, so there is no need to adjust when he encounters the next cavalletti in the line.

TTeam, a Nontraditional Training System

The training method known as TTeam, developed by Linda Tellington-Jones, is the most thorough and horse-friendly basic training system available to today's horseman and horsewoman. It is especially suited to educating any horse who might have learning difficulties due to poor handling, injury or stress issues, or simple inherited conformational bio-mechanical issues. The system is divided into body work, work with the horse on the ground and mounted work.

"TTeam addresses the pain, soreness, fear and tension in a horse's body which is very often responsible for their resistance and/or their undesirable behavior," says Tellington-Jones in her large, excellently illustrated book *Improve Your Horse's Well Being*. "TTeam allows you to change your horse's behavior and influence his personality without force, by using non-habitual, non-threatening movement and special ground exercises."

The best way to become acquainted with the system is to learn it first-hand from its masters: Linda Tellington-Jones, her sister Robyn Hood or the practitioners trained and certified by them. The Feldenkrais Method, a world-renowned system designed around the human body, is the foundation of TTeam work. It does require patience to learn and refine, but the rewards are well worth it. Performance horses in every discipline,

Riders working through a TTeam labyrinth.

from endurance horses to Olympic dressage and jumping horses, have shown improved performance with the use of the TTeam training system.

The Tellington-Jones Equine Awareness Method and *The Tellington TTouch* are two other books that offer information about the method. It is the system that most honestly fulfills today's rising imperative of being able to enjoy and partner with horses in a way that produces comfort and confidence in horse and rider, and a spiritual connection as well.

Expanding Your Horse's Education on the Trail

In one sense, training your horse by riding him out of the arena on the trail can be viewed as another training system. This is especially true when the trail you choose presents problems and biomechanical demands by offering varied topography. Nature and gravity then become your training assistants, helping you address your horse's balance and body use issues. It is easier for you to help your horse select the most efficient muscles to use when climbing (which is strength training) and descending (which uses the same muscle groups used to *collect* his gait) when the horse can understand the necessity of handling the terrain before him.

Trail time can be used to make any type of performance horse more fit, and usually has the added benefit of refreshing his mental state, especially if he has spent a number of years going round and round in an arena. Before using the trail as a classroom for your horse, though, you must prepare your lesson plans with the following in mind:

- If you are going to spend hours on the trail, your equipment must be carefully fit to your horse and selected to provide safety and comfort for *both* the horse and rider. A saddle that "almost fits" may be all right for riding in an arena, where you will spend an hour or less on the horse's back each time you ride. But when you put from two to eight hours of constant pressure on your horse's back, the difference between an okay fit and a good fit can mean the difference between a happy horse and a sore horse.

- A saddle that stays in place without the use of a breastplate or crupper on the flat may shift when riding up or down hills. If this happens at an awkward moment, it could easily cause a serious accident or make your horse arrive home sore and uncomfortable. Learning this particular lesson through experience is not fun and could easily leave your horse with a sour attitude toward any further trail work.

- Even well-trained horses can become excited or frightened on the trail, especially on their first few outings. If your horse's normal headgear happens to be a mild snaffle bit, be sure you can control him when his mind is distracted by thinking he's about to be eaten by a "rock monster" (or cow, biker, hiker, flock of birds flying out of a bush, etc.), or you could be inviting a wild and dangerous ride back to the barn or trailer.

- If you plan to explore your horse's potential in competitive trail or endurance riding, be sure to give some consideration to the type of shoes he will need for the different types of terrain you will encounter. A correct shoe will offer secure footing and protect your horse's feet. Many Thoroughbreds and some Quarter Horses have sensitive soles that are easily bruised by rocks. If you're riding a horse of one of those breeds, you will want to take precautions to prevent a stone bruise rather than have your horse sidelined for six weeks to six months with a foot abscess caused by stepping on a sharp rock his first time out.

- Do things in small steps. Don't pick the hottest or windiest day of the year to tackle your first trail ride or to go on the longest trail ride you've ever attempted. On your first few outings, try to avoid going by yourself or with another rider who's never been on trail. Instead, ride with an experienced rider whose horse is calm and quiet. His example will help instill confidence in your inexperienced horse or help settle a horse who is hot.

Using Trail Riding to Condition the Competition Horse

Each horse is an individual. Just as you would not expect the same exercise routine to be good for both a four-year-old and a 64-year-old person, it is necessary to take your horse's specifics into consideration as you plan your goals and design a conditioning schedule. Factors to be considered are age, present physical condition, personality type, experience, footing, temperature, humidity and topography. Conditioning your horse for any discipline requires thought, time, patience and practice, but unlike the arena, the trail seldom invites boredom.

Young horses are often energetic, but if they are under five years of age, their bones, tendons and ligaments may not be fully mature and strong enough to do any type of sustained work. Since youth is notoriously associated with exuberance, it may not be easy to tell when your young horse has reached his limit. His enthusiasm or nervous energy may make it seem as if he could go all day. It will only be in the following days, weeks or possibly even years that you will fully understand the consequences of heeding a brash young horse's opinion of himself.

It is important to progress slowly through any program, and include rest time between major efforts. Never increase more than one type of workload at a time. Preparing an event horse for cross-country is as much about conditioning, so he doesn't make mistakes at fences halfway through his round because he's tired, as it is about teaching him to jump the solid, cross-country obstacles.

Horses respond best to learning when you follow the KISS method (keep it simple, silly). For instance, if you want to prepare your show horse for trail competition and you are used to doing a seven-mile pleasure ride on weekends, you could begin increasing his fitness for trail competition by adding two three-mile trail rides, mostly at a walk, during the week, spacing them one or two days apart. After about four to six weeks of this schedule, you could increase your weekend ride to 10 miles, add one five-mile ride during the week and keep the middle ride distance at three miles.

The next change you might add would be to increase speed. For example, you could increase the amount of trot time on the 10-mile ride by 10 percent, and increase the trot time on the five-mile ride by 20 percent, while keeping the short training day at a relaxing walk.

Consider the Circumstances

Weather, topography and footing surfaces are among the daily conditions that many a rider has failed to take into consideration, with the result being a less than desirable outcome to the day's work. These three important factors are reason enough to make a generic conditioning schedule—whose formula may be delivered in miles to be ridden, circles to be made or sliding stops to perform—a risky prescription. Take, for example, a show-fit hunter you want to try in the lowest division of a horse trial. You might normally ride this horse five to eight miles (approximately one and a half to two hours) per week on the trail just for fun. You decide to increase the distance to 15 miles as a part of his conditioning program. Ordinarily, this would be acceptable. But if you haul to a new trail site that consists of primarily sandy footing, when you have previously only been riding on grassy fields or in a groomed arena, or if your new trail has significant altitude gain and descent in those 15 miles when your previous route was composed largely of mainly flat or gently rolling terrain, or on the day of the ride your normally dry, moderate climate turns out to be 15 degrees hotter *and* humid, then you would need to *cut back* your planned workload rather than increasing it, to avoid overworking your equine partner.

It is also important to remember that mental work uses energy. A horse who is nervous or agitated for any reason is using more energy than a calm horse. In addition, the emotionally charged horse is seldom using his biomechanics efficiently, so he is using half again as much energy as the calm horse to do the same job. That emotional energy expenditure must be taken into consideration when planning a training program. Otherwise, you run the risk of having a metabolic problem, such as tying up, when you haven't yet reached your mileage schedule and indeed, without leaving the arena. This *emotional factor* is something that can change in the middle of a ride or a work session, if your horse becomes frightened or frustrated. Once that happens, it is easy to overwork his body and put him in metabolic danger.

Saddle Fit and Training

The critical importance of a correct saddle fit to successful training can't be overstated. Even forgiving horses become less likely to perform, lose their edge, display behavior problems and become emotionally stressed if they must perform their daily workout in tack that isn't comfortable.

In today's market, with all the brands and types of saddles, it ought to be easy to find one that fits the rider, the horse and the discipline—but it isn't. Cost alone will not guarantee fit, just as big advertising budgets don't guarantee an accurate or honest description of a product.

Before buying any saddle it is best to know what discipline you and your horse want to pursue (dressage, jumping, eventing, polo, trail riding, etc.), because all saddles are tweaked in some way to help the rider and horse perform their specific job more easily. You can talk to other riders and ask what type or brand of saddle they use, how they like riding in it, and so on. Be sure to ask if they've had any problems with the saddle they now own or any previous saddles they may have used.

Part of the problem of good saddle fit lies in the logistics of acquisition. When you're buying a new saddle, it is imperative to ride in it. The problem is, most stores don't want marks on the merchandise if you have to return it. A five-minute ride in your arena is not a fair trial and won't tell you all you need to know about fit—unless, of course, the fit is *really* bad. Buying a brand name is no guarantee you will get a good fit either, since despite what manufacturers would like us to believe, one Stubben or Circle Y is not necessarily just like every other Stubben or Circle Y, even when the style of the saddle is the same.

When you embark on the great saddle hunt, these tips may help.

- Before even putting a saddle on your horse, turn the saddle upside down and sight down the center line (the part of the saddle that sits over the horse's spine), comparing the two side of the saddle to see if they are symmetrical in structure and padding. Saddles with twisted trees can often be identified this way. Of course, used saddles should always be checked for a broken tree, which can be done by applying pressure both lengthwise and widthwise and feeling how much give there is in the tree (or saddle frame). English saddles, built on a spring tree, will have a slight give, but should not collapse between your hands. Western and most Western-type endurance saddles should have little or no give when pressure is applied.

- Look for even sweat patterns and avoid anything that leaves large dry patches on your horse's back.

- The saddle should never touch the horse's withers or rest on the spine. The general rule is that you should be able to insert two to three fingers between the top of the horse's withers and the fork or gullet of the saddle. A saddle that sits too high off the horse's back (four fingers or more) will have a tendency to roll on a round-backed horse, making it very unstable and necessitating a very tight girth or cinch to compensate.

- Check to make sure the saddle will allow the horse to move his shoulder without pinching or gouging. To do this, slip your hand under the saddle, palm toward the horse, and trace the edge of the shoulder blade with your fingertips. Your fingers should be able to slide downward easily, without getting stuck between the saddle and the shoulder. Repeat this test with the rider in the saddle. Saddles are often placed too far forward, with the front edge of the saddle covering too much of the horse's shoulder. When you place the saddle on your horse's back, picture the horse's shoulder blade and notice if the saddle is resting on top of it. Another way to check this is to notice if the girth is up against the horse's elbow. On a correctly positioned saddle, you should be able to place three to four fingers between the horse's elbow and the girth or cinch.

- The panels or bars of the saddle should conform smoothly to the horse's back along the *entire* length of the muscles on each side of the horse's spine. Many saddles only make contact on the front and at the rear of the tree, something called *bridging*. Bridging is a sign of a poor fit and a definite recipe for trouble, especially for the trail rider or fox hunter who spends hours on her horse.

- Putting a thick pad under a saddle can disguise a poor fit, filling in the gaps between the saddle and the horse's back. However, while it may dull pressure points, it will not remove them entirely, and eventually your horse will pay the price in his performance or his soundness.

Finding a saddle to fit you and your horse takes attention to detail, time and effort. Expense is secondary, since a poorly fitting saddle that was cheap will later be quite expensive because of lost training or competition time when the horse ends up with a sore back. Some horses translate back discomfort into tight joints and impaired movement long before they show signs of having sore back muscles, putting excess wear and tear on their legs and joints, which in turn means you'll be paying your vet the money you saved by buying a cheap saddle—and then some.

When buying from *private* saddle makers, rather than through tack shops, first find out if they offer a money-back guarantee if you are not satisfied with the saddle; many don't.

As an all-around horseman or horsewoman you will probably need more than one saddle in your barn. Hopefully, you can find a few good ones that let you and your horse perform in comfort and style without the experience turning into your worst nightmare.

The Role of Auxiliary Equipment in Training

Technically speaking, a saddle might be considered auxiliary training equipment, because it is possible to train a horse to carry a human without a saddle. But for the purposes of this book, I will consider the most common equipment used when handling and training horses, such as a halter, lead rope, basic head stall, plain snaffle bit, reins, breastplate, saddle and pads, to be *standard* equipment, and everything designed to produce or facilitate a specific posture in your horse to be auxiliary equipment.

Ever try to fix a car or a sink, or anything else for that matter, without the right tools? If you're innovative as well as practical, you'll no doubt get the job done, but whether it will be simple and easy is another matter entirely. A large part of training a horse lies in teaching him how to carry a rider efficiently and easily (if you make your horse's job easier, you will make your horse happier). A horse who elevates his back (giving a rounded appearance over his top line when in action), engages his hind legs under his body and carries some of his weight, as well as some of the rider's weight, on his hind quarters, is the horse who will be freer in the shoulder, lighter in the front end, easier to steer and stop and more comfortable to ride. Having said that, the question arises, "How do I make this Tiger Woods of equine athletes?"

Well, if your horse has well-balanced conformation, a mellow personality, is a naturally free mover and you're a rider who is fluid and balanced (so you can deliver your instructions to your horse through aids that don't annoy the horse, including making contact with the bit without your hands bouncing on his sensitive mouth), *and* your equipment fits well and doesn't make the horse uncomfortable, *then* you could just ride classical gymnastic patterns and up and down transitions, working in the arena or on the trail with and without contact with your horse's mouth. Pretty soon, your horse would begin to accept your hands and legs and let you *shape* his body into the most efficient posture for carrying you. That posture would include a relaxed, swinging back, a neck that is supported by the muscles along the top, rather than being held up by the muscles at its base, and a head that is positioned near or on a vertical plane because the horse is willing to soften his jaw muscles and the muscles around his poll in response to the pressure applied by the rider's hands through the reins and bit. It would also mean the horse moves efficiently, not using more energy than necessary to do his job. Such a horse would gradually develop the muscles that enable him to carry more of his weight on his hind legs. The end result of all this would be a better balanced, efficient athlete, at all speeds and over all topographical challenges and footing conditions.

Sound too good to be true? It is, except for a very few master horsemen and horsewomen. Good horsemen and horsewomen the world over know that the best training happens through clear communication with the horse and requires not much more than good horsemanship skills, correct and through knowledge of how the horse's body works and how the horse thinks, plus patience and time. Patience and time are all too often affected in the horse's world by monetary considerations. In noting this fact, I am simply pointing out that anyone riding and training a horse will inevitably experience at least moments during the training process when he or she will consider using something more than what is listed here as standard training equipment.

For those who do not, or have not used any auxiliary equipment and have produced well-rounded equine athletes who express their power and majesty through a sport or discipline, happily and soundly, you are among the elite of horsemen and are also very limited in your numbers. For the rest of us, knowing our equipment, understanding its design purpose and its function, as well as any inherent limitations its use might build into our horse, is the best the reality of time and circumstances may allow us.

A great array of mechanical contraptions have been invented over the years to "help" a rider gain a horse's cooperation about such things as letting the rider dictate how the horse carries his body or positions his head and neck. Some are useful, some are harmful. All, including the mildest, can be abused by a rider to the detriment of the horse. It doesn't take a genius to figure out an electric skillsaw, and in the right hands it can make a construction job go a lot faster and produce a cleaner, neater job than if all that wood had to be cut with a hand saw. But you'd better know your equipment before you start hacking away or you might come up with some missing fingers, a badly mangled leg or even a severely injured eye—and the saw could certainly be damaged as well.

The simplest, probably the oldest, and certainly the most commonly seen and used piece of auxiliary equestrian equipment is a **running martingale**. The job of this device is to keep the horse from raising his head and thus avoid control of the rider's hands. At its best, it can keep you from getting smacked in the face by the neck of an unruly, noncompliant horse. The device is generally made of two straps, each with a ring at the end, through which the reins are threaded. The straps are fixed usually in the area of the horse's chest by being attached to a breast collar or their own support system of straps. A running martingale is connected to the snaffle rein. It only comes into play, exerting a downward pressure in the horse's mouth, when the rider is holding the reins in such a way as to make contact with the horse's mouth. When you release contact by letting your reins go slack, the martingale immediately deactivates, exerting no further pressure whatsoever.

A horse who, for whatever reason, moves with his head stuck up in the air is also moving with the muscles of his back in a contracted, rigid state. It is not possible for the horse to stiffen or tighten the long muscles that comprise what is known as the back and loin without all the

WHEN ENOUGH IS ENOUGH

Just because a little pressure may produce a desired result, a lot of pressure will not necessarily improve the picture or produce the desired result if the horse is extremely resistive. Indeed, it can and has done irreparable harm, both physically and mentally.

Knowing *how much* and *for how long* to apply any pressure to a horse in the name of training, from a natural aid to a training device, is a process of understanding:

• Equine biomechanics

• The nature of the horse

• The requirements of the job

• The drawbacks inherent any time pressure is used to overcome a horse's resistance

joints in both the forehand and the hindquarters losing some of their range of motion. These tight muscles, tendons and ligaments that surround the horse's joints reduce the joints' ability to flex or extend to the degree that would be dictated by the skeletal conformation of the animal, creating unnecessary wear and tear on the horse's body, which in the long run will hasten his deterioration. Using a martingale in the process of training such a horse could be justified, as it offers an increased margin of control and safety for the rider and perhaps a greater chance at long-term structural soundness, if not immediate comfort, for the horse.

Another piece of auxiliary equipment that can encourage a horse to use his back correctly is known as a **chambon**. This is a French training device that rewards the horse when he extends and lowers his head and neck, thereby stretching and raising the muscles of his back and freeing the leg joints, especially in the hind legs, which can then reach further under the body as the horse moves and can also drive against the ground with greater force, propelling the horse both upward and forward to a greater degree.

A note of caution is appropriate here for the amateur considering using this particular piece of equipment: The chambon should never be

BETHANY CASKEY

Even a longe line can be used in such a way as to qualify as auxiliary equipment. Rigged to a horse in the manner shown in this drawing, the longe is used not only to guide the horse on the circle, but also to draw his head inward toward the handler, encouraging him to give his neck, helping to supple him through his body as he moves around the longe circle.

activated (hooked up to the bit) on any horse who has not first been taught to release his head downward when pressure is applied in the area of his poll! This cannot be stressed strongly enough. Once the chambon has been put in place, if a horse panics and throws his head in the air, the pressure on the bit and poll will only increase as the horse lifts his head and will cease only when the horse lowers his head. This increase of pressure could cause a horse in panic to flip over backward.

The chambon in no way restricts the horse's ability to extend his nose. It therefore allows a horse to relax the area of the throat latch, as opposed to other mechanical devices that pull the horse's nose toward his chest and can kink the horse's neck or force the throat latch area to become tight and cramped.

The chambon should only be used while longeing the horse or while working him freely in a round pen. It can also be used to help rehabilitate horses who, for one reason or another, have short, tight, hollow backs or overdeveloped muscles of the lower neck through resistance or incorrect carriage. A horse can be worked in all gaits in the chambon.

When adjusting the set or length of the chambon to influence the height the horse is to carry his head while working, the device should not be tightened or shortened too quickly. Start by adjusting the chambon so the horse feels only a little pressure when he carries his head in his accustomed position, no matter what that might be. As he responds to the pressure exerted by the chambon over several weeks, gradually lower the head and neck carriage by tightening the device *slowly* over a period of four to eight weeks, until your horse can maintain the relaxed head and neck position on his own and begins to build the correct muscles.

An interesting feature of the chambon is the effect it has on a horse's mental attitude, often calming and quieting him as it influences and changes his balance and carriage.

Draw reins are also commonly used to control where a horse places his head. Draw reins are nothing more than elongated reins that fasten to the girth, either between the horse's front legs or on each side of the horse, just below the saddle flap, or they can be secured to the D rings of a Western cinch. The reins are then run through the rings of the snaffle bit and back into the rider's hands.

Draw reins lower a horse's neck, but also force the horse's nose downward and backward toward his chest. A little bit of this device goes a *long* way, and while it provides a very strong counterforce for horses who pull against a rider or toss their heads, overuse can easily put a horse on his forehand. It can also teach a horse to evade the bit by tucking his chin to his chest—a very undesirable thing. When used correctly, in conjunction with a regular rein and by not using them to make your horse position himself with his nose to his knees, the draw reins can be an effective tool to help relax a horse's neck and back and help the horse move in a rounded, more efficient frame. To produce the best effect with draw reins, a rider must use an interplay of leg and rein aids, and not rely solely on the mechanics of the draw reins.

No matter what device you choose to help solve temporary training and carriage problems, remembering to make haste slowly and closely monitoring the progress of your equine partner (including his mental state and any signs of physical soreness) on each and every ride will help you avoid of the hidden pitfalls of these and other training devices.

Chapter 7

When to Ask for Help (and How and Where to Find It)

*E*veryone is capable of learning; the trick is knowing what you need to learn. So it is with horses. But frequently, with horses, when you don't know much you also don't know what you need to know. In other words, not only may you not know the answers, but you may not even know which questions you should be asking—until it is too late.

If you own or ride a horse, you probably know there are a million opinions for just about everything having to do with horses, from care and handling to training and riding. Everyone has an opinion, and most will think theirs is, if not the *only* answer, then certainly the *right* answer. To make matters more confusing, many well-known clinicians, trainers, instructors and even equine medical professionals seem to express opinions or theories that oppose one another. Part of the problem lies with the industry. Horse professionals largely fall into one of several categories:

- Knowledgeable, dedicated horsemen and horsewomen

- Horse lovers

- Horse traders

- Rodeo cowboys, jockeys and polo players

- Philosophers who teach the art of living with the help of the horse

What they all have in common is a strong sense of independence. Unfortunately for the general consumer of equestrian services, that independent spirit has deterred many equine service industries from testing, certifying or licensing their practitioners. If you put your life on the line with a surgeon or a pilot, you have some assurance knowing they passed state and/or national exams to prove they are capable of performing their jobs within a basic standard—minimizing the risk to you. Equestrian consumers tend to forget that, just like going into surgery or getting on an airplane, you are putting life and limb at risk every time you are around or on a horse. Those who think I'm exaggerating can check the emergency room statistics of the American Medical Association, or the companies who assign insurance rates relative to risk factors. But if you do, be prepared for some sobering answers.

It is therefore ridiculous, when you think about it, that there is no mandatory national licensing of equine professionals, other than within the equine medical profession(s). There are some organizations, such as the American Riding Instructors Association, that offer voluntary testing and certification, and some farrier associations that grade and license members. But even with a college degree from an accredited equestrian program, there may still be a great variation in the *quality* of service, if not in the basic philosophy and techniques used by the service provider.

Common Sources of Information

The following list of information sources will help you know where to go to begin, not just to get answers to your questions, but also to learn what the right *questions* are in the first place.

Magazines
Offer:

- Informative articles on all aspects of horse care and training.

- Personality articles that offer insights into how other horsemen and horsewomen reached their goals or handled crises.

- Information on the competitive disciplines, trends, rule changes, etc.

- Breed articles that highlight special attributes of the various breeds of horses.

Advantages:

- Because magazines are published frequently, the information is usually up to date, and especially in the medical field, this can be vitally important to your horse's health. Prime examples are the recent outbreaks of such disabling or life-threatening diseases as EPM and West Nile virus.

- Scanning advertisements can quickly update you on what's new and currently popular in the industry.

Disadvantages:

- Storing and preserving important information, and finding it again after a few months or years, is not easy.

- The quality and accuracy of material can vary greatly among magazines, from issue to issue, and even within a single issue.

Books

Offer:

- Information on all aspects of horse health care, maintenance, ownership preparation and problems, training, riding, breeding and competing.

Advantages:

- Mountains of information from many authors, both old school and new and innovative.

- Reading about a topic can better prepare you to understand it when you have the opportunity to experience the same information kinesthetically.

- Books give you a chance to review different opinions on the same subject in the privacy of your home.

RED FLAGS THAT MAY SIGNAL
A NEED FOR A PROFESSIONAL'S HELP

- Horse is underweight.

- Horse is difficult to bridle.

- Horse tosses head when ridden.

- Horse runs backward.

- Horse pulls back either when tied or when being led.

- Horse drags you around when being led.

- Horse won't pick up or hold up feet.

- Horse is difficult to shoe.

- Horse is a picky eater.

- Horse won't stand still when being saddled or mounted.

- Horse is "cinchy" or holds breath when being girthed up.

- Horse drops or sinks down in the back when rider lowers her weight into the saddle.

- Horse is lame.

- Horse won't load in trailer.

- Horse's body is sore or horse has lost quality of gait or movement.

- Horse is sluggish when under saddle.

- Horse is agitated or nervous when under saddle.

- Horse won't bend body laterally.

- Horse won't give to the bit or leans on the rein in one or both directions.

- Horse is difficult to stop or slow down in any gait.

- Horse won't walk out going downhill.

- Horse tries to rush up hills.

- Horse is difficult to clip.

- Horse kicks, strikes, bucks, balks or rears.

- Horse exhibits an aggressive attitude toward people or other horses.

- Horse is extremely timid.

- Horse has unbalanced movement, heavy on the forehand.

- Horse stumbles.

- Horse has a crooked body, unbalanced muscle development.

- Horse carries head excessively high when ridden.

- Horse is barn sour.

- Horse won't pick up correct lead in one direction.

- Horse won't longe or will only stay out on circle when going in one direction.

- You've been riding regularly for six months or more with the same instructor without making any progress.

- Your fear or tension levels have increased rather than decreased during your lessons with your current instructor or trainer.

- You are experiencing increasing levels of physical pain when you ride.

- Authors are generally required to have solid qualifications in order to get a book accepted for publication.

- Books are easier to store and access than magazine articles, as the years go by.

Disadvantages:

- Long production time can make some information obsolete.

- To make use of books on training or riding, you've got to be able to read a written description of a physical action, then accurately reproduce or translate that word description into a physical action you perform or produce in your horse. This restructuring of information from mental to physical is a skill you must also learn.

Videos

Offer:

- Information on most aspects of horse handling and care.

- Visual examples of the form of winning horses and riders in many of the various performance disciplines.

Advantages:

- Moving visual input often better clarifies spoken or written instructions than photos or drawings would.

- Slow-motion features allow for detailed study of the mechanics of how a horse and rider perform a particular routine or task.

- Tapes can be watched over and over again to reinforce the rider's mental focus for later work in the saddle.

Disadvantages:

- Videos are often expensive, unless you can rent them.

- Information can become outdated pretty quickly.

- Production quality can be poor, creating a frustrating rather than an illuminating experience.

Lectures

Offer:

- New information, or extended information on a topic you are already familiar with.

- Many lectures are community affairs sponsored by local horse clubs or organizations, so they are also a good place to meet other horsemen and horsewomen from your area or in a specific discipline interest, who may then become a source for additional local information sources.

Advantages:

- Usually inexpensive, often close to home and an average of one to two hours long.

- Good lecturers are both knowledgeable and entertaining.

Disadvantages:

- It is a mistake to assume that every speaker is equally qualified to lecture on a topic, and if you are relatively inexperienced in the world of horses, you may have a hard time assessing the validity of material being presented.

- You can't revisit the information when desired, unless you are a very good note taker.

- Limited presentation time often curtails critical topic details, the lack of which can leave an unbalanced picture.

College Courses

Offer:

- New information.

- More in-depth information on a topic you are already familiar with.

- Continuing education credit.

Advantages:

- Usually local with reasonable registration fees.

- Excellent venue for getting classroom-type information, especially business-oriented classes that can make the difference between being successful and losing your shirt in the horse business, whether you are boarding, breeding or training.

Disadvantages:

- Extended time commitment requires a flexible work or family schedule that allows for six, eight or twelve weeks of regularly scheduled classes from one to five days a week.

- Registration is sometimes oversubscribed when these types of classes are offered at community colleges.

- You may be required to buy several expensive textbooks.

Seminars and Clinics

Offer:

- New information.

- Extended information on a topic you are already familiar with.

Advantages:

- Usually given by experienced, nationally recognized horsemen and horsewomen.

- Frequently includes hands-on or mounted work with a horse.

- Longer time allows for more detailed information and possibly more participant-presenter interaction, so specific questions on the topic can be asked and addressed.

- A great way to learn, especially when you choose a topic that is consistent with your need and current level of achievement or equestrian experience.

- An invaluable avenue for improving personal and horse-related performance skills for those who cannot readily or easily find the professional services of a good instructor or trainer in their local area.

- Even if you have a regular instructor, attending a clinic recommended by your instructor can often provide the stepping-stone to a new level of personal achievement for you or your horse. Perhaps it is the clinician's ability to see you with fresh eyes, or perhaps it will be a particular turn of phrase that will allow your mind to grasp a concept and your body to reproduce it precisely, or perhaps it will simply be riding a new exercise that will facilitate your ability to do something you've been trying, with little success, to get right for awhile. No matter what does the trick, when it happens to you, you will come away deliriously happy with your horse and yourself.

Disadvantages:

- More expensive then club-sponsored lectures and college courses.

- Often involves a fair bit of travel, increasing your costs with travel expenses and accommodations for both you and your horse if the clinic is two days or longer.

- Generally, groups are fairly large; six to eight riders constitutes a small clinic, and groups of up to 25 riders are average. The number of participants in the riding group will limit the amount of individually focused instruction possible.

- Without guidance from someone who is an experienced horseperson, sorting through conflicting concepts presented by various clinicians can become confusing and can potentially cause frustration for both rider and horse.

Riding Instructors

Offer:

- Help with improving your riding skills.

- Supervision while you're getting comfortable with handling a horse on the ground and in the stable, or while handling a new or difficult horse.

- Help in buying a horse.

- Coaching for competition.

- Assessment of current skills and performance level of both horse and rider and recommendations for the best ways to achieve current and future goals.

Advantages:

- A good instructor can lead students to both personal and competitive success, helping them develop their confidence and skills.

- A good instructor can open the door to the vast world of possibilities within the horse industry.

- Good ones act as mentors, guiding horse lovers to safer, more rewarding interactions with their horse, while helping them explore the many performance disciplines and styles of riding open to them.

Disadvantages:

- The cost of a *good* instructor is never too high. Having said that, cost may certainly be a factor for some riders considering regular instruction.

- There is no mandatory licensing of riding instructors in the United States (except in Massachusetts) at this time. Anyone can claim to be a riding instructor and charge money for lessons. The ability to ride and/or train a horse well is only one of many skills required in a good instructor. When you realize you are putting your safety and possibly even your life in the hands of your riding coach, finding a qualified person to fill the job is as important as deciding how you will fit the cost of instruction into your budget.

- It is not unusual for instructor and client to become friends, but, just as in public school, it is highly unlikely that the perfect teacher for you in kindergarten will also be the best teacher for you (and your horse) when you have progressed to college-level riding. It sometimes takes thought and tact on the part of both student and teacher to keep a professional relationship that has evolved into a friendship from flattening your learning curve.

- It's especially tough to find a top-quality, qualified instructor who is willing to pass you on, when the time comes.

Horse Trainers
Offer:

- Help with starting a young horse.

- Help with educating a horse who is under saddle already but is not a reliable, enjoyable ride for your level of experience.

- Help with improving a specific discipline skill or preparing you or your horse for competition, or advancing to a higher level in competition.

- Help with changing a horse's performance specialty.

- Help to correct a horse's behavior or attitude problems.

- Help in assessing your horse's talents and selecting a performance specialty.

- Help with rehabilitating a horse after a serious injury.

Advantages:

- A good trainer will not only teach your horse to be good at a specific job, he or she will give your horse confidence; teach him manners (how to behave around humans so as not to endanger either the human or himself); build him up physically, making him stronger and better able to withstand the rigors of his work; and finally, instill pride for a job well done, so your horse can be happy with his job and his life.

Disadvantages:

- As is the case with riding instructors, there is no state or national licensing system that can assure you that the person in whose hands you are about to leave your equine friend has the knowledge to choose from among the multitude of methods available for performance training, those that best suit your horse's individual emotional and physical requirements and will allow your horse to thrive, not just achieve, and remain sound over the long haul.

- Many professionals can lay claim to results, including many awards in competition, yet they use "quick result" methods that are not always in the best interests of the horse. It is difficult for an inexperienced rider to know how their horse is being handled every day when they are not present, or to know, until it is too late, that the pressure put on the horse during training was too great, either for his mind or his body. It is therefore wise to have your needs and expectations recorded in a training contract before leaving your horse in the hands of any trainer or agent. A professional trainer will spell out what will be done with your horse during the time he is in training, how often the horse will be ridden or worked and by whom, what he will be fed, what the charges are for those services and whether there can be additional charges for such things as hauling and showing. The contract, if it is a good one, will also spell out what the legal responsibilities are for each party, and what steps will be taken and at whose expense if the agreement is not kept in good faith. Since many states allow the seizure of a horse for unpaid bills, you are best advised to know in advance that you could lose your horse if financial calamity struck.

- Trainers come in all shapes and sizes and in all sorts of specialties, and it's not always easy to know which is best for you and your horse. To select the right trainer for your situation, you need to consider your horse's age, breed and temperament, your present and future training and/or competitive goals, your desired level of participation in your horse's education, your budget and your own gut feeling when you interview your prospective employee (the trainer).

- Most reputable trainers with experience command a substantial fee for their time and services—as well they should. A trainer risks injury and death each time they mount up, especially on green or problem horses. When the amount of time it takes to properly school a horse is combined with the time it takes to prepare them to be ridden and then care for them after exercise, few if any trainers can claim an hourly wage that even comes close to the one earned by the mechanic at your local garage, and he doesn't risk his life every day performing his job.

ON TRAINING AND TRAINERS

Training is mercurial. A well-trained horse, ridden or handled poorly, may quickly become "untrained." The horse is constantly learning from his environment and the people in it, and will manifest those traits or behaviors that are reinforced or allowed. Money invested in training is only well spent if the lessons learned are constructive and you will be able to continue to make the horse perform his job(s) in the desired manner.

A good trainer might be able to get a talented horse to perform advanced maneuvers in as little as 30 to 60 days, but it takes a year to confirm the lessons, and if the horse is asked to do work he is not physically prepared to do comfortably, his performance will soon deteriorate and his soundness will quickly follow suit.

Weeding Out the Bad Ones

Knowing when to holler "uncle" and ask for help is only part of the solution to the inevitable challenges you are going to encounter. The other, equally important part of the equation is *finding* that help. Looking at ads in magazines, tack shops, feeds stores or on the Internet can give you an introduction to the professionals or service providers who are in your area and who supposedly have the expertise to address your needs and the needs of your horse. But remember, after locating someone who provides the desired service, you still need to know the right questions to ask so you can assess at least some of their qualifications before you put your horse, yourself and your money into their hands or trust them with your dreams. Try the following quick quizzes to help you separate the chaff from the wheat.

Farrier

Each *yes* answer is worth three points. Questions in bold are extra value questions and are worth five points each. Total the points for all the *yes* answers to find the score.

1. The farrier has trained at a school accredited by either the American Farriers Association, the Brotherhood of Working Farriers Association or the Guild of Professional Farriers.

2. The farrier has served a minimum two-year apprenticeship with a master farrier.

3. The farrier arrives on time.

4. **The farrier keeps his or her appointments.**

5. **The farrier has an eye for a balanced, level foot, but also uses apparatus to run a double check.**

6. **The farrier has an eye for movement and understands how hoof angle, shoe weight, toe length, heel height, etc., affect stride and impact.**

7. The farrier returns your calls within 24 hours.

8. **The farrier stocks a wide variety of shoe types and sizes and a variety of shoes to correct defects or movement problems.**

9. The farrier attends seminars and/or lectures periodically to keep his or her skills current.

10. **The farrier "reads" horses well and handles them in a respectful and kindly manner, in accordance with their needs.**

11. The farrier takes a little extra time with oldsters, youngsters and difficult to manage horses.

12. **The farrier never loses their temper with a horse.**

13. **The farrier is willing to work with a horse's owner/rider/trainer and the horse's veterinarian and/or chiropractor when it comes to decisions affecting the performance and welfare of the horse, i.e. how the horse should be shod.**

14. The farrier keeps up to date on new industry techniques, developments and products and regularly shares this information with his clients.

15. **The farrier takes the time to educate the owner and rider of the horse about such things as shoe wear patterns, breakover patterns, follow-up care of the hoof and seasonal hoof maintenance.**

16. The farrier will notify the client if an abnormal wear pattern presents itself.

17. **The farrier can recommend various approaches to problems such as sheared heels, shelly walls, quarter cracks, abscesses, overreaching, brushing, contracted heels, navicular problems and laminitis.**

18. **The farrier can hot shoe and is willing to draw clips.**

19. The farrier finishes clinches to remove any burrs.

20. The farrier avoids removing excess hoof wall as a rule.

21. **The farrier does not "short shoe" a foot to avoid returning to replace a pulled shoe.**

22. The farrier carries a variety of nail sizes and lengths.

23. **The farrier will return promptly to replace a pulled shoe.**

24. The farrier picks up nails and nail tips and cleans up when done.

25. The farrier is a member of the American Farriers Association, the Brotherhood of Working Farriers Association or the Guild of Professional Farriers.

Scoring

60–70	Your horse is hard to catch on shoeing day.
71–80	Cowboys shod their own horses and nobody complained.
81–90	Welcome to the 20th century.
91–100	Diamonds are not a horsewoman's best friend; farriers who rate in this category are!

Veterinarian

Each *yes* answer is worth three points. Questions in bold are extra value questions and are worth seven points each. Total the points for all the *yes* answers to find the score.

1. The vet and/or the office staff know and can give accurate cost estimates for treatment, medication, lab work, follow-up services and so on before procedures or programs are begun.

2. The vet follows through with callbacks.

3. The vet returns non-emergency calls in reasonable time.

4. **The vet is open to owner input.**

5. **The vet is open to or recommends alternative therapies when applicable.**

6. The vet knows and can refer you to specialists when needed.

7. The vet will work with your farrier when circumstances require.

8. The vet knows and will refer you to an equine dentist.

9. The vet or office sends you vaccination reminders.

10. The vet explains procedures in understandable layman's terms.

11. **The vet will accommodate special circumstances when euthanasia is necessary.**

12. The vet treats animals with respect and kindness.

13. The vet offers enough information and options to give you a choice of treatment programs whenever possible.

14. The vet takes the time to instruct you in the correct procedures for simple treatments or administering drugs your horse needs for treatment.

15. The vet has superior horse handling skills

16. The vet participates in professional continuing educational opportunities.

17. The vet stays up to date with new procedures and treatments.

18. The vet has superior observation and gait analysis skills.

19. The vet remains calm and can handle difficult horses in critical situations.

20. The vet inspires confidence.

21. The vet has a good "bedside" manner.

22. The vet will neuter at least one barn cat at no charge.

23. The vet is willing to extend both time and services rendered beyond the call of duty in critical care situations.

24. The vet leaves clearly written, easy to understand instructions for necessary follow-up treatment.

25. The vet's office staff and assistants are courteous and efficient and relay telephone messages in a timely manner.

Scoring

65–70   If you're gambling your horse's life, the odds should be more in his favor.

71–80   OK, but it would be nice to do better.

81–90   Have a pot of hot coffee and warm cookies on hand the next time this vet arrives at your place.

91–99   Put the veterinarian on retainer.

Riding Instructor or Clinician

Each *yes* answer is worth two points. Questions in bold are extra value questions and are worth four points each. Total the points for all the *yes* answers to find the score.

1. **The instructor is certified by the American Riding Instructor's Certification Program or the British Horse Society.**

2. The instructor is a professional who teaches full time.

3. The instructor has studied riding and teaching in a formal school setting and/or served at least a two-year apprenticeship teaching under the guidance of a qualified, certified professional instructor of riding.

4. The instructor has taken college level classes to enhance their teaching skills.

5. The instructor is certified in cardiopulmonary resuscitation (CPR).

6. The instructor has a printed price list for the services they offer.

7. **The equipment used during lessons is clean and well maintained.**

8. **The lesson horses are well trained, happy and in good physical condition.**

9. Students are mounted on horses suitable to their needs and skill level.

10. Lessons are given in a safe environment.

11. Unleashed dogs are not allowed in the lesson area.

12. Every student receives instruction in basic horse handling skills, including catching, haltering, leading, grooming and tacking up the horse, or has been checked by the instructor and found to be accomplished in these skills.

13. The size of the saddle fits the size of the student.

14. The instructor can recommend books or videos to support the lessons, if requested.

15. The instructor will accompany students to competitions.

16. The instructor encourages students to participate in or audit different types of horse-related events and clinics to expand their student's knowledge and experience.

17. The instructor is a good communicator.

18. The instructor uses multiple techniques (visual, auditory, tactile) to help students grasp and understand concepts.

19. The instructor never leaves a class or a student unattended to talk on the phone or talk with other clients who are not involved in the current lesson.

20. The instructor never smokes while teaching.

21. The instructor can easily identify the primary source of a student's problem.

22. The instructor never uses sarcasm or screams at students.

23. The instructor knows and uses (has students perform) a variety of exercises to help improve their seat and position and control skills.

24. The instructor is respected by other industry professionals.

25. The instructor treats students and horses with respect.

26. The instructor puts the welfare of the student and their horse above the importance of winning.

27. The instructor regularly attends clinics or events to expand and update their own riding and teaching skills.

28. The instructor knows how to "read" and deal with the age and type of person who makes up the majority of their clientele.

29. Lessons begin and end on time.

30. The instructor willingly answers students' questions.

31. The instructor willingly "graduates" students to other qualified instructors when it is time to do so, or when it is in the student's best interest to do so.

32. The instructor is proud to see their students grow beyond their own accomplishments.

33. The instructor can explain the methods they use and know there is usually more than one way to solve a problem or reach a goal.

34. The instructor never loses their temper.

35. The instructor arrives to the lesson, clean, neat and appropriately dressed.

36. All students must wear protective head gear when mounted.

37. The instructor will help students find and buy a horse who meets their needs, if requested to do so.

38. Students are required to wear appropriate footwear when on or around horses.

39. The instructor is equally effective and comfortable giving private or group lessons.

40. The instructor has a sense of humor and uses humor to help students relax and learn.

Scoring

60–69   Knowledgeable guidance in a sport where risks include the possibility of serious injury and death is not a luxury, it is a necessity. You can do better.

70–79   Your ability to enjoy horses will depend on your ability to understand them and get along with them, both on the ground and mounted. An adequate teacher is okay, but don't give up the search for excellence.

80–89   A good, knowledgeable professional who has his or her students' best interests at heart.

90–100   You have found an instructor of outstanding quality. Count your blessings.

Horse Trainer

Each *yes* answer is worth two points. Questions in bold are extra value questions and are worth four points each. Total the points for all the *yes* answers to find the score.

1. **The trainer works full time at their profession.**

2. The trainer has graduated from an accredited equestrian program or college, or has spent a minimum of two years apprenticing full time with a professional trainer.

3. **The trainer's printed price list for services offered is available to customers and is posted in plain view somewhere in the trainer's office or tack room.**

4. The trainer requires a contract between trainer and owner that outlines services, fees, responsibilities of both owner and trainer, and the intended goals of training.

5. **The trainer maintains training equipment in good condition.**

6. **The trainer offers a safe training environment for both horse and client.**

7. **The trainer can recognize signs of stress, lameness and illness in the horse and knows when veterinary assistance is required.**

8. **The trainer has the knowledge to accurately assess both equine and owner skills and temperament in relation to the stated training goals.**

9. **The trainer is willing to give an honest appraisal of both the horse's and the rider's capabilities and potential in respect to the stated goals.**

10. The trainer or their staff updates that initial appraisal on a timely, ongoing basis.

11. **The trainer or staff keeps the owner informed of the horse's progress.**

12. **The trainer or staff adjusts training schedules to accommodate the horse's mental as well as physical needs.**

13. **The trainer puts the welfare of the horse over any competitive demands.**

14. The trainer has an open-door policy for owners who want to watch training sessions and visit their horse.

15. **The trainer and staff treat all horses with respect.**

16. The trainer and staff understand horse body language.

17. The trainer can produce a horse suitable to the rider, provided the horse and rider's capabilities are reasonably matched.

18. **The trainer has a respected standing among other industry professionals.**

19. **The trainer and staff are knowledgeable about the nutritional needs of performance horses and adequately provide for those needs while the horse is in their care.**

20. Any assistant allowed to work with a client's horse is supervised by the head trainer and is required to give daily progress reports on the horses they are responsible for working.

21. If an assistant is a part of the horse's training team, they are included in the decision-making discussions between the head trainer and the horse's rider/owner.

22. The trainer attends clinics, seminars or other educational events every year to advance skills and knowledge.

23. **There are qualified personnel in change of any horses left at the home barn at all times when the head trainer is absent or on the road.**

24. The trainer offers support services at shows (coaching, grooming, warm-up, etc.) if the horse and rider are being prepared for showing.

25. **The trainer will refer horses and clients to another industry professional when the required or requested work is beyond their skills or area of interest or expertise.**

26. The trainer allows play time for horses in their care.

27. The trainer offers a list of references when asked.

28. The workspace is free of clutter, organized and suited to the job.

29. **Horses in the trainer's barn care seem content and well cared for.**

30. **The trainer and staff can explain the methods they use and give an overview of the expected logical progression as a direct result of their use.**

31. The trainer and staff can read a horse's personality and intent and respond with firmness or kindness appropriate to the needs of each individual situation.

32. **The trainer and staff never lose their temper with a horse under any circumstances.**

Scoring

60–69   A horse represents a substantial investment of time and money, so it is best to stick with quality all the way around. You should do better.

70–79   A utilitarian program may be inexpensive, but if you or your horse incur medical bills and time off from your respective jobs, what you saved can be quickly erased.

80–89   Experienced, caring guidance is one of the greatest ways to ensure that you and your horse continue to enjoy each other and reach your goals.

90–100   Professionals in this category are like treasured friends; their first concern is the best interests of both you and your horse, and they find a way of telling the truth even when it may be tough for you to hear.

Retail Tack Shop

Each *yes* answer is worth three points. Questions in bold are extra value questions and are worth five points each. Total the points for all the *yes* answers to find the score.

1. The store offers a varied inventory.

2. The staff knows their merchandise, the performance history of the products it carries and comparative values

3. The store stands behind the merchandise it sells.

4. The store offers a professional discount.

5. The staff knows where to refer customers to find services or items they are unable to provide.

6. The store carries a variety of similar products that offer customers a range of prices.

7. The store offers periodic sales with discounts on all merchandise.

8. Regular customers get first-chance sales notices.

9. The staff is courteous and friendly.

10. The store only takes a modest markup on necessity items such as fly spray, wormer and basic medical supplies.

11. The inventory suits the needs and interests of the local equestrian community.

12. The store stocks new and innovative products.

13. The store promotes consumer education and awareness.

14. The store carries quality merchandise.

15. The store supports the local equestrian community by sponsoring or contributing to nonprofit horse-related programs.

16. The store hosts periodic equestrian-focused social events or fundraisers.

17. The store offers a limited inventory of companion animal items for the shopping convenience of customers.

18. The store has a consumer-friendly policy and sincere attitude regarding returned merchandise.

19. The store has educational videos for rent.

20. The store has a variety of equestrian books and periodicals for sale.

21. The store carries seasonal equestrian-related cards and gift items.

22. The store has a community bulletin board.

23. The store provides space for informational flyers on competitions, clinics, seminars and other equestrian events.

24. The store carries veterinary supplies (vaccines, medications, surgical scrubs, etc.).

25. The store is open convenient hours.

26. The store takes used tack on consignment.

27. The store has a large inventory of new and used saddles.

28. The store has someone on staff who is knowledgeable about saddle fit.

29. The store has a qualified, experienced saddle fitter or repair department.

30. The store takes a reduced consignment percentage on a used saddle consigned by a customer who has purchased a new one at that store.

Scoring

60–75   OK, but this place could do more for its customers.

76–88   Service oriented and probably a good place to do business.

89– 99   Goes the extra mile for the benefit of both horse and rider.

More Tips to Help You Find the Right Instructor

The goal of being an all-around rider means you want to get an excellent basic education in equitation. It is generally easier to go from the English disciplines to the Western than vice versa, so finding an instructor who can teach you what is generally referred to as a *balanced seat* would be a good place to start. Once you're solid on the basics, move on to acquiring or polishing your skills for jumping, if any of the events you want to try require it. Finally, get some coaching from a good stock seat or Western coach.

Make a list of instructors and facilities in your area, but remember, if you cannot find good quality instruction locally, you are better off traveling to the best instructor you can afford, even if it means taking your

---

QUESTIONS TO ASK

Other things to consider include:

- The distance of the instructor from your home or work, including travel time

- The price of lessons

- Whether discounts are offered for multiple lessons, and whether there are any cancellation charges for missed lessons

- The length of lessons (is saddling time included in that time block?)

- The instructor's specialty and number of years teaching

- What facilities are available (indoor arena, jumps, trails, trail course, cattle, school horses, etc.)

- Any specialized equipment you may need

- Additional programs available to student and clients, such as coaching on the trail, schooling shows or the possibility of using school horses to get experience showing in a new discipline

lessons in intense segments, such as a multiday clinic, or arranging for several days of multiple sessions with a specific coach before you return home. When possible, get your work (both regular instruction and, periodically, your practice sessions) videotaped and arrange time to review the tapes with your instructor.

Be sure to choose an instructor with whom you feel comfortable. If you can't understand an instructor, if you are worried about being dressed down if you make a mistake, if the demands of the lesson leave you feeling defeated and drained, you won't advance your skills very quickly, if at all.

If you must force your body into positions that cause actual physical pain, your body will respond by defending itself with tension patterns. And once imprinted as habits, those patterns will be hard to break. So learning correct techniques from the beginning is as important to your ultimate health and welfare as it is for performance success.

Before putting yourself in the saddle with any instructor, clinician or coach, audit a couple of their classes or clinics to get a feel for how they are run. Try to observe classes of students whose riding abilities or discipline is the same or similar to your own—or to the one you are exploring. Spend some time talking to some of the students after the lessons. Ask things like, "How long have you been taking lessons with this instructor?" and "Do you feel your riding has progressed during that time, and if so, how so?"

Avoid instructors who swear, smoke while teaching, whose attire is dirty or sloppy and who scream or use sarcasm in their teaching.

A teacher must be able to put himself in the student's place and communicate clearly what he knows. Top riders and trainers long ago committed what they do to unconscious memory. But to communicate those skills to a student, the instructor must remember all of the details that go on while riding. Good teaching requires patience and the ability to communicate by building pictures in the student's mind with words, and good teaching skills are usually the result of *many years of practice of both riding and teaching.*

An intermediate or advanced rider who studies with an advanced coach doesn't need to have a lot of time focused on his or her body issues. When changing disciplines, ask your coach to explain any variation in application of the aids that might apply. A coach who works with advanced riders will focus primarily on giving you feedback about what your horse is doing relative to what he needs to do so you can be successful in that specific discipline, and what routines, exercises and patterns you can use to reach your desired performance level.

As an intermediate or advanced rider, you may be expected to periodically ride challenging horses, to help advance your skills. If this happens, the ultimate responsibility for your safety rests with you. Any time you feel a horse or an exercise is more than you can handle, or you feel you are in a potentially dangerous situation, *speak up*! Tomorrow may be another day, but you need to follow your instincts to get there. If your basic skills are strong, few horses who are not truly dangerous will threaten your security, so if you *do* feel threatened, reconsider your timing, return to the basics and wait to test yourself until your skills make you feel confident when faced with the challenge, whatever it is.

Fitness and Your Body's Role in Reaching Your Goals

If you've ridden all of your life, never had an accident on or off a horse, don't have any inherited body issues, such as scoliosis, short leg, etc., don't spend eight hours a day in a job that emphasizes repetitive, one-sided motions or body positions and are reasonably fit, you will have little trouble performing the work required to become a better rider and to acquire the skills of a new discipline—at least until you enter your 50s. Many people, however, have body issues caused by at least one of the items I've just listed, and experience blocks, caused in part by those issues, which slow or prevent them from acquiring a desired riding skill or goal.

It is not uncommon to be unaware of your body issues (except perhaps for noticing the normal aches and pains of living, working and aging) until you try to perform a specific skill. If this happens, you can end up struggling for months, making little progress and becoming more and more frustrated with yourself, your horse and your instructor. Should this happen to you, it may be time to look outside the equestrian industry for help. Chiropractors, Alexander practitioners and Feldenkrais practitioners are all focused on alignment, and the last two specialize in efficient use of the body during movement.

You can cross-train in yoga, for stretching and flexibility, and work on your aerobic fitness with swimming, but control of your skeleton, for balance, security and as a communication tool, requires some highly discipline-specific muscles, known as *core* muscles. To develop those, the best cross-training program for equestrians is the one known as Pilates. Denise Montagne, a licensed physical therapist and certified Pilates instructor in Reno, Nevada, works with equestrians and offers the following thoughts about this particular approach to acquiring or improving the skills of riding.

Horseback riding affects many systems of the body, including the musculoskeletal system, the cardiovascular system, the vestibular system and the reflexes. Normal rider training is done *on* the horse, but there is a great deal you can do to enhance your physical ability out of the saddle that will enable you to move more fluidly with your horse and improve your ability to communicate clearly with him.

Most human bodies are unbalanced or asymmetrical to some extent. This could be the result of a previous injury, genetic predisposition or postural habits. Some muscles may become weak or too tight, while others compensate and become too strong. Muscles need to be balanced in both length and strength to function efficiently. If the proper balance is not there, it can predispose you to injury, fatigue or pain, as well as the inability to perform.

There are several kinds of exercises that are beneficial for equestrians, including aerobics, weight training and yoga, but I have found the best exercise program for riders is Pilates. Popular in health clubs, private studios and physical therapy centers for fitness and rehabilitation, Pilates exercises focus on strengthening the core muscles of the rider's trunk—the *powerhouse,* as it is called. The work produces strength, stability, flexibility and postural alignment of the spine and trunk muscles, but also includes the hips, shoulders and extremities. The system is based in yoga and involves breathing coordinated with movement. It develops long, sleek and flexible muscles rather than muscles that are bulky, short and tight. Pilates movements are done slowly, with precision, intent and grace, to enable your mind and body to come together. A session with a trainer should leave one feeling invigorated and peaceful, not fatigued and sore.

For equestrians, strengthening the core muscles is essential, as it is this area of the body that provides the muscular ability to collect a horse. A strong trunk helps prevent injuries and back pain, improves posture, allows a stable yet independent seat and enables you to ride for a longer period of time without early onset of muscle fatigue. In addition, proper alignment and coordinated and integrated movement facilitate the delivery of the proper aides from rider to horse in a subtle manner, without communication overkill.

There are numerous Pilates books and videotapes on the market, but finding a qualified and experienced instructor, especially if you have a history of injuries, is the best way to be introduced to this valuable cross-training technique. Once properly learned, a Pilates floor routine can be performed in your own home in less than 20 minutes, four times a week.

Riding regularly and correctly will maintain your general fitness level, but it is always a good idea to think about preparing yourself as well as your horse when you intend to step up the difficulty of your specialty or change to one that requires a higher degree of fitness. Riding over a course of hunter fences is not the same as riding an eventing cross-country course, and a casual two-hour trail ride does not make the same demands on your fitness as a 50-mile endurance ride. If you are relatively young and reasonably fit, you may be able to push the edge of your envelope, dealing with the soreness and stiffness you'll inevitably feel if you ramp up your performance without preparation. But as you tire, you are a less able partner for your horse and can even become a detriment to his performance. So if you really want success, make the extra effort to ensure that both you and your horse are physically prepared for the challenges you choose.

SUSAN HARRIS

Chapter 8

Where the Road Can Lead

Competitions on the Trail

Trail Trials

Best type of horse: Any horse or pony

Object of the game: Test your horse's obedience, bravery and training by negotiating various predetermined natural or manmade obstacles set along a measured, marked trail route. Obstacles can range from simple, such as a log stepover or mounting and dismounting, to complex, such as hoisting a human-size dummy onto your horse's back and rescuing the "injured person" by leading your horse a set distance with the dummy draped over his back. Each obstacle is judged individually, usually by a different scorekeeper or judge. Awards are decided based each horse and rider's cumulative obstacle scores. The pace is usually a walk or trot.

Choose it if you like: A fun day on the trail with friends, with periodic challenges to your skills as a rider and to your horse's training

Compatible disciplines: Competitive trail riding, an endurance ride in the limited distance division

Governing organization: Usually, state horsemanship organizations

Competitive Trail

Best type of horse: Any breed of horse or pony. The best horse is one who is calm and obedient with good recovery time and a low heart rate.

Object of the game: To cover a set distance, usually from 15 to 40 miles in a day (some events are two or three days long), demonstrating your understanding of pace and control of your horse by arriving at various checkpoints along a marked route, within specific time frames. The horse receives a score for his physical condition before, during and after the ride. Horses are also scored for trail manners, while riders receive a score on their horsemanship and general handling skills. In some areas of the country, obstacles are also included at intervals during the ride, and horse and rider are scored on their work through these obstacles.

Choose it if you like: To spend all day with your horse and your riding friends on the trail. To challenge your ability to pace your horse, riding him in a way that gets you both over the distance in the required amount of time, while conserving his energy and soundness.

Compatible disciplines: Trail trials and endurance riding

Governing organization: North American Trail Ride Conference, www.natrc.org

Upper Midwest Endurance and Competitive Rides Association, www.umecra.com

Eastern Competitive Trail Ride Association, www.ectra.org

Magazines with coverage: *Trail Blazer Magazine*, *The Trail Rider*, the monthly or bimonthly publications of the governing organizations

To learn more: *NATRC Rider's Manual—A Complete Guide to Competitive Trail Riding*, by the North American Trail Ride Conference; *Problem Solving, Volume I: Preventing and Solving Common Horse Problems*, by Marty Marten, Lyons Press

Competitive trail riding can be a challenging day out in the country.

Endurance

Best type of horse: Most breeds that trot, as well as some of the gaited breeds; most winners are Arabians.

Object of the game: Covering distances from 25 to 100 miles in 24 hours or less. The first horse across the finish line is the winner, but all horse and rider teams to successfully finish a ride in the allotted time receive an award; "to finish is to win" is the motto of the governing organization. All horses must meet and pass multiple veterinary inspections for soundness and metabolic rate before the ride, along the ride route and at the finish line.

Choose it if you like: Runs the gauntlet from a personal best challenge to a great way to spend the day with your horse, to a grueling, complex, athletic test of horse and rider, to an adrenaline-pumping flat-out horse race.

BECKY SILER

Without skipping a beat, an endurance rider "goes fishing" for water with his sponge. He'll put the water on his horse's neck to help cool him. (In this photo the two horses are aligned so that it looks as if there are two riders on one horse.)

Compatible disciplines: Competitive trail, foxhunting

Governing organization: American Endurance Ride Conference, www.aerc.org

Magazines with coverage: *Endurance World* and the monthly governing organization's magazine *Endurance News*

To learn more: *The Complete Guide to Endurance Riding and Competition*, by Donna Snyder-Smith, Howell Book House; *Go the Distance*, by Nancy Loving, DVM, Trafalgar Square

Ride and Tie

Best type of horse: Any trotting breed; most winners are Arabians.

Object of the game: Teams of two riders using one horse cover a specified distance in the fastest possible time. One team member runs, one team member rides, switching as they go through the course. The first team across the finish line wins. As in endurance riding, horses must pass periodic veterinary checks before, during and after a race.

Choose it if you like: Running and riding

Compatible disciplines: Endurance riding

Governing organization: Ride and Tie Association, www.rideandtie.org

Arena Disciplines

Dressage

Best type of horse: Any of the trotting breeds can perform tests; the favored breed is the Warmblood.

Object of the game: Perform a predetermined series of geometric figures and movements in various gaits, known as a *test,* in a flat arena approximately 66 feet wide by 198 feet long. Movements are begun and ended at specific letter markers throughout the arena. The horse is judged using a numerical score from 1 to 10 by judges who grade on the accuracy of the movements, the correctness of the

THE CHRONICLE OF THE HORSE/NICOLE LEVER

Dressage presents both mental and physical challenges to horse and rider.

work and the overall beauty and harmony of the picture presented by horse and rider.

Choose it if you like: The challenge of getting a 1,000 pounds of muscle and bone to become so linked to you that he feels like an extension of your body and mind. This is a complex discipline that attracts those who like mental as well as physical challenges and enjoy dancing with a horse as a partner.

Compatible disciplines: At its basic levels, dressage is a gymnastic foundation for all other disciplines, because it prepares a horse to carry his rider in a self-preserving, athletically maximized way.

Governing organization: United States Dressage Federation, www.usdf.org

Magazine with coverage: *Dressage Today*

To learn more: *Dressage Formula*, by Erik Herbermann, J.A. Allen & Co.; *The Complete Training of Horse and Rider*, by Alois Podhajsky, Wilshire Publishing; *Dressage With Kyra*, by Kyra Kyrklund, Trafalgar Square; *The Athletic Development of the Dressage Horse*, by Charles deKunffy, Howell Book House; *Dressage for the 21st Century*, by Paul Belasik, Trafalgar Suqare; *The Competitive Edge: Improving Your Dressage Scores in the Lower Levels*, by Max Gahwyler, Half Halt Press

Pleasure and Equitation Classes (English, Western and Saddle Seat)

Best type of horse: Any breed of horse or pony

Object of the game: Demonstrate the quality and consistency of your horse's gaits within the class or breed specifications, in front of a judge in an arena setting.

Choose it if you like: Dressing up and showing off your horse and your equitation skills.

Western equitation gives you and your horse a chance to really dress up.

Compatible disciplines: Pleasure riding, trail riding, dressage

Governing organizations: USA Equestrian, www.equestrian.org

Breed organizations such as the American Quarter Horse Association and the American Paint Horse Association

Magazines with coverage: Association magazines, and general interest horse magazines such as *Horse Illustrated, Practical Horseman, Horse & Rider* and *Performance Horseman*

To learn more: *Centered Riding 2: Further Exploration,* by Sally Swift, Trafalgar Square; *Hunter Seat Equitation,* by George Morris, Doubleday; *Western Horsemanship,* by Richard Shrake, Lyons Press; *101 Horsemanship and Equitation Patterns,* by Cherry Hill, Storey Books; *Anatomy in Motion II: Visible Rider* (video), with Susan Harris, Trafalgar Square

Showmanship

Best type of horse: All breeds

Object of the game: An immaculately groomed, physically conditioned horse and a well-turned-out handler work together to show the quality of the horse's conformation and the aptitude of the handler at positioning and controlling her horse, to present the horse in the best light to the judge.

Choose it if you like: Showing off your horse

Compatible disciplines: Halter class, flat classes, longe line classes

Governing organization: USA Equestrian, www.equestrian.org

Various breed organizations

Reining

Best type of horse: Quarter Horses have the edge, but Arabians, Paints, Appaloosas and others can also be competitive, especially within breed shows.

Object of the game: The horse and rider team performs stylized maneuvers or patterns in an arena. The maneuvers originate from skills required to work cattle, with the rider in complete control,

THE CHRONICLE OF THE HORSE/JOHN STRASSBURGER

Controlled speed is the name of the game in reining.

and include spins and rollbacks, flying lead changes, slow lope, fast gallop and sliding stops. The horse should be guided by his rider with no apparent resistance. A judge or panel of judges scores the horse and rider team using a numerical system, based on smoothness, finesse, attitude, quickness and controlled speed.

Choose it if you like: Speed, agility, adrenaline, thrilling stops

Compatible disciplines: Working cow horse, team penning

Governing organization: USA Equestrian, www.equestrian.org

National Reining Horse Association, www.nrha.com

National Snaffle Bit Association, www.nsba.com

Various breed organizations

Magazines with coverage: Association magazines, *NRHA Way to Go*

To learn more: *Reining*, by Al Dunning, Lyons Press; *Fundamentals of Judging*, (video), National Reining Horse Association

Barrel Racing

Best type of horse: Quarter Horses and other breeds

Object of the game: Horse and rider race a cloverleaf pattern around three barrels set in a triangle approximately 70 to 90 feet apart. The fastest horse takes the prize.

Choose it if you like: Lots of speed and hairpin turns

Compatible disciplines: Gymkhana speed games such as pole bending and keyhole, reining

Governing organization: National Barrel Horse Association, www.nbha.com

Magazines with coverage: *Barrel Horse News*, *America's Barrel Racer*

To learn more: *The A.R.T. of Barrel Racing*, by Sharon Camarillo, www.sharoncamarillo.com; *Barrel Racing: Training the Wright Way*, by Ed and Martha Wright, Equimedia

Hairpin turns at hair-raising speed are the hallmarks of barrel racing.

Trail Horse Class

Best type of horse: Any trotting breed

Object of the game: Demonstrating your horse's agility, obedience and calm disposition over a series of obstacles, including walkovers, backthroughs and gates. The work through each obstacle is scored by a judge. The best score wins the class.

Choose it if you like: Slow, precise work that requires and rewards your horse for listening closely to your aids.

Compatible disciplines: Pleasure, equitation, Western riding, dressage, pleasure driving

Governing organization: USA Equestrian, www.equestrian.org

Various breed organizations

Magazines with coverage: *Horse & Rider, Performance Horseman*

To learn more: *Training for Trail Horse Classes*, by Laurie Truskauskas, Alpine Publications

Agility, obedience and calm are required for the trail horse class.

Western Riding

Best type of horse: Any trotting breed

Object of the game: The Western riding class is a bit like a Western dressage class. Horse and rider perform and are judged on a preset pattern that includes transitions, walking, jogging and loping over and around obstacles, a serpentine pattern with flying changes and a halt and backup. The class is scored numerically with smoothness and overall pattern accuracy among the scoring criteria.

Choose it if you like: To test yourself and your horse on your basic handling and the smoothness of your horse's responses to your aids.

Compatible disciplines: Trail class, Western pleasure, lower level dressage, team penning

Governing organization: USA Equestrian, www.equestrian.org

Various breed organizations

To learn more: *Western Training,* by Jack Brainard, Lyons Press

Pleasure Driving

Best type of horse: Most trotting breeds can be driven; commonly seen breeds are Morgans, Arabians, Saddlebreds, Hackneys and Warmbloods, as well as several of the pony breeds.

Object of the game: Enjoying your horse from the seat of a carriage, testing your skills as a driver, enjoying time travel back through history for a couple of hours or a day.

Choose it if you like: A sense of history, dressing up in costume, a peaceful afternoon at a slower pace

Compatible disciplines: Combined driving

Governing organization: USA Equestrian, www.equestrian.org

American Driving Society, www.americandrivingsociety.org

Various breed organizations

Magazines with coverage: *Carriage Journal, Driving Digest*

To learn more: *Carriage Driving: A Logical Approach Through Dressage Training*, by Heike Bean and Sarah Blanchard, Howell Book House; *Competition Carriage Driving on a Shoestring*, by Jinny Johnson, J.A. Allen & Co.; and *Teach Your Horse to Drive* (two-video set), with Mary Ruth Marks

Contests Involving Jumping

Hunter

Best type of horse: Thoroughbreds and some Warmbloods, but most trotting breeds have individuals who can jump well enough to complete, at least at the lower levels.

Object of the game: Getting around the course and over the fences cleanly while making it look effortless

Choose it if you like: Mild thrills (more excitement than a flat class), tests of your equitation skills

Compatible disciplines: Jumpers, foxhunting and eventing

The best hunter rounds look clean and effortless.

THE CHRONICLE OF THE HORSE/TRICIA BOOKER

Governing organization: USA Equestrian, www.equestrian.org

Various breed organizations

Magazines with coverage: *Hunter & Sport Horse, Practical Horseman, The Chronicle of the Horse*

To learn more: *Schooling to Show: Basics of Hunter-Jumper Training,* by Anthony D'Ambrosio, Viking Press; *Training Hunters, Jumpers and Hacks,* by Harry Chamberlin, Putnam; *Anne Kursinski's Riding and Jumping Clinic,* by Anne Kursinski, Doubleday

Hunter Hack

Best type of horse: Any trotting breed; Thoroughbreds are the top choice in open competition.

Object of the game: This is like a pleasure class with two low jumps. Riders show their horses on the rail in three gaits and hand gallop, then individually jump two fences. Judges look for brilliance, manners, performance and the ability to jump cleanly, obediently and smoothly.

Choose it if you like: Pleasure classes, but want to try showing over small jumps

Compatible disciplines: Flat rail classes and hunter classes

Governing organization: USA Equestrian, www.equestrian.org

Various breed organizations

Jumper

Best type of horse: Warmbloods and Thoroughbreds, but any trotting breed can produce horses who can jump, especially at heights below five feet

Object of the game: Clear all the fences in the course in the shortest amount of time

Choose it if you like: Adrenaline, roller coasters, excitement, clever and aggressive riding

Compatible disciplines: Eventing, hunters

Exciting, aggressive riding is required in jumper competition.

Governing organization: USA Equestrian, www.equestrian.org

Various breed organizations

Magazines with coverage: *Practical Horseman, The Chronicle of the Horse, Hunter & Sport Horse*

To learn more: *Classic Show Jumping: The De Nemethy Method,* by Bertalan deNemethy, Doubelday; *101 Jumping Exercises for Horse and Rider,* by Linda Allen, Storey Books; *Anne Kursinski's Riding and Jumping Clinic,* by Anne Kursinski, Doubleday

Eventing

Best type of horse: Thoroughbreds and Warmbloods excel at the top levels, but many different trotting breeds are successful at the lower levels of the sport.

Object of the game: This test is divided into three sections: The first section, dressage, tests the horse's basic training and obedience. The second section, speed and endurance, tests the courage, fitness and athletic skills, cleverness and intelligence of horse and rider. The third section, stadium jumping, tests obedience and athleticism.

Choose it if you like: Mental as well as physical challenges, high adrenaline levels, precise riding, tests of courage, incredible highs

Compatible disciplines: Jumping, dressage, hunters, point to points, foxhunting

Governing organization: USA Equestrian, www.equestrian.org

United States Eventing Association, www.eventingusa.com

Magazines with coverage: *Eventing, The Chronicle of the Horse*

The author on Appaloosa stallion Medicine Man on cross-country at Ram Tap, on the way to winning the Reserve Championship in the training level division.

To learn more: *Training the Three-Day Event Horse and Rider,* by James Wofford, Derrydale Press; *Gymnastics: Systematic Training for Jumping Horses,* by James Wofford, Compass Equestrian; *Give Your Horse a Chance,* by Lt. Col. A.L. d'Endrody, Trafalgar Square; *Practical Eventing,* by Sally O'Connor, Half Halt Press; *Cross-Country Masterclass With Leslie Law,* by Leslie Law, David & Charles

Contests Involving Cattle

Team Penning

Best type of horse: Quarter Horses and stock horse type horses are favored, but any trotting breed can do it with the right training

Object of the game: A team of three riders and horses enter an area with a herd of 30 cows. Each cow has a number on it. Each team of riders must cut out the three like-numbered cows from the herd and move them down the arena and into a small holding pen. Two minutes are allowed to pen the three cows. The shortest amount of time to get all three cows in the pen wins the contest.

BECKY SILER

While many participants in the Western disciplines do not regularly use safety head gear, I recommend that all riders wear approved safety helmets when mounted.

Choose it if you like: Working with team members in a strategy game, tests that demand fast and accurate control of your horse; you've got a horse who thinks it's fun to chase cows.

Compatible disciplines: Reining and working cow horse classes

Governing organization: American Quarter Horse Association, www.aqha.com

Team Pen America, www.teampenamerica.com

United States Team Penning Association, www.ustpa.com

Magazines with coverage: *Western Horseman*, association magazines and Western general interest horse magazines

To learn more: *Team Penning*, by Phil Livingston, Lyons Press; *The Penning Tape* (video), with Peter Brown, Handshake Films

Working Cow Horse

Best type of horse: Stock or ranch type horses do the work best, with Quarter Horses leading the parade to the winner's circle most often; most trotting breeds can perform the routines

Object of the game: The test is divided into two sections, both scored by judges: a reining pattern and working a cow. Each phase has equal importance and the winner is decided by the highest combined score. The reining pattern varies, but consists of demonstrations of slow lope and fast gallop, flying lead changes quick, sliding stops, fast turns (spins and roll backs) in both directions, and a backup. In the cow work, the horse must demonstrate his ability to *hold* a cow, like a cutting horse, as well as demonstrating he can control the direction of a moving cow.

Choose it if you like: The experience of riding a cat, excitement, the fun of the chase, the feeling of 1,000 pounds of living Ferrari between your legs and hands.

Compatible disciplines: Reining, cutting and team penning

Governing organization: USA Equestrian, www.equestrian.org

National Reined Cow Horse Association, www.nrcha.com

Various breed organizations

The horse should always appear to be guided by his rider and offer no resistance.

Magazines with coverage: *Western Horseman, Horse and Rider,* association magazines and Western general interest horse magazines

To learn more: *Win With Bob Avila,* by Juli Thorson, Lyons Press

Cutting

Best type of horse: Quarter Horses excel; other breeds, including Arabians, Paints and Appaloosas, are also represented.

Object of the game: Match the mind of your horse against the mind of a cow. The rider cuts one cow away from a group, then horse and rider must keep it from returning to the herd. The horse should seem to work on his own with a minimum of signals from the rider. The performance is scored numerically by a judge or panel of judges.

Choose it if you like: Working with a supremely athletic equine partner who likes outthinking a cow; riding thrills and fast movement

Compatible disciplines: Working cow horse, reining

Governing organization: National Cutting Horse Association, www.nchacutting.com

Magazine with coverage: *Cutting Horse Chatter,* association magazine

To learn more: *Training and Showing the Cutting Horse,* by Lynn Chamion, Lyons Press; *Cutting, One Run at a Time,* by Barbara Schulte, Barbara Schulte Press

Roping

Best type of horse: Quarter Horses and ranch type horses

Object of the game: In team roping, you break from a chute after a calf or a steer and get your rope on his head or heels as quickly as possible. In calf or tie down roping, the rider must then dismount, lay the calf down and tie three of his feet together. This is a timed event.

Choose it if you like: The historical significance of the cowboy skills of roping, the challenge of making a good rope horse partner, the feeling of riding through history into the present day

Compatible disciplines: Working cow horse, ranch horse trials

Governing organization: Professional Rodeo Cowboys Association, www.prorodeo.com

United States Team Roping Championships, www.ustrc.com/Home/

Magazines with coverage: *Spin to Win, Ropers Sports News, Western Horseman,* Western discipline general interest horse magazines, association magazines

To learn more: *Team Roping With Jake and Clay*, by Fran Smith, Lyons Press; *Calf Roping*, by Roy Cooper, Lyons Press

If you always wanted to be a cowboy, roping is for you.

Other Events

Drill Team

Best type of horse: Any breed

Object of the game: Precision riding maneuvers in groups of from 4 to 40

Choose it if you like: Fun, the thrill of entertaining a crowd with your horse, the challenge of the sometimes intricate figures, which can demand precise control of your horse

Compatible disciplines: Pleasure and flat classes, reining, dressage

Governing organization: United States Dressage Federation, www.usdf.org

State horse organizations such as the California State Horseman's Association

Magazines with coverage: *Western Horseman*, general interest horse magazines

Precision riding maneuvers can be an interesting challenge for you and your horse.

Combined Driving

Best type of horse: Most trotting breeds; top-level competitors include Warmbloods and Morgans.

Object of the game: In horse driving trials and combined driving events, there are three phases: the dressage phase, which is very similar to a ridden test; the marathon phase, where horse and driver go off-road, cross-country, meeting and handling a series of obstacles, known as hazards; and the cones phase, back in the arena, where the driver must maneuver her horse and cart through a series of pairs of cones in a prescribed order, without dislodging the balls that rest on top of the cones. Scoring is done by accruing penalties, and the team with the lowest penalty score wins.

Choose it if you like: Thrills, precision control, enjoying a view of the countryside from the seat of a cart, being connected to a sense of history and the historical importance of the horse

Compatible disciplines: Pleasure driving, dressage, trail riding

Governing organization: The American Driving Society, www.americandrivingsociety.com

USA Equestrian, www.equestrian.org

Magazine with coverage: *The Whip*, association magazine

To learn more: *American Driving Society Handbook*

BECKY SILER

Combined driving can connect you to the historical role of the horse.

Foxhunting

Best type of horse: Thoroughbreds and Warmbloods, but any trotting breed that shows a talent for jumping can participate.

Object of the game: Getting together with other foxhunters, riding to the hounds for four to six hours on brisk fall days; having a brave, reliable horse who will jump any obstacle he encounters in the field.

Choose it if you like: Fast gallops, the thrills of jumping and the chase, being on a horse's back for most of the day, an occasional nip from your flask on a chilly day, during a cast

Compatible disciplines: Trail riding, cross-country jumping

Governing organization: Masters of Foxhounds Association of America, www.MFHA.com

Magazine with coverage: *The Chronicle of the Horse*

To learn more: *Riding to Hounds in America*, by William P. Wadsworth, MFH, Chronicle of the Horse

Chapter 9

Six Fun Things You Can Do With the Same Horse

W hen you're deciding among the multiple challenges you can explore as an equestrian, your own interests will lead you. But be aware your horse may have his preferences as well, and you will want to consider his opinion if you want a *great* partnership. It is best to begin your competitive career with basic skill tests, such as trail riding, and pleasure or equitation classes in the show ring, for example, before moving into something more advanced that demands greater versatility, athletic talent (such as jumping) or an inherited predisposition (such as cutting).

If you start your journey toward an all-around goal as a basic pleasure or trail rider, with either a hunt seat, Western or saddle seat focus, it would make sense to choose the pleasure and/or equitation divisions as your first contest events, or pick competitions that take place on the trail. In almost any venue, competitions are divided into several levels, including the experience level of the horse or rider (maiden, green, novice, limit, open), age of the rider (junior, young riders, senior, Jack Benny), and sometimes by professional status and ownership (amateur, adult amateur, amateur owner).

Pleasure and Equitation

The pleasure and equitation divisions call for and reward a horse and rider team who can present a judge with a well-balanced, good mover in all three gaits. To win a ribbon in the English divisions, your horse needs to be well schooled in a balanced, forward moving trot, a regular, relaxed walk and a semi-collected, round, three-beat canter. Since some advanced pleasure classes call for work at the hand gallop and the extended trot, it is a good idea to work your horse on these elements at home, until he can make a smooth transition both upward and downward within his gaits, as well as between them.

The desired head and neck placement of the English horse may vary within the pleasure and equitation classes between open and breed shows. For instance, in an open hunter show the horse who displays a relaxed, *natural* neck carriage, while offering the nearly vertical head position suggestive of a horse *on the bit*, will make the best impression on the judge. Your horse would need to display the type of long, low, stride generally associated with Thoroughbreds. A short, quick, or choppy way of going and any tendency to fall on the forehand during transitions would need to be improved with gymnastic schooling before you can expect your horse's performance to win.

If you are showing in a breed show, your horse's head and neck carriage and the arc of his leg movement (flat or elevated) will be determined by specific breed rules and breed characteristics.

No matter what the breed, a pleasure horse is one who displays good movement, good balance, calm, prompt responses to his rider's aids and whose disposition makes him appear to enjoy the work, including standing quietly in the lineup at the end of the class and backing readily in a straight line at the judge's request. It is also worth noting that a horse who uses his ears well (rather than pinning them while performing) always offers a more pleasing picture, and while it is hard to train this characteristic, it is one of the signposts you can use to measure your horse's interest and enjoyment in his work.

Ringsmanship can definitely play a part in a winning ride. If you find yourself in a large class, you cannot allow your horse to be constantly positioned three deep on the rail, where he will be invisible to the judge. The smart competitor remains aware of what the other horses and riders in the class are doing, especially those who are in close proximity. If the horse in front of you covers less ground than your horse in trot or canter, and you're not aware of that fact until it is too late, you can get boxed in, especially in a large class. If that happens, your horse may break gait. At the very least, you will not have the opportunity to show him to his best advantage. If you find yourself temporarily stuck in just such a situation, riding deeper into arena corners can buy you some extra space and maybe save you from disaster long enough for you to find an opening to move through. If your horse is a big mover, on the other hand, you cannot afford to find space by spending all of your time on the second track, because you will end up lapping all the other horses in the class, making your horse appear to be moving too fast.

Correct attire for a hunter seat rider: solid, conservatively colored hunt coat; complementary "ratcatcher" shirt with choker; black velvet hunt cap with safety harness in place; tan or canary breeches; tall, black, English dress boots and dark gloves.

The ability to change lanes smoothly and quickly is one of the necessary skills of a winning pleasure team. Make your horse appear to be an enjoyable, effortless ride, remembering the judge is most probably asking herself which horse in the class she would most like to ride.

Equitation is basically conducted in the same manner as a pleasure class, only the *rider's* skills are the judge's primary focus. The horse's performance still influences the outcome, since a wrong lead, rushing, rough transitions or other problems reflect on the rider's skill at getting a good performance from her horse. When riders are called out for individual tests in equitation classes, the pattern is designed to let the judge get a look at how well and effortlessly the rider uses her aids to perform the required movements.

Trail to Ring, Ring to Trail

If you have decided to cross over from the show ring flat class divisions into a trail riding competition, your show horse will require additional conditioning to bring his fitness up to the desired level, even for the novice divisions of a competitive trail or endurance ride. Since he may well drop a few pounds or turn it into muscle during conditioning, it is best to time your crossover into trail disciplines near the end of a show season (before his winter rest) or at the very beginning of one—making him muscular and fit, then adding the weight necessary for the show ring.

While a show horse may feel very confident in the relatively restricted confines of a show grounds and an arena, and be calm and obedient when ridden there, you should be prepared for the possibility he may become an agoraphobic when ridden on the trail, especially the first time or two. The same can apply in the other direction: The confident trail horse, especially if he's used to being ridden alone or in the company of only one or two companions, may freak when asked to canter around the small, restricted (to his mind) space of a ring, with 40 other horses. Patience and practice, through *slow, incremental* exposure, will allay the misgivings and fears of all but the worst cases of equine show nerves or wild frontier jitters, transforming your equine into a potential winner on either stage.

If you are reversing the sequence, taking a pleasure or competitive trail horse to the show arena, you will need to spend time in the ring, polishing and balancing your horse's gaits and transitions, getting prompt, smooth responses and getting him to perform in a more rounded frame then he would on the trail. You will also need to be sure he will give to the pressure of the bit and allow you to adjust the way in which he carries his head.

To be successful in the show ring, your horse will need to carry his nose close to the vertical, on a loose rein (in Western) or a light contact (in English) without becoming frustrated or excited. If you don't practice with your horse, he may become cramped in his neck, making him toss his head repeatedly or try to evade the bit by inverting his neck and lifting his head. All of these behaviors are considered severe faults and will end any chance you might have of earning a ribbon in the class, even if your horse's gaits and manners would otherwise put him on the judge's list of finalists.

If you and your horse spend a lot of your training time on the trail, you could easily begin to acquaint him with jumping by encouraging him to jump small logs or obstacles encountered during your rides.

Jumping small logs on a trail is a good way to get your horse used to jumping.

Western to English, English to Western

After mastering the pleasure and/or equitation divisions and perhaps a trail competition, before you leap to the next level of difficulty, why not just change your clothes and try riding the pleasure and equitation classes on the other side of the fence—in the Western division or English division? A winning head position on a Western horse is significantly lower than that of his English cousin, so if you are planning to cross over, you will need to school your horse in this new, lowered poll position before you can expect him to win. In addition, the Western gaits, known as jog and lope, are considerably slower and cover much less ground than those of a good English horse and most trail horses, so you will want to know if your horse is comfortable collecting his gaits so he can travel slowly in jog and lope.

If you are moving from the Western division to the English division, you will want to increase the animation and impulsion of your horse's gaits, raise his head and ask him to come more on the bit instead of behind it, lengthening rather than quickening his stride. A well-balanced equine athlete can shorten and lengthen his stride considerably, and while the Western jog is not a true collected trot, it doesn't take horses long, once you can collect them, to teach them to relax and jog with reduced impulsion—rolling and dropping their hips rather than driving through the hocks.

Neither Western nor English pleasure or equitation classes permit the use of martingales of any kind. While English equipment has very little difference between a working saddle and a show saddle, most Western show saddles are decked out in varying amounts of silver. Rules stipulate a lack of silver is not to be counted against the horse and rider in a performance class, but if you want to run with the big dogs, sooner or later you'll want your equipment to showcase the quality of your horse's performance.

As a Western enthusiast, it may take you a little longer to acquire sufficient English equitation skills to be competitive; the laws of gravity being a bit less forgiving of someone sitting on a postage stamp, rather than on a couch. But with work and dedication you can succeed.

After exploring the pleasure and equitation classes, you will want to challenge yourself and your horse with a more demanding test of skills, such as Western riding, trail class or a class over fences. All of these tests ask more of you and your horse than a basic pleasure class. You can add work over cavalletti to your training sessions to prepare yourself and your horse to handle low fences, like the ones encountered in a hunter hack class, where horse and rider are asked to jump two small fences.

Western riding requires flying changes. Trail classes favor calm horses who have inquisitive, active minds, which are happiest when busy. Putting them to work solving the various puzzles offered by the different types of obstacles will engage their attention and interest. Training time must be allowed for the horse to be *slowly* exposed to objects he might otherwise consider frightening, but once your horse trusts you, you can teach him that solving a trail obstacle or jumping over a series of obstacles is part of the fun of this new game you are playing together.

If English or Western pleasure or arena riding is your home base, including at least one outside trail contest in your all-around repertoire

A horse and rider appropriately and nicely dressed for a Western pleasure or equitation class, with a Western hat, vest and matching chaps. Note that the show saddle and bridle are enhanced with silver.

is good for both you and your horse. If you first master the skills of a winning performance in pleasure and equitation, then move to a trail challenge, the timing will be right and you will find work on the trail will refresh your horse. You will also reap the benefits of thoughtful conditioning over the varied topography of the trail, which will increase your horse's fitness and improve his muscling. Trail contests, both competitive and endurance, have a very relaxed dress code—an added benefit if you're on a budget. A heavy Western show saddle is not an advantage as the miles mount up, but if a Western saddle is where you feel most comfortable, there are lightweight barrel racing and synthetic

Endurance riders modeling the standard dress: vented lightweight safety helmet, T-shirt, riding tights, half chaps and either running shoes or jodhpur boots.

Western saddles that will serve quite well for trail disciplines. Fans of English-style saddles will find many trail riders who use dressage and all-purpose saddles. Besides a comfortable pair of riding tights, any clothing that suits the weather and your comfort is acceptable. The same goes for footwear, so there is no need to have a big budget to compete in a trail discipline.

Dressage

Another discipline that, when practiced correctly, is guaranteed to improve the performance of horses in any contest is dressage. Don't let the formal appearance of dressage competition intimidate you. If you think about it, at the lowest levels dressage is little more than a combined test of rider equitation skills and the basic training that makes any horse a pleasure to ride. *Tests*, as they are called, are rather like individual patterns in an equitation class—made up of straight lines, curved lines, circles and half circles of various sizes, and varying gaits. They test the skills and training of both rider and horse.

You will know your test long before you have to perform it, so you will have plenty of time to memorize it. And just in case you forget something, you can have a friend, known as a reader or caller, read the prescribed test aloud to you as you ride through it with your horse. Each of the movements will begin and end at letters that are set around an arena and that never change location, so once you memorize where they are, you will have a road map of the dressage arena forever. Your horse's performance of the test you have chosen to ride is scored numerically by a judge who sits just outside the arena in the judge's box at the center line, watching you and your horse perform.

At what is known as the introductory level, the test has 10 movements with a possible score of 1 to 10 for each of them. When you and your horse have finished exhibiting your skills and training, the judge also then gives a score from 1 to 10 in four additional categories, called the collective marks. Here your horse is scored on things like the freedom and regularity of his gaits, his desire to move forward and the relaxation

Don't let the formal appearance of dressage competition intimidate you.

Dressage letter markers; the judge's box is at C.

of his back, his attention to you and confidence in you, as well as the harmony, lightness and ease of his movements and his acceptance of your aids. Finally, there is a score given for your seat and position, and the correctness and effectiveness of your aids.

A distinct advantage of competing in dressage is that every rider receives a score sheet on which the judge's secretary has entered the judge's scores and comments on each movement you and your horse performed. After the class is placed, you may have your score sheet to take home, meaning each class can become a mini-clinic in what you and your horse did well and where you still need to improve your performance. Few if any other show classes offer that type of immediate, valuable feedback from the judge.

Since schooling your horse to be able to perform well in a dressage test through second level will also make him a better athlete, bringing out his talent by improving his strength, his straightness, his suppleness and his ability to listen to your aids, dressage is a highly recommended competitive choice for the all-around horse and rider.

A dressage rider's attire consists of tall, black, English dress boots, white breeches, a black hunt jacket or shadbelly coat and either a top hat or a standard black velvet hunt cap (at the lower levels). Your horse's attire includes an English saddle (dressage type is the most common, but is not demanded by the rules) with a plain (usually white) pad and an English headstall with a snaffle bit.

The placement of competition numbers varies from discipline to discipline. Pleasure and equitation riders tend to wear them on their backs. Some show classes allow or require them on the saddle pad. Competitive trail and the cross-country phases of combined driving and eventing have "pinnies" that the riders wear which display the team's number on both the rider's chest and back. Endurance rides number competitors in water-resistant grease pencil on the horse's rump. Dressage competitors commonly put their competition number on their horse's bridle, as shown in the photo above.

High-Performance Events

If you're cowgirl through and through and your horse's heritage favors the Western side of riding traditions, you may want to choose a contest that includes working cattle as you climb the ladder of performance challenges. Cutting and roping are highly specialized skills, and may

BECKY SILER

If you love the thrill of jumping, try adding classes over fences.

require a great deal of time and practice to develop a winning performance, even in talented horses. But the skills necessary for team penning, a contest that also involves cattle, can be taught to a smart, well-broke horse in a reasonable amount of time with quiet work. Finding partners to make up your team will most likely be a bigger challenge then getting your horse to play the game, once he understands it. But if you have a group of like-minded riding friends, or a large, horsey family, your team is at your fingertips.

Riders who favor the English disciplines and find they have a thirst for the adrenaline rush that accompanies jumping can choose to move to the next rung of the competitive ladder by adding classes over fences. Disciplines involving jumping can range from the relatively staid, straightforward course of an elegant hunter round to the faster, more aggressive riding demanded in jumper classes. Just like the Western high-performance specialty classes, such as reining, cutting and working cow horse, you need to leave plenty of time to prepare for contests that involve jumping, to ensure the soundness and safety of both horse and rider. A focus in any of these high-performance events is best accomplished with the assistance of a specialty coach—one who is proficient in training both horse and rider.

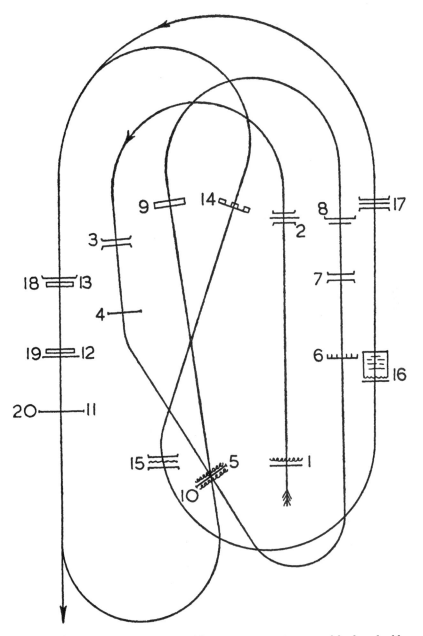

An example of an open jumper course with oxers, a water jump, and both a double and a triple combination.

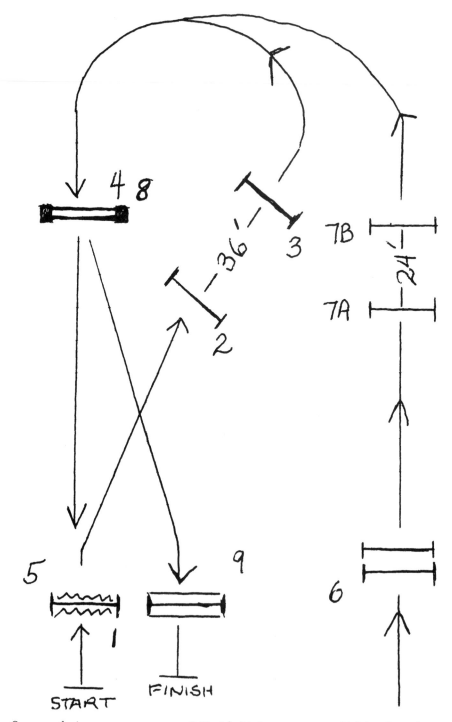

Compare the jumper course on page 247 with this hunter course, which has fewer jumps and more straight lines.

Three-Day Eventing

For real adrenaline junkies there is always the invitation to step out of the arena and try one of the great tests of the all-around horse and rider, the military three-day event. Eventing, as the discipline is now called, tests the mettle of horse and rider in three events, usually held over three days. A dressage test on the first day demonstrates the horse's training and obedience. On the second day, a speed and endurance test asks horse and rider to gallop many miles cross-country, jumping tricky, sometimes multilevel, solid obstacles that challenge the nerve of the pair and the athleticism of the horse. On the third day, an arena test over fences, called the stadium jumping phase, tests the horse's fitness and willingness to remain obedient to his rider after the long and tiring effort demanded during the cross-country course.

Driving and Drill Team

For your sixth event, try Robert Frost's "road less traveled" and consider driving your horse. (Be sure to consult a professional if you have never driven a horse before and/or taught one how to drive.)

Or think about joining a drill team. This is a fun activity that offers the added thrill and reward of entertaining an audience.

A cross-country jump.

You get to be a real showman in drill team.

More Than One Road Leads to Rome

If you start your journey as a:

Western pleasure rider, try:

1. Pleasure or equitation

2. Western riding

3. Western trail

4. A trail riding competition (now change clothes and test yourself in . . .)

5. English pleasure

6. Either English equitation or dressage

Hunter hack.

English pleasure rider, try:

1. Pleasure or equitation

2. Hunter hack

3. Dressage

4. A trail riding competition (now change clothes and test yourself in . . .)

5. Western pleasure

6. Western riding

Trail rider, try:

1. Trail trials

2. Competitive trail

3. Dressage

4. Endurance riding

5. Drill team

6. Barrel racing or team penning

Hunter over fences.

Hunter rider, try:

1. Hunter pleasure

2. Hunter hack

3. Hunter over fences

4. Dressage

5. Trail riding competition

6. Show jumping

Jumper rider, try:

1. Show jumping

2. Medal seat class

3. Trail riding competition

4. Dressage

5. Eventing

6. Barrel racing

Dressage can be the starting point to a number of disciplines.

THE CHRONICLE OF THE HORSE/ NICOLE LEVER

Dressage rider, try:

1. Dressage

2. English pleasure

3. Hunter hack

4. Trail riding competition

5. Western pleasure

6. Quadrille or driven dressage

Eventer, try:

1. Eventing

2. Dressage

3. Jumping

4. Endurance riding or trail riding competition

5. Fox hunting

6. Show hunters

Cowgirl, try:

1. Barrel racing

2. Team penning

3. Working cow horse

There are many possible disciplines for the Western enthusiast.

4. Trail riding competition

5. Drill team

6. Western riding

Cowboy, try:

1. Team roping

2. Team penning

3. Working cow horse

4. Reining

5. Trail riding competition

6. Calf roping

Reiner, try:

1. Reining

2. Working cow horse

3. Cutting

4. Team penning

5. Western riding

6. Trail horse class

Driving enthusiast, try:

1. Driving

2. Dressage

3. Trail riding competition or endurance

4. Drill team

5. Hunter pleasure

6. Western pleasure

Fox hunter, try:

1. Hunting

2. Endurance riding

3. Show hunters

4. Eventing

5. Dressage

6. Show jumping

Better yet, dream up your own list and see where it takes you and your horse. The most important things to remember: play hard, have fun, stay within reasonable safety risks, grow in skill, grow in confidence, get help when you need it, never overface your team, enjoy your success, don't rest on your laurels, and most important, enjoy your horse and the journey!

Chapter 10

Three All-Around Horses and Their Riders

One Very Smart Quarter Horse Stallion, by Carol Harris

As a breeder, I was always searching for the good movers with the good minds; everything seems easier for these horses. I tried through hard work to get to know all my young horses so that, by the time they started training, I had personal round pen knowledge of their pluses and minuses. I must admit I have been bit, kicked and hammered into the ground on more than a few occasions, and I definitely learned to respect every young horse I ever touched. They were inclined to give me the moon when I did things right and send me *to* the moon when I misread them. But if you have a good eye, the talented horse seems to pop right out and let you know that for him everything is easy.

My best experience with an all-around horse has to be with a bay 15.2-hand American Quarter Horse stallion named Rugged Lark. The American Quarter Horse Association (AQHA) recognizes the amazing versatility of the breed and annually presents a coveted award at their World Show in Oklahoma City to recognize all-around equine talent. It's called the Super Horse Contest.

What I ever did to deserve Rugged Lark I will never know, but in 1981 he came into my life. I was about to become a senior citizen and was no longer showing many horses myself except at halter and pleasure. However, I remained extremely active in all my horses' early training. At home I was still riding yearlings and two-year-olds, and running a fairly profitable breeding farm called Bo-Bett Farm in Ocala, Florida's beautiful horse country. I specialized in AQHA halter horses and performance horses, and on the side I bred a few Thoroughbred racehorses.

My job kept me moving at a fast pace from one morning to the next, but I loved every moment of it. My resident trainer was Mike Corrington, a diehard reining horse trainer. I appreciated Mike because with his foundation in reining, I knew my horses would be thoroughly broke and would not be hurt or intimidated. One of Mike's first equine students at Bo-Bett Farm was an exciting yearling colt named Rugged Lark. He had the qualities we search for in a horse and was also exceptionally good looking. Mike took to him at once and describes him in the following quote from Rugged Lark's book, written by Rebekah Witter. "From the start Rugged Lark learned so quick; you'd just show him something one time and that was it. I could almost hear him say, 'Well, I got that, what's next?' He made my job very easy."

Lark got Mike thinking a lot about equine intelligence. Working with Rugged Lark convinced him there is more to it than most people know or are willing to acknowledge. As Mike explains, "By him being so easy to get along with, I could allow him to use his own mind and natural talents. For instance, I didn't have to teach him how to change leads, I just taught him to change leads when I wanted him to. I didn't have to teach him to turn around, all I did was teach him when I wanted him to turn around. We didn't have to teach him how to do anything, I just added cues to aid his own abilities because it was all there naturally. Then, with his mind being so agreeable all the time, there was never a conflict. He trusted us, and we trusted him; it was kind of a 50-50 deal. From the very beginning we had no reason to mistrust him and he had no reason to mistrust us."

Because Lark always seemed to put Mike in a good mood, Mike would save him for his last training session of the day. "It was just a joy to ride Rugged Lark because he never disappointed me," Mike said. "He was always in a good mood, so I always rode him last because I knew when I quit, I'd be in a good mood too."

Mike hauled Lark to shows as a two-year-old to give him exposure, and occasionally showed him in Western pleasure classes. Early in 1984, while he was still being trained for reining, Lark completed his Superior Title in Western pleasure (60 AQHA points). In the fall of that year Lark won the reining pre-futurity in Louisville, Kentucky. He was then favored to win the big reining futurity at the All American Quarter Horse Congress, but, unfortunately, a pilot error in this futurity destroyed everything and Lark was disqualified. Because Mike was so disappointed in himself, he walked out of Lark's life forever. It was devastating at the time, but today we are reminded that God moves in mysterious ways.

Yes, Lark messed up in the Congress reining futurity, but for some strange reason, I had also nominated him to the hunt seat futurity. With only one hour to get ready, his sliding plates were removed, his mane braided, tack switched and his catch rider, Lynn Palm, was dressed and ready. She rode Lark into the arena and, without benefit of a warm-up, won the class over an entry of 132 horses.

Rugged Lark and Lynn Palm winning the 1984 hunt seat futurity.

I can say right now that no reining horse had ever done this before, and I'm quite positive none ever will. The word *versatility* immediately took on a new meaning. From that time on, I turned over Lark's training to Lynn, feeling certain that he would be in safe hands and would benefit from her experience in some brand new events.

My decision turned out to be a good one. Lark thrived on Lynn's philosophy, which permitted him to relax and enjoy life while acquiring additional skills for his growing repertoire. Lynn said, "A very important training technique that I believe in and follow religiously is to have fun with your horse. Not just for the great times it allows, but for the more important sake of variety and expanding the horse's mind by introducing new situations and challenges. I don't care whether the animal's main training discipline is Western, hunter, jumper, dressage, amateur, Olympic or what! Get out and have fun with that horse!" When Lark came to Michigan with Lynn, she said, "I not only broke him to pull the sleigh, but we went swimming in ponds, forded streams, did hill work, etc. On the trail we'd practice upward and downward transitions, increasing his speed, slowing his speed, and on straightness of lines. The horse enjoys it because he's not having to do the same things over and over, in the same spot, the same arena." Doing lots of different things keeps both horse and rider fresh, which starts building a sound horse in mind and body who is going to last a long time. "Regardless of what we did, Lark was always a good student," Lynn continues. "Now I've had horses that retain well and enjoy their work, but with Lark, many times I'd find myself stopping in amazement, saying, 'Lark, you shouldn't be doing this well yet!' Then I'd have to reward him by putting him up. To this day I haven't had another horse who was that quick."

What followed was three full years of successful competition, mainly in seven different events and sometimes even nine. Lark didn't seem to care how many classes we entered him in. His ears always stayed forward and he easily adjusted from English to Western. He nailed the all-around championships most everywhere he went, including the 1985 All-American Quarter Horse Congress. He also dominated the Congress versatility class, and as a junior horse at the World Show won the 1985 Super Horse Contest. In 1987, his show career ended with his second Super Horse Title with 53 points, which is a record.

At retirement, my intentions were to take him home to Florida and stand him at stud. However, in 1988 Lark received an invitation to make

Rugged Lark demonstrates his skill in a trail horse class.

a guest appearance at the All-American Quarter Horse Congress. From that point on, his new life started and his career became entertainment.

It didn't take long for Lark to become a star. It was obvious he forged friendships with everyone he met. Countless fans hung his portrait in their living room or displayed his book on their coffee table. They wrote to him, sent him boxes of his favorite treat, Fiddle Faddle, played his videotapes and collected his memorabilia. Now, at age 22, Lark and I have been immortalized in a beautiful life-size bronze statue by artist Maritta McMillian. Called *Ambassadors,* this statue welcomes all visitors at the front door of the American Quarter Horse Foundation and Museum in Amarillo, Texas. Perhaps Lark's popularity developed because I let him be accessible to everyone who wanted to touch him, hug him or take his picture. I'm so glad I did all that, because I realized how much his fans loved him and it would have been selfish not to want to share him. They also idolized Lynn Palm, who rode him in almost all his competitions and exhibitions. Lark's babies became in demand, not just because they were beautiful but because they had become a symbol of the all-around Quarter Horse that everyone wanted to call their own.

One might wonder why he merited this adulation. Was it because he did a little bit of everything? He did some jumping and dressage without a bridle, did a few tricks without a whip, dressed up and went to parties to drink wine with his friends, but he also excelled as a show horse, in Western pleasure, reining, Western riding, trail, barrel racing, working hunter, hunter hack, hunter under saddle and pleasure driving. Whatever it was, he did it all so easily and at the same time was a popular breeding stallion who could be trusted in the house with crowds of children around him. Yes, Rugged Lark was definitely an all-around kind of guy. He's still the only Super Horse to sire Super Horses: The Lark Ascending in 1991, Look Whos Larkin in 1999 and Reserve Super Horse Regal Lark in 1993.

Being Lark's owner, I remember it all so well and must say that the association I personally developed with Mike and Lynn was very special. I respected their talents as only a horsewoman could, and admired the ease and grace with which they perfected their work. Their respect for me and my horse was phenomenal and everything that I felt for Lark I truly believed they felt double. This horse never could have been the ultimate all-around horse without our relationships, and even after Mike was gone, Lynn and I could always rely on Mike's basic teachings to help us with something new that we cooked up for Lark to try.

In our world of specialization, it is difficult to find riders and trainers who can take one horse and do justice to him in diverse disciplines. Generally, several specialized horsemen are needed. This is why I never attempted the cattle classes with Lark. I did not know any cutting horse trainers who would put up with the standards for training that Lynn and I felt were essential. I always feared that some trainer unintentionally might undo some of the pure willing innocence that had been carefully developed in Lark. The cattle classes are extremely specialized. Riders involved in them have little interest in or time for other events. Also, I believe a good all-around horse must be highly competitive in all his events, not just so-so. I'm not sure Rugged Lark could have ever been a great cutting horse. He never showed me enough spook or reaction to surprises. Lark was much too brave.

Looking back 20 years on Lark's career, I feel that most everything he accomplished can be traced back to the beginning when Mike started

ENDEAVOR GRAPHICS

Rugged Lark with owner and breeder Carol Harris, looking for his Fiddle Faddle.

him and Lynn continued by changing nothing. She wisely advanced his education by building on the trust that was already there, and in 2003, at age 22, Rugged Lark is still a youthful, beautiful animal with a strong back, no soundness problems nor a single blemish on his legs or body. As always, he is fun to live with and appears to enjoy everyone who comes to see him.

[Author's Note: *America's Super Horse, The Story of Rugged Lark*, written by Rebekah Witter and available at www.bobettfarm.com, is an intimately personal book, filled with wonderful stories, photos and mementos reflecting the love, laughs, enchantment and excitement of Rugged Lark, and captures his charisma, uncanny sense of humor, honest heart, quiet confidence, gentle nature and generous spirit. You'll also discover some of the training secrets of Rugged Lark's owner, Carol Harris, a lifelong horsewoman, whose eye, judgment and personal philosophy brought her unparalleled success in the demanding show world.]

A Brave Haflinger Combined Driving Mare, by Peggy Brown

I have to credit 4-H for establishing my love for and interest in a good all-around horse. I began riding as a teenager, and along with my equine accomplice, savored the freedom of riding miles of roads and trails around the farm.

The moment I was able to taste competition and the show ring, I became hooked for life. The more classes I could enter, the happier I was. I was blessed with a large pony who patiently endured one tack change after another, and a wonderful father who generously paid what were then the $1 entry fees. What a joy to have a pony who could run a blazing set of barrels and then immediately walk over to another ring to do a quiet, winning trail class! We would then do a quick clothes and tack change and head for the hunter ring. Some days were great, others not so good, but we sure had fun.

After spending my teen years on the back of a horse, it was a logical choice to share my love of the sport, and of horses, with others by becoming a riding instructor and teaching riding and driving. My farm is a small operation, so my show horses must double as lesson mounts. My champion mare, Ulie, who is a speed demon in combined driving, is usually the horse I'll start a beginning driver with.

When I look for a good all-around horse, I select a horse who is careful of himself and avoids behavior that will result in injury to himself. I believe this sense of self-preservation tends to carry over to help keep the rider safe as well. The best choice is an animal who is interested in training, willing to work and willing to learn. I want an animal who is aware and curious about his surroundings—who knows what is going on around him and is not constantly taken by surprise. I try to select a horse who is athletic, forward and bold, yet conserves his energy to have enough left for later. I want to ride or drive a horse who I feel I could take with confidence into a raging battle, if I were a horse soldier long ago.

But I did not buy my Haflinger mare, Ulie, with forethought like that at all. In fact, I was not even in the market for a horse. Ulie came to me quite by accident. My family had purchased two weanling Haflinger ponies back in the 1980s, because the Haflinger breed had a reputation as a good, versatile family pony; large enough that even the men in the family could ride and drive in comfort. Our original Haflingers were gems. They were easy to train and worked well for lessons and shows.

As a family, we have won hundreds of ribbons with our Haflingers in draft driving, pleasure driving, jumping, contesting, trail, dressage, pleasure—you name it. But best of all was that we could do all the events with the same ponies. The young children could go in walk-trot, grandma and grandpa drove in the Jack Benny classes, and the Haflingers carried my husband and my brother through speed events as well as hitch classes. What wonderful all-around ponies, and what a joy to be able to show our ponies as a family!

The Haflinger breed originated in the mountains of the Tyrol, which is south of the Alps. A part of northern Italy, the area is a mountainous region whose inhabitants developed a smaller and lighter horse for riding and draft work. The first Haflingers were imported into the United States in 1958 by Temple Farms in Illinois. Since then the breed has evolved into two types: the heavier draft type used in farm and logging work as well as hitch classes and pony pulling; and a taller, lighter, free-moving sport type pony used in a wide variety of disciplines both under saddle and in pleasure harness and combined driving. Haflingers range in size from 54 inches (13.2 hands) to 60 inches (15 hands), and are known for their wide range of chestnut-colored coats with flaxen or white manes and tails.

As I said, Ulie came to me by accident. I had no intention of buying a horse that fateful day. I was at a Haflinger breed auction buying a Haflinger for a friend when Ulie walked into the ring. She was nine months old and a most sorry, wormy, rough-coated little filly. But did that ugly little filly have a walk on her! I leaned over to my husband, Ben, who said to me, "Do you see the walk on that filly?" I did, and I brought that ugly, wormy little filly home. To this day, when we look at old pictures of her we have to laugh. I'm sure people at that sale thought we were nuts. Today I feel I could ride her boldly into a furious battle, knowing she would not easily allow a bullet to mar either her silky coat or mine. She is brave and bold and has carried me through many a situation that would unnerve other horses. She has traveled thousands of miles with me for eight years, competing in riding and driving events, attending clinics and sometimes serving as my demo horse for the visible rider and centered riding demonstrations I do with Susan Harris at clinics and trade shows around the world.

A little powerhouse at 14 hands, she was the 1997 Reserve Champion Versatility Haflinger. At the 1999 Haflinger Nationals, Ulie brought home the blue ribbon in preliminary driven dressage, second level ridden dressage, Western pleasure, English pleasure, open jumping, barrels, as well as the versatility class. In pleasure driving she has taken me to Walnut Hill and the Canadian Classic Shows, and in 1997 won a bronze medal in the North American Pleasure Driving Championship in Large Pony Division. I have also shown her successfully in ridden dressage shows and we are now training Third Level. Just for fun we once entered a combined training event, where we easily took second place, outjumping many of the big horses.

Our latest endeavor is combined driving. Ulie loves it, as do I! She won the Great Lakes Challenge in the Training Division, and in 2002 won The Laurels and Southern Pines in the Preliminary Division. This past year we have taken the big leap into the Advanced Division and have competed at Gladstone, The Laurels, Fair Hill and others. The sport and the competition are grueling but exhilarating! Combined driving is a sport I never dreamed I would participate in, and I am having the time of my life in the process of learning and competing. The big walk of that scruffy little filly comes in handy again and again in the driven dressage test and in what I call "the walk section" on marathon day.

In between driving competitions, Ulie and I continue to build and improve our skills and vary our work between riding, driving and groundwork. We are models of cross training. We practice our jumping, both in the ring and outside. We trail ride many miles. We work at our contesting skills and continue to practice our show ring obstacles. We take long walks on some days, on others we build condition and endurance, and on others take long gallops. We continue to refine and improve our dressage training. What a joy it has been to be able do it all with one miraculous horse!

While on the road, Ulie walks proudly off her trailer and confidently follows me to whatever stall is hers for the night. Strange dogs, front-end loaders, Ferris wheels, balloons and carpeted floors through the middle of a trade show mean nothing to her, except as a curiosity. Ulie acts very much the diva in her shiny fur coat. She does not mind strange surroundings in the least, but she does hate strangers looking in at her and especially touching her! After a day or two of people walking past her stall and reaching in, she becomes angry and can really work herself into becoming an evil little golden dragon. While she likes to perform in the ring, she expects privacy in her stall. From the day I brought her home as a baby, she has always greeted me (and most everyone else) with her ears laid flat down and looking like an attack horse. It is her style, and I think almost an aura she creates around herself. She will come to greet me with those flat ears and evil eyes and then gently nuzzle or hold my hand between her teeth and her eyes become soft. I don't think I would ever accept this strange behavior in any other horse. Yet with Ulie it is part of her diva personality, and strange as it is even to me, I accept it. The more fit and conditioned she becomes the more the diva seems to come into play. I have learned to handle her with care and good humor, and in spite of all her nasty grimacing, she is always a solid companion—sure of foot and careful of me. I trust this fiery little dragon more than I have ever trusted another horse.

I started Ulie lightly under saddle in the fall of her third year. While many driving trainers start young horses in harness, I prefer to start them first with light round pen and groundwork, and then under saddle, before I introduce the harness and cart. I want to have a horse well grounded in the stop and stand commands before I ever strap a vehicle behind him. My initial work under saddle involves mostly walking. I like to use this time to begin to work simple transitions and trail obstacles, and build confidence and balance. I'm interested in a horse who is sensible and safe. The get up and go will come later! I want the stop, stand and wait commands right from the beginning.

I believe that for all horses, both ridden and driven, English or Western, dressage training is the key to developing balance, rhythm, impulsion and engagement as well as obedience. All horses and ponies benefit from the systematic training and development that dressage has to offer. You do not have to own special tack or build a special arena to train dressage. What is more important is to work your way slowly up the dressage training pyramid. Give both the horse and yourself the time to learn and gradually develop both mentally and physically as you progress. The basic components of step-by-step dressage training will serve you well in whatever direction you and your horse decide to go.

I firmly believe that a key to having a happy, as well as a physically and mentally sound performance horse is providing that horse with a variety of work. A horse drilled day in and day out in the same arena or in the same discipline will inevitably become bored, and possibly even physically uncomfortable. A horse who is bored or sore may respond by developing soundness issues or evasion tactics. All of my ponies and horses have benefited from variety; many call it cross training. The variety builds and conditions different muscles every day.

For myself, centered riding has been an outstanding means of improving my technique, balance and independent seat. While dressage is

Peggy Brown and Ulie competing in the marathon phase of a combined driving event.

step-by-step training of the horse, centered riding is step-by-step train-ing of the rider. For me to continue to compete and enjoy my horses and ponies, I have to continually work on myself as an athlete. Only when I can ride and drive with a balanced independent seat, using what Sally Swift calls "clear intent," can I be effective in following my horse's movement and clear and conversational with my aids. I try to devote the majority of my attention to myself and what I am doing as a rider or driver, and leave Ulie alone to do what she does best. So much of my training with Ulie involves training myself to communicate with her and follow her movement. As a rider I work to find the balance and move-ment of each individual horse I ride. It is my job as Ulie's rider to first accept who she is and how she moves, before I begin to develop and pol-ish her to her best advantage.

A great deal of our progressive training is what I'll call strength and flexibility training. I have had to build Ulie and myself athletically each step of the way before we could progress to the next step. It would be unfair of me to ask my horse to perform a task that he is physically unable to do. For instance, the slow jog and lope of Western pleasure can be extremely physically taxing on a horse who has not had the necessary conditioning work. Jumping asks for different skills and form. Contesting and hazards in combined driving require another kind of strength and agility. Flying lead changes waited until Ulie was physically able to do them. We constantly to go back to training and refining the basics, as well as moving on to new skills.

The Haflinger is a breed known for its longevity and I hope that I will be able to continue riding and showing Ulie for many years. I do know that having brought her along slowly, I have not compromised her soundness by trying to do too much at a young age.

Conditioning the horse properly plays a big part in success in combined driving, and moving to the advanced level has really taken that commitment to the max. I am asking Ulie to pull around 700 pounds at speed for 12 to 16 kilometers, often over rough terrain, to complete the marathon phase of the event. The conditioning process has been ongoing for several years. Ulie trains on a variety of surfaces and over a variety of terrain. We sometimes work in the heat of the day and sometimes work with a sleigh in deep snow. Ulie's favorite work is cross-country riding and driving, as she likes to trot out and see the sights of new places. We've been fortunate to be able to drive and hack in so many beautiful parts of North America together!

Ulie and I never set out intentionally to do versatility work. It was something I enjoyed and did with my other horses and ponies. As it turned out, it is something Ulie enjoys as well. Sometimes temperamental, with very strong opinions, she has not always been easy to work with, but she does like to work and seems game to try anything. She is the type of pony, however, whom you can not force. She must decide she wants to play or she simply won't. Her personality challenges me, as her training partner, to find new ways to keep her interested in the work we must do, but when we catch those magic moments of perfect connection, the power and the communication between us is the greatest thrill one can achieve with a horse. I live for those special days!

Ulie is incredibly brave. Competing at Gladstone in the advanced division, one of the hazards had an enormous slide hill with an option to take the slide or backtrack to take an easier but longer route. I repeatedly walked the hazard each way, not making a decision on that big slide until I knew the footing and how well Ulie would run on marathon day. On marathon day I passed through the gate and opted to take the slide route. Without hesitation Ulie dropped down that hill on her haunches.

From where I was perched in the driver's seat, she literally disappeared beneath me and I felt as if I was suspended in midair sliding down the roof of a house. I remembered to ground my feet and seat in the marathon vehicle, and down the hill we slid. Balance the mare, keep the vehicle straight, don't interfere until (phew!) we were back on level ground. Quick now, balance for a sharp right turn, then let's go! That's the sport of combined driving!

While in Aiken, South Carolina, I had the opportunity to ride my mare in the famous Hitchcock Woods. Some brilliant cross-country jumps are set up in the woods. Ulie was in her glory, as jumping is one of her favorite activities. We galloped through the woods, neatly taking the fences. The feeling of controlled power and confidence she gave me is indescribable, and I shall never forget it.

I love to ride, I love to drive, and I cannot decide which I love more. There are those who say that if you do not pick one discipline and focus just on that, you will never be really good at anything. But how does one choose? I play with this discipline and that, and enjoy every moment I spend with my horses. I intend to continue to learn and grow until the day I die. It has been Ulie, and my other wonderful all-around versatility horses, who have enabled me to enjoy so many of the opportunities and so many of the people and communities the horse world has to share.

A Big Little Connemara Stallion, by Karen Vicencio

When I was very young, I was introduced to the Connemara breed through the book *The Blind Connemara* by C. W. Anderson. Impressed with the mind and the talent of the fictional horse in his story, I wanted to meet a real Connemara pony. But they were rare in the United States, particularly in California at that time. You may imagine my joy when I began taking lessons at a local riding stable, only to find one of the lesson horses was a gray Connemara pony named Blazer. I finally got my wish to see and ride a Connemara pony!

Blazer, who had been given his name because he had hunted with the Galway Blazers in Ireland before he was imported to the United States, was 14.2 hands, and, true to his breed, could he jump! I eventually got to show Blazer in local hunter and jumper classes, where a lovely, large gray pony stallion who was winning both hunter and jumper classes caught my eye. Captain Cricket, I soon discovered, was a Connemara too.

My interest was piqued. I started reading more about Connemaras. I learned the breed was several hundred years old and had originally been bred for riding, driving and as farm and pack horses. Raised on rough, rocky ground with scarce food, they became very hardy, displaying excellent bone and feet, and able to live on small amounts of poor-quality feed. Their steady temperaments suited them to the work of plowing fields and carrying turf to be burned to heat the home. On Saturday, they took part in the weekend's relaxation, carrying the man of the house over hill and dale, jumping large stone walls on awful footing while foxhunting. On Sunday, they were hitched to the cart to take the family to town and to church. Even stallions were expected to work, hunt and pull the cart, so their temperaments had to be as tractable as those of the geldings and mares.

While Connemaras are no longer bred as draft ponies to be used for farming, they are still bred to be driving ponies (they are popular for combined driving events), to jump (in the FEI pony jumpers, they often jump courses of four and a half feet), and they are often used as foxhunters, keeping up with full-size horses in the field. Their good movement makes them popular for dressage as well. One of the most famous is Dundrum, a 15-hand pony who holds the world record for a high jump, clearing seven feet two inches.

When he was young, I showed Brannigan in hand at sport horse shows and in hunter breeding classes. He went best young pony at many shows, and several times was the highest-scoring pony at the sport horse shows due to his good conformation and his fabulous movement. His normally calm temperament was most impressively demonstrated each year as the breed representative in the Cavalcade of Horses at the California State Fair, with one million visitors in 18 days, exotic animals and fireworks every night.

The first time I rode Brannigan was at the state fair. Late one night I took him out into an arena full of 4-H riders who were preparing for their championship show the next day. He was so unconcerned with the other horses, I went ahead and climbed on. He walked and trotted around, as if he had done it many times before. When the nightly fireworks exploded at 10 o'clock, many riders had to dismount and hold on to their spinning, fearful horses. Brannigan made one small jump at the first big boom, then decided it was nothing to be worried about. That is the attitude he has maintained for the rest of his life.

Karen Vicencio and Brannigan receive yet another award.

Not long after, I started riding him in dressage, where he scored in the 60s and 70s in training and first level. My 12-year-old student, Noelle Lenhard, rode him in the hunter divisions, winning numerous show and series championships, while I rode him in jumper classes, which he also won.

I had driven extensively, running a commercial carriage company for several years, but hadn't started a driving horse on my own before. Worried about making a mistake, I asked a friend, a well-known and respected draft horse driver, Randy Parnell, to help me start training Brannigan to drive. I started by ground driving him, dragging a tire. Brannigan accepted the work with his usual aplomb, so I took him to Randy's place to hook him to the cart for the first time. Randy long lined him a little, pulled a tire, decided he was ready and hooked him to the cart. We were very cautious at first. I had a lead line on Brannigan in case he was frightened of the cart bumping behind him, but we needn't have worried. Randy and I ended up driving him all over the ranch that day. Randy was impressed with how good Brannigan was, and proclaimed that he must have been a driving horse in a former life, as he already knew what to do.

Two weeks after his first time being hooked to a cart, he went to his first driving show and won the pleasure driving class. He went on to win many driving classes, in pleasure, reinsmanship, driven dressage and obstacle driving.

One of his most memorable wins for me was at the West Coast Connemara Show, where he had won the championship the year before. Seven-year-old Riley Sexton desperately wanted to drive him in a class, so I told Riley she could drive Brannigan in the reinsmanship class. She was very excited, but had only driven a few times. Although she was only seven, she was fearless. She would ride any pony, and the few times she had driven I had spent a lot of time saying, "Slow down!"

The day before the driving classes at the WCCS, I gave Riley another driving lesson. After the lesson, where she had driven at a sedate walk and trot, practicing turns and halts and circles, she wanted to do some driving on the polo field. My friend Paul McNamara, a wild Irishman, offered to ride in the cart with Riley so I could go school some other ponies. A few minutes later, I saw a frightening sight. Brannigan was at a full gallop going across the polo field. I thought perhaps he had run away. But a closer look proved that was not the case. Although galloping, Brannigan was in complete control, being driven by Paul. Riley was holding onto the railing of the cart, screeching in delight at their great speed. Paul slowed Brannigan down a little and handed the reigns to Riley. She did zigzags and figure-8s at the gallop, while Brannigan appeared to be greatly enjoying himself.

The next day I rode Brannigan in several jumper classes, where, making a tight turn, a stirrup leather broke and I came very close to falling. Brannigan slowed down, giving me a chance to get back in the middle of him, jumped the next jump (which had been only two strides away), and then packed me around the rest of the course. Immediately following the jumpers was the driving. We took off the riding tack and harnessed him up. Riley got in the cart, and off we went to do her reinsmanship class. All the ponies entered the arena and worked together. They were asked to walk, trot, change directions, extend the trot and halt. Then the judge asked everyone to exit the arena so they could do individual tests. The obstacles from the cones class were still up in the arena. The judge told the drivers that each person had two minutes. They had to trot a circle, do an extended trot, a figure-8 and a halt. They also had to do a serpentine through the cones, drive through a gate and drive through an L. They could go at any speed they wanted and could do the test in any order, so long as they did all the elements of the test and were safe. The judge told the drivers to "show me what you've got."

Most of the drivers drove the course at a sedate pace, showing very little lengthening. Some horses had trouble with the halt. Others had problems with the shape of the circle. When Riley's turn came, she decided to show the judge she and Brannigan could outdo everyone. She went in at a *very* forward trot and sped through the obstacles, slowing just enough in the tight turns to safely negotiate them. Her circle and figure-8 were perfect, then she put Brannigan into his huge extended trot and precisely at X, asked him to halt. He did, perfectly square. She waited five seconds, then trotted quietly out of the arena. The seven-year-old child driving the 14.1-hand stallion had indeed showed them how it was done, and won the class.

Brannigan won the driving championship for the second year in a row. He also took home the Orchard Hills Funny Princess trophy, a performance trophy given to the horse who won the most points in the hunters, jumpers, driving and Western classes at that show.

Being a true all-around horseperson at heart, I love team penning too. My Connemara had been my team penning horse, and I wanted to do it again, so I started penning with Brannigan. He quickly figured it out, and in no time at all he was tracking the cow. I had to make sure I was ready, because if that cow turned, Brannigan was going to turn with it. Our greatest day team penning was at an exhibition. We had a pony team (Brannigan, a Welsh stallion and a Connemara mare), a team of professional cutters, another team of champion team penners, as well as several other teams. We got a lot of teasing from the cowboys about our ponies. The teasing ended when our ponies were the only ones to pen both sets of cattle, winning the first round in the fastest time, and being the only ones to pen the slightly wild cattle in the second round.

Brannigan's even temperament, athleticism and intelligence made him my horse of choice whenever I wanted to try something new. I decided tricks looked like fun, so I taught him to bow, do a Spanish walk, stand on a pedestal, wave at the crowd and lie down on command. We have done many exhibitions, including doing the tricks without bridle or saddle, and at liberty. Once there was a man riding a buffalo, which scared Brannigan to death, until he realized the buffalo was just a big, hairy cow. After that, Brannigan was used to escort the buffalo to events in different arenas, because the sheriff's horses were terrified of the animal.

When I got invited to go foxhunting, Brannigan became my hunt horse. I wanted to dabble in Western pleasure, so he learned how to neck rein and to jog and lope, and we won many Western pleasure classes. I also barrel raced him and rode him in parades.

Brannigan earned his certificate of excellence in hunters; won the Ann Tostal Perpetual Trophy (a national award given to the stallion who has done the most to promote the breed); was reserve champion AHSA zone 10 Connemara Hunter; earned certificates of achievement and year-end awards in jumpers, driving, dressage and in hand; and won in Western pleasure classes, driving classes, team penning and barrel racing. He has participated in parades, wagon trains, store grand openings, trick horse exhibitions and fox hunts. It takes less time to tell people what he hasn't done than what he has done.

When my students ask me now who my favorite horse of all time is, the answer is easy. It's Brannigan, a very big little horse.

Pop Quiz Answers

The Horse's Mouth

Novice: True, True, False

Intermediate: True, False, False

Advanced: True, False, True

No Foot, No Horse

Novice: True, True, False

Intermediate: False, True, True

Advanced: True, False, True

Why Diet Is a Four-Letter Word!

Novice: False, True, False

Intermediate: False, True, False

Advanced: True, True, True

Home Is Where the Barn Is

Novice: True, False, False

Intermediate: False, True, False

Advanced: True, False, False

Tack and Equipment

Novice: True, True, True

Intermediate: False, False, False

Advanced: False, True, False

About Donna Snyder-Smith

*A*s a professional equestrian coach, national clinician, successful competitor and freelance industry journalist (my first published article appeared in *Western Horseman* magazine in 1965), I have spent over 50 years with horses. During this time, my natural curiosity about everything equine, led me to the barns and teaching seminars of some of the very best minds in the industry in the past half century, in a variety of disciplines. In Virginia in the late 1950s, I was exposed to the wisdom of the grand dame of hunter seat equitation, Jane Marshall Dillon. Three years of very formal dressage lessons in a riding school in Augsburg, Germany, left an indelible mark on my understanding of riding and training principles. A move to the West Coast, allowed me the opportunity to work with respected, international dressage judge Hermann Freidlander, and being accepted to the USDF's National Vi Hopkins Instructor's Seminar, meant getting exposed to the training philosophy of Kyra Kirkland's coach, Anders Lindgren, whose input has influenced my teaching style and some of the exercises I use through the present day. Last (but by no means least), a fortuitously timed month of study at the Potomac Horse Center in Maryland, allowed me the opportunity of observing the master Nuno Olivera, training and riding horses eight hours a day, for an entire week!

Not satisfied with restricting my learning to English disciplines, I sought out and rode in reining clinics with the great Monte Forman, and more than once have sat glued to my seat watching "horse whisperer" Harry Whitney work his round pen magic in his clear, quiet way.

The early '80s brought with them the opportunity to study the Alexander-based Centered Riding techniques under Sally Swift and her staff, as well as the unique TTeam focus and techniques for working with horses, learned from contemporary horsewoman, Linda Tellington-Jones and her sister Robyn Hood. The innovative approaches to teaching riders and training horses conceived and modeled by these remarkable women were to prove as invaluable to my teaching career as my dressage training, eventing and jumping experience had for my understanding of the athletic capacity and biomechanics of horses.

This eclectic education, then, augmented through the years with competitive experience in jumping, eventing, dressage, Western riding disciplines and endurance riding, has shaped my priorities as a teacher and horsewoman, and so shapes the contents of this book.

Receiving the American Riding Instructors Association's first Lifetime Achievement Award in 1991 for my contributions to the industry as both an instructor and a journalist was the icing on the cake of a long and satisfying career.

Index